THE BONZ DOO-DAH BAND

JOLLITY FARM

The story of the Bonzos in their own words

Text by Bob Carruthers

Edited by David Christie

About David Christie:

David is undertaking a project known as the Doo Dah Diaries. The aim of the project is to compile the detailed history of the original Bonzos from the 1960's to the present day. Look up the Doo Dah Diaries on the web or write to the Doo Dah Diaries, PO Box 255, Wallington, SM5 4WL for more information.

ANGRY PENGUIN
LIMITED

Published by Angry Penguin Ltd. Minshull House, 67 Wellington Road North, Stockport, Cheshire SK4 2LP. Catalogue number AP3106   ISBN: 978-1-906783-21-1

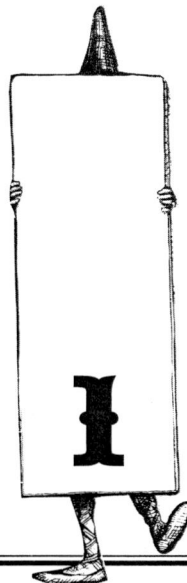

Now look at 40 years and celebrate,
Overwhelmed I try to condense
My careers to three words *Paradox, The Absurd and Process of Change.*
'Ere, that's more than three words.
So it is, but you know what I mean.
Something like Better Left Alone then? The real meaning of
"A man of few words, who doesn't suffer fools
Gladly," the journalistic conclusion of a 1968 interview.
Enough! Plus ca change, plus c'est la Meme chose.
Taciturn one, is it not time to quit whilst you're ahead?
Hey, but I'm so far ahead it's beautiful!
Is it just left then to become a sax-exile, and to
  fantasise
Something like, Rodney pulls his beret-
  basque to a rakish angle,
Ties a string of onions to his
  handlebars
Immaculately, and pedals
Majestically, and
Emotively into a glorious
  Borehamwood sunset
  Au revoir tout le monde.
  Au revoir Rodney.

**Rodney
Desborough
Slater**

**Co-Founder Member
Strategic Therapist
Jazz Saxophonist**

*"Nom de Dieu!
J'ai marche dans
la merde!"*

Photo by long time friend and
collaborator, Richard Waterhouse

(Onions grown by R. Slater)

Former member Rodney Slater's contribution to the Pour l'Amour des Chiens booklet.

2

CONTENTS

Throughout this book you'll find cryptic clues and graphic puns concealing a number of classic Bonzo numbers and one album title. If you can't solve them, you can dive straight to page 205 for the answers.

1. DRAWING BORED 4

2. GORILLAS AND DOUGHNUTS 31

3. URBAN SPACEMEN 74

4. WRESTLE POODLES... AND WIN! 107

5. TRAGIC MAGIC 122

6. ...AGAINST A WALL 142

7. HEIGH HO 158

8. I'LL REPEAT THAT... 165

APPENDIX ONE: A BONZO DISCOGRAPHY
1966-1971 BY CHRIS WELCH 175

APPENDIX TWO:
POUR L'AMOUR DES CHIENS 200

APPENDIX THREE: THE ANSWERS 205

CHAPTER ONE
DRAWING BORED

O ver the course of a forty-five year time span memories will inevitably become hazy as the events of yesteryear are revisited once again. There are a great many facts concerning the Bonzo Dog Doo-Dah Band which have sadly been forgotten and more than a few that have become confused in the telling. As the reader progresses through this volume it will become clear that there are now a number of differing recollections concerning even some of the main events in the history of the band. Elsewhere the chronology has become somewhat mangled as a natural result of being processed through a pretty disparate bunch of craniums. There is however crystal clear recollection with regard to the exact date on which the first seeds of the idea that would grow into the Bonzos were sown. Fortunately for posterity, and to the delight of Bonzo completists everywhere, Rodney Slater has kept the exact date when the idea of the Bonzos was first conceived firmly locked in his memory for almost half a century.

The year was 1962 and Rodney Slater was at the time an art student living in rented digs in London. In common with the rest of the country he was eagerly awaiting the late night radio broadcast of a much anticipated boxing match; but shortly after closing time Mr Slater's life was destined to be changed forever. Unbeknown to Rodney, the man enjoying a few drinks with Tom Parkinson, (who was then Rodney's flatmate), was an eccentric figure bent on a path of merriment, booze, jollity, brilliance… and more booze. This was, of course, the one and only Vivian Stanshall. Like Rodney, Vivian was an art student and their forthcoming chance meeting would have a dramatic effect far beyond the narrow confines of the world of art colleges and herald the birth of the Bonzo Dog Doo-Dah Band.

"It came about on the 25th September 1962," says Rodney Slater, "when I was sitting up late in my flat waiting to hear a transatlantic

broadcast of the boxing. Everybody listened to it in those days. This particular fight was scheduled for three o'clock in the morning. It was the famous bout between Sonny Liston and Floyd Patterson. About twelve o'clock, after the pubs had closed, in walked my flatmate, Tom Parkinson and he had brought Vivian Stanshall with him. Although we had not spoken before, I had obviously noticed this great big geezer in a frock coat and a huge red beard. I remember seeing him for the first time at a party in a church on Westbourne Grove, where he got up in the pulpit and was acting away all night". A police raid interrupted the party and stopped the opportunity for conversation, but on that night of the famous boxing bout a life-long friendship was established. "We hit it off right away," recalls Rodney, "and we sat and talked for three hours, 'til the fight came on, it lasted two minutes! But the Bonzo Dog Doo-Dah Band, which was formed that night as a direct result of that conversation, lasted eight years. Other notable members of the band joined at various points from one, two, three, four years later, but Viv and I were the only two people that actually were in it right from the start."

Fortunately for the history of popular music in Britain, the pact made between Rodney Slater and Vivian Stanshall was no mere passing fancy conceived in an alcoholic haze. Soon after, Vivian moved into the house in West Dulwich, which Rodney shared with fellow student Tom Parkinson. Vivian Stanshall later recalled that, "the whole place was littered with sarrusophones and helicons, and so I would pick any damn thing up and honk it or strum it." The new partnership was based on a genuine commitment and the pair soon began to set about achieving their vision of an anarchic fusion of jazz, vaudeville, surrealism, nostalgia and general lunacy. There is no doubt that Vivian felt the group was a continuation of the Dada concept into the performance arena as he later confirmed to Phil McMullen for Ptolemeic Telescope. "I felt this was a bloody sight more fun. Moreover, I couldn't see any difference!" In fact the band was all about having fun, as Vivian described those early days. "30 or so people who got together to fool around. It was just a release from college. We had no idea it was going to become as big as it did."

Initially the arrangement was strictly amateur and the ranks of the band were filled from among fellow art students. With little at stake financially there was no reason to fix a firm line up and there was inevitably a large amount of movement as different faces moved through the ranks of the band. There were so many players in the early incarnation that many have

5

been lost to posterity. Unfortunately the date of the very first gig with both Rodney Slater and Vivian Stanshall in the band is not recorded, but it is most likely to have been at the Royal College of Art. As Vivian recalled: "Rodney had this bloody great band at the Royal College of Art. I don't know, about forty or fifty of them." That was where the band played even though Rodney actually studied at St Martins, however there were members of the loose-knit band that did attend the Royal College, plus other budding musicians from St Martins.

Rodney Slater later recalled the chaotic early days of the band. "Well, there were loads of people initially. We did three months with some guys who were from art schools and we used to play and rehearse at the Royal College, where Roger Wilkes and Trevor Brown were the representatives of the college. We had some more from St Martins; Tom Hedge, Chris Jennings and Tom Parkinson, and then a few odd floating members that filled it out and whatever. That first line up split up after Christmas, it just blew apart".

> "He had brought Vivian Stanshall with him whom I had not previously met, but we hit it off right away."
>
> Rodney Slater

Things may well have rested there in the gentle wake of the Bonzos less than auspicious first stab at fame and fortune, which had lasted all of sixteen weeks. As far as we can tell, the original line up of what was then known as the Bonzo Dog Dada Band was something like Rodney Slater on clarinet, Vivian Stanshall on tuba and vocals, 'Happy' Wally Wilkes on trumpet, Tom Parkinson on sousaphone, Chris Jennings on trombone, Claude Abbo on saxophones, Trevor Brown on banjo and Tom Hedge on drums. This was probably the most representative line up, which seems to have crashed and burned during the first brief flowering of life for the Bonzos.

The reason for the sudden dissolution of the band lay with the fact that Vivian Stanshall, Rodney Slater and Tom Parkinson, now sharing communal digs, had all too eagerly embraced the artistic creed, which revelled in the power of art to shock its audience. This particular attempt to shock was led by Vivian and had taken the form of painting a full sized Third Reich swastika design in red, white and black all over the front room ceiling. The landlord had indeed been duly shocked especially as the emblem was clearly visible from the street below. He was clearly unprepared to view the work through the prism of the influence of Man Ray or Duchamp. He was more inclined to the "bloody liberty" school of art criticism and the artists were unceremoniously kicked out of their shared accommodation, which brought a sudden halt to the activities of the band.

However both Rodney Slater and Vivian Stanshall were conscious that

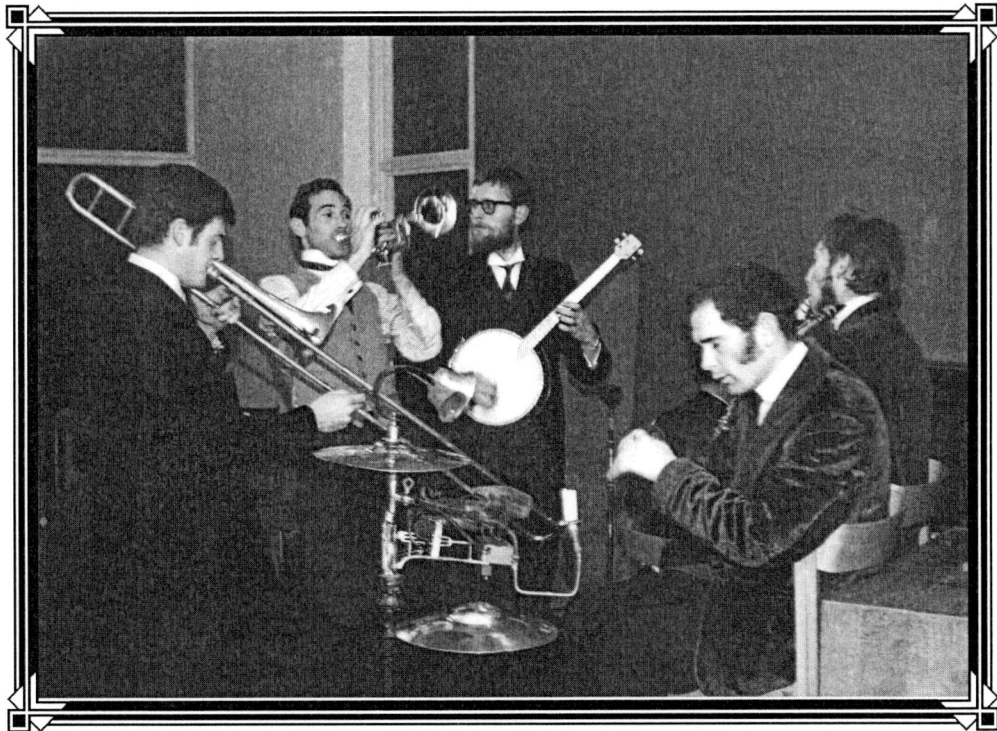

One of the earliest shots of the Bonzos in action. Featuring left to right, Chris Jennings, Wally Wilkes, Vernon Dudley Bowhay-Nowell, Sam Spoons and Rodney Slater. Photo courtesy of Vernon Dudley Bowhay-Nowell.

there was the germ of a very good idea in the wreckage. It was clear to both of the key players in the unfolding Bonzo saga that there was definitely something unique and original about what they had seen in that short-lived flowering between October 1962 and January 1963. Rodney in particular was keen that the new venture should not die and he was already acutely aware of the huge potential in his new found colleague. There was no doubt about it that Vivian, (or Vic as he was known to many old acquaintances), was touched by some kind of genius. "I went off and worked on a farm in Lincolnshire", recalls Rodney, "and Viv carried on at Central. But we used to correspond and promised each other to get the band together again sometime, and eventually we did."

These were the real formative years of the band, with constant changes to the line-up, as Vivian Stanshall remembered. "People kept saying, 'we're sensible, we're painters' and dropping out. So it came down to about thirty or forty." However, as Rodney Slater recalls, "That second attempt brought in some key members, especially Neil, of course, who came recommended by Vernon because although everyone else was still a student, Vernon was actually lecturing at the college and Neil was his lodger."

7

ENTER VERNON

The aforementioned Vernon is better known to the world as the splendidly monickered Vernon Dudley Bowhay-Nowell. Originally our hero was just plain Vernon Dudley but on meeting with Vivian Stanshall he was immediately dubbed with the wonderfully vibrant triple barrelled name by which he is still known today. Vivian Stanshall did not take the run of the mill view of names. For him names were not, as most of us meekly accept, a life long tag

> Vernon is certainly one of the more colourful characters to emerge from the ranks of the Bonzos.

bestowed on each of us by our parents and locked in place, there to remain rigid and unchangeable. Vivian was a Dadaist and was quite prepared to take a long hard look at ordinary everyday life and challenge convention. For him sticking with a given name one disliked was a sign of surrender to the humdrum world he feared. In Vivian's opinion if a name was unacceptable to the owner, then it was perfectly acceptable to change it. Vivian had done this himself, he had actually been christened Victor Anthony Stanshall and was to be known all his life to many friends and acquaintances as Vic. Vivian was a name that the young artist felt reflected the more cosmopolitan artistic world to which he aspired. There was also a darker twist to the switch. Bizarrely the change was also prompted by a desire to live a life that was a mirror image to that of his father. In short it was a bit of a wind up. Vivian's father had actually been christened Vivian George Stanshall, however the upright and conservative Vivian, (senior), felt that the name Vivian was effete and unmanly. He therefore changed his own name by deed poll to Victor, a proper masculine name derived from the Latin and associated with winning and conquerors. In due course Stanshall (senior) also christened his first son as Victor, thus establishing the Victor christian name and extinguishing the memories of the hated 'Vivian' forever – or so he thought. Stanshall, (junior), had other ideas and he not only revived the Vivian christian name taking it for himself, but he too changed it by deed poll switching from Victor to Vivian, thus reversing all of his father's plans!

Given what had gone before, it was no surprise therefore that Vivian Stanshall sought to enhance and magnify those aspects of Vernon Dudley's persona which most amused him by the simple expedient of tinkering with

Vernon's surname. Vivian was a genius with language and he understood the poetic concept of economy with words. There is nothing inherently funny about Vernon's new name, there's no double entendre or overt silliness, but Vivian knew instinctively what was needed and the slight tweak in name was all that it took to transform his new band colleague into an altogether more windswept and interesting individual.

Vernon Dudley Bowhay-Nowell is certainly one of the more colourful characters to emerge from the ranks of the Bonzos, or indeed any band. Blessed with a fantastic sense of the ridiculous and a highly honed sense of just what is right for the band in visual terms, Vernon has always had a strong grasp of the unwritten code that defines what is, or isn't, suitable for the world of the Bonzos. From the very outset of the band Vernon was able to balance a keenly developed sense of the absurd with a maturity that provided a genuine glimpse into a vanishing England.

Vernon Dudley Bowhay-Nowell was an instant hit with Vivian Stanshall. Vivian hailed from the suburban sprawl of Southend and he was the product of an ordinary respectable family background, but somehow by the age of eighteen Vivian emerged to embrace life as an artist with a wonderfully rounded faux old Etonian accent, which stayed with him for the rest of his life. He thoroughly enjoyed the phrases of the public school world, which had played no part in his days at Southend High School. Vivian adopted phrases like "dear boy", as his own idiom and made a concerted effort to keep alive the vocabulary and fruity pronunciation, which evoked the vanishing world of Oscar Wilde and Noel Coward. Vivian's plummy accent was later to become an essential ingredient in the Bonzo mix. In a number of interviews however, Vivian maintained that he originally spoke with a distinctly East End accent, which he was forced to change by his father. There were clearly a number of issues between Vivian and his father who pushed Vivian towards more manly pursuits and openly despised his artistic aspirations. In many interviews Vivian was highly uncomplimentary concerning his father. One obvious example is the interview given by Vivian to Phil McMullen published in Ptolemeic Telescope's Winter 1992 Edition. "I was clearly an artist. There was

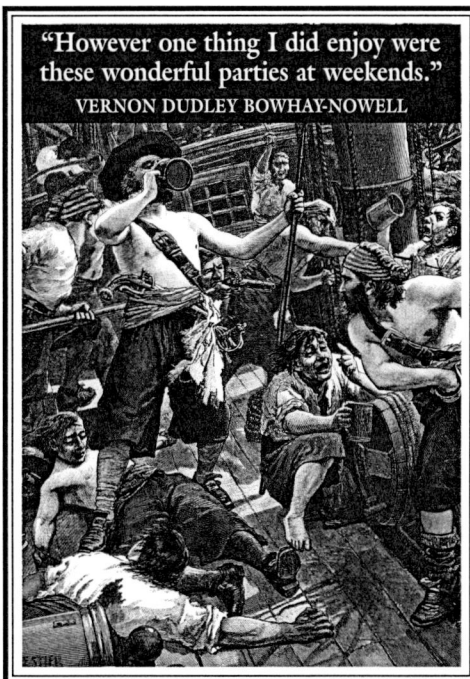

"However one thing I did enjoy were these wonderful parties at weekends."
VERNON DUDLEY BOWHAY-NOWELL

9

> "Originally we would play two or three numbers and we would be asked to leave, so that was extremely good training for the hard knocks to come."
>
> VERNON

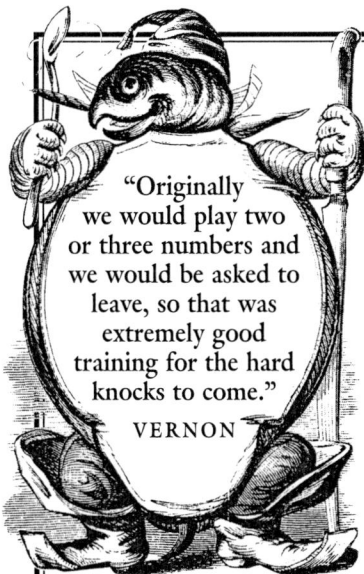

no question of my being anything other. I tried, dear God! Although I don't sound it, I'm an East-Ender. Grove Road. My father came back from the war full of swank, determined that he was officer class, - which he wasn't!"

Vivian Stanshall maintained that it was his father who had forced the change and frequently described how he would be forced to use one accent to conform to his father's prejudices and another to fit in with his peers. Vivian enjoyed his life as a young Teddy Boy, hanging around the seaside resort and the famous Kursaal amusements, however speech patterns modelled on Oscar Wilde were not likely to prove a natural fit with his fellow Teddy Boys, as Vivian recalled. "So I went through this horrible period when I went out speaking in an East London accent otherwise I was gonna' get hit, and when I got home it was "Hello Mama" and "Hello Papa". To some extent I forgive him that. What I don't forgive him is his intolerance. At the time the BBC had a commonality of speech, you didn't hear accents or dialects. Although he's been dead for two years I'm still terrified of him now..."

It was no surprise that Vivian Stanshall loved Vernon Dudley Bowhay-Nowell's old fashioned mode of delivery allied to his very proper English accent. Vernon's manner of speaking quite naturally encapsulates the hallmarks of the vanishing language that, for Vivian, conjured up echoes of the Raj and exotic lives led in far-flung corners of the Empire. Vernon's polite delightfully enunciated tones and quaint turn of phrase for Vivian evoked pictures of that softly mannered and genteel England, which Vivian in particular had a great longing to be a part of. Vernon was therefore an immediate favourite for inclusion in the band heartily championed by Vivian who enjoyed this link to a different, half imagined world which seemed both genteel and richly eccentric. Eventually Vivian's love of cultured expression would find its ultimate manifestation in the world of 'Sir Henry' and the 'Rawlinsons'. It is significant that Vernon was the only Bonzo invited to make an appearance in the film.

In 1963 'Sir Henry' still lay a long way in the future and Vernon Dudley Bowhay-Nowell later recalled those early events, which led to his first meetings with Vivian Stanshall. "I was older than everybody else, I'd done National Service and I was supposed to be going in to train as an architect, but faced with the thought of seven years being supported by the old man, I decided that that was really too much, and so having tried a variety of jobs I went into teaching. In those days you could go into teaching without a degree, but one needed to get a degree to stay in it, so after three years of teaching I applied to go to Goldsmiths. The principal at the

10

Are you sure these men were single?

time very kindly allowed me to teach a half a day a week and get on the full degree course. In those days you could live quite comfortably on three quid a week: – thirty bob for your lodgings, and thirty bob for your other necessities. And, of course, you could work in the holidays, but a great advantage was to play a musical instrument because then you were invited to all the parties."

There are, of course, a great number of art students with a genuine artistic talent, but the lure of the art world has also proved a powerful draw for the louche, the undecided and the fey. To Vernon Dudley Bowhay-Nowell's mind the tiny pool of those who were likely to ever profit from their art were somewhat outnumbered by the sheer volume of students who were merely filling in time in a rather less than pressured environment. This did have its advantages, one of which was the relative preponderance of female students and a large pool of willing participants for the endless cycle of parties, which provided a diverting counterpoint to the realisation that there was little real prospect of gainful employment in the art world. "I suppose art schools still are considered a place for young ladies to go as a finishing school more than anything else, because other than teaching, the prospect of a decent employment at the end of your course is pretty remote; unless you have a little third party support. However one thing I did enjoy were these wonderful parties at weekends, and if you played a musical instrument and like me actually had a car, you were always being invited to weekend parties in the country where you could stuff yourself with food, which was a welcome bonus indeed. Eventually one got more and more into the playing business and in my case, of course, comedy. Comedy is much nicer to be in than anything else, and you meet a better class of people, but in my case I eventually met up with the others!"

It wasn't just the young ladies whom Vernon Dudley Bowhay-Nowell was destined to meet and eventually a wide circle of his future colleagues were all associated with various art colleges. In 1963 Vivian Stanshall and Larry Smith were attending Central London Art College, Sam Spoons was at the Royal College, Rodney Slater was at St. Martin's, Roger Ruskin-Spear was still unknown to the others, but was studying art at Ealing College and Neil Innes was at Goldsmiths.

11

NEIL INNES - PIANO

Neil Innes lodged with Vernon Dudley Bowhay-Nowell and Vernon soon became aware of the fact that his lodger was not only a promising student, but he was also a gifted pianist, fledgling philosopher and composer. In addition to a highly honed set of musical sense and a fine appreciation for the world of art, Neil also brought an interest in philosophy to the band. It was he who would be responsible for widening the palate further to include yet more influences to the eclectic melting pot of the Bonzos. Soon hints of Baudrillard, Russell and Stuart Mill would be entering the mix alongside Man Ray and Duchamps. It was inevitable that the world of Neil and Vernon was soon to collide with Rodney Slater and Vivian Stanshall. Many years later Vernon recalled the circumstances of the first meeting. "The Royal College common room on Friday night was where anybody who was anybody went, and there were wonderful bands performing there like the Temperance Seven and the Alberts. On other nights you could get up and play and that was where I met up because Viv was at the Central, and I think Rodney was there too originally."

Vivian Stanshall certainly made an impact when he first met the new band members, as Neil Innes recalled. "We first met in a pub in New Cross, he was 22, I was 20. He was then rather overweight and was wearing this frock coat and Billy Bunter trousers, which was an outfit he loved. He was also wearing these little tinted oval Victorian glasses perched on his nose, a weird violet colour. He had a euphonium under his arm and was also wearing these horrible pink false ears."

Vernon Dudley Bowhay-Nowell first got to know the Bonzos before the first split, but didn't actually become a member until Rodney Slater and Vivian Stanshall had resurrected the band later in 1963. Vernon is quick to pay tribute to the fact that it was Rodney's persistence which had kept the flickering flame alive. By this stage the group had taken its first uncertain steps out of the closeted world of the college and into the harsh commercial glow of the pubs. The results were not always terribly successful as Vernon succinctly recalled. "Rodney was very dedicated because he moved back to Peterborough and used to come down especially on Friday nights for our sessions at the Royal College and then we tentatively started playing in the local pubs. Originally we would play two or three numbers and we would be asked to leave, so that was extremely good training for the hard knocks to come."

The music was of course the vital ingredient that drew the band together, but there has always been something unique about the Bonzos. It lies with common

interest in art, comedy and philosophy. The magic of the Bonzos relies upon the communal ability of the artists to draw on their love of performing to produce an amazingly coherent statement, which combines elements from the world of comedy, theatre, vaudeville, poetry and above all, the world of art. A particular influence was a common reverence for Dadaism, the early twentieth century anti-art movement, which took everyday objects and looked at them in a completely different way. It was this influence which was to have a huge effect on the visual stamp of the band as Neil Innes later recalled. "As art students we all thought in visual terms. I think we all quite liked Duchamp, he was the band pin-up amongst all the artists. Dadaism in general was a major influence, and I liked Man Ray a lot, and I know the others did too. It certainly had an influence on the visual side of the band. In fact, there's still a little corner of the Tate Modern where they have some of these original things, like Man Ray's 'Cadeau', the flat iron with the tacks glued on it. Just wonderful kind of simple ways to make you re-think, re-adjust the furniture in the mind. You can see how some of the Bonzo presentations grew out of that."

Vivian Stanshall also explained to John Platt in his 1979 interview given for the highly respected Comstock Lode magazine how Dadaism had been an element of the make up of the group from its very inception. "There were instruments all over the place at Rod's house and he said, 'Do you think you could play tuba?' And so I started with that. They didn't have a vocalist and I started posturing at the front, got the smell of it and started dominating a bit, singing lyrics out of newspapers. All very Dada." As Vivian clearly recalled on many occasions the Dada movement definitely inspired the band's name. "For a start we were to be called The Bonzo Dog Dada Band, but then we decided that nobody had heard of the word or knew what it meant. We changed it to 'Doo-Dah' because we heard a lot of people use it by saying: 'Where's the doo-dah', meaning something that you couldn't put your finger on. We didn't want to be limited."

Neil Innes later confirmed the importance of the relationship between art and music to the band and confirmed Vivian Stanshall's version of events. "So the word Dada was definitely intended to be part of the name, but if you try and explain in a short time that your band has this strange name because it's at least in part inspired by an affinity for "a turn of the century anti-art movement", it can make for a rather awkward conversation. So we thought, "Oh, let's just change it to Doo-Dah; let's not go there.""

SAM SPOONS - RHYTHM POLE

Despite the fact that much of the inspiration and influence came from those who had strived to present a higher level of expression, there was still the ordinary everyday business of finding the right personnel to consider. The

Little Sir Echo was another of the novelty songs rescued from the thirties which became a mainstay of the set. The song was accompanied by a wonderful visual gag in which Sam would assume the role of a ventriloquist's dummy and perch upon Vivian's knee.

Bonzos were always on the look out for performers that were novel and visually entertaining and could be added to the act. Rodney Slater remembered how the next piece had fallen into place with the arrival of Sam Spoons. "So once Vernon and Neil had joined, the band had a much more solid shape to it, the next bit of luck came with Sam. Sam we sort of found wandering around the Royal College with some cutlery, making percussive noises. He did it with various bits of cutlery, especially the spoons. Everyone thought that was quite brilliant and would make a great addition to the band, so we had him along and he's still known as Sam Spoons to this day."

Although the meeting with Sam Spoons was a piece of good luck for the Bonzos, good luck was in terribly short supply for the spoon player himself. Sam's affairs had reached a pretty low ebb. "I was having a very difficult time at the Royal College of Art and I had absolutely no money. I couldn't even afford a half pint of beer in the bar, but I knew that there were all sorts of embryo bands in this particular college, because it was the place to be. It was the Mecca and people would turn up and you'd hear all sorts of music going on. I eventually got a job washing up, just two evenings a week to begin with, and that meant that suddenly I had a bit of money to spend and so I actually could afford to go to the bar and there I heard this ridiculous sort of jazzy noise going on which was the Bonzos, of course. I thought, right, I'll get a pair of spoons, which I'd just washed up, went up there and started playing the spoons."

Yes you read it right, the Bonzos found their first recorded drummer as a result of an improvised session with a near desperate washer upper who had just dried up his own instruments! Outside the rarefied world of the Bonzos, the spoon is obviously not the natural instrument of choice for aspiring musicians. Let's face it, it's a pretty unorthodox option and inevitably the question, which eventually springs to even the least enquiring mind is: "So what led you to the spoons Sam?" It's a question that Sam has had to provide an answer to countless number of times over the years. So once more for the record ... here we go again. "I've always played the spoons as a party piece and everybody would go 'yeeaah', and it's so stupid. It's a stupid thing to do, but I loved it for

14

the audience reaction. My dad managed a big shop and I can remember at staff Christmas parties and so forth, he had a couple of porters play the spoons, and another one sang a bit, and at all these various social functions they'd get up and do it. Everybody else dreaded them doing their turns, but I used to really look forward to it, and this guy taught me the rudiments of the spoons. I thought, 'this is so ridiculous, I must have a go at this.' So I got in the kitchen one day, got the spoons out and got going. So there I was… – there was always a party going on somewhere and that was my party piece and I loved the reaction. It's not something you see too often and everybody thought it was pretty cool." In 1963 The Sam Spoons haberdashery extravaganza was indeed considered to be a "cool" addition to the developing set by the new core of the Bonzo band and Vivian Stanshall, Rodney Slater, Vernon Dudley Bowhay-Nowell and Neil Innes were soon augmented by the impecunious Sam.

Fortunately for Sam Spoons the band was by now beginning to earn what were for the first time some pretty respectable engagement fees and Sam in particular welcomed the opportunity to augment his meagre income with the fruits of the heady new world of professional music. "So having passed a kind of audition upstairs, I was invited to do my first gig at the Imperial College, which was just down the road from us, – and that was a kind of Bonzo gig. I didn't know if it was actually called Bonzo Dog or anything, I didn't know it was a proper band. I'm not sure it was then, actually, - but anyway we fooled around in front of a whole load of engineering students at the Imperial College and I can remember getting paid five pounds – and I thought, "Oh, wow!" I mean that was my week's rent in those days and a bit extra too. So that was that really."

Sam Spoons was pleased to be a full member of the band, but joining a band is a fairly informal experience at the best of times, it's not like joining the army there are no forms to sign and induction can feel like a bit of an anti-climax. It certainly did for Sam who had gone from the heady wine of earning a week's rent to the realisation that he didn't even know who else was in the band. "I didn't see any of the blokes the following week. I had no idea where they all came from. None of them were Royal College students. I think one of them was a trumpet player called Wally Wilkes. I think he was in the Furniture Department. I did bump into him by chance, a few days later."

It's no surprise that Sam Spoons found things were a bit loose. Rodney Slater and Vivian Stanshall had an inkling they had the recipe for a successful formula, but there was as yet no real structure to the group, no leader, no programme of rehearsals and certainly no clear idea of where they were all going. The whole project was just rolling along grabbing opportunities as they rolled by. This was one of the reasons why the experience for a fledgling Bonzo could be a somewhat tentative experience as Sam recalled. "Well, it wasn't really a band

The Bonzo Dog Doo-Dah Band on stage during 1965.
Photograph courtesy of Vernon Dudley Bowhay-Nowell.

then. They had got a few gigs but then it sort of folded and two or three of the band kept in touch. I think Rod Slater came all the way from Peterborough for practice sessions and gigs and a couple of other people decided they would do this gig at the Imperial College. They were short of other players and they thought I'd fill a vacant spot. Then I discovered the percussionist at the time was coming up to his third year and didn't want to do it any more, so I was asked, "Would I take over on the drums?" Only problem was, of course, I didn't own any drums. So I got a bit of a kit together as best I could, I went up to Portobello Road and bought a whole load of old drums and stuff and got an old cast iron bed leg and something and strapped it all together so that I had something in front of me that I could sort of hit. It wasn't really a

16

band that was together, as far as I could make out, because there were different personnel turning up at the various rehearsals. There was no regular gig, which was frustrating. Finally I did get a regular gig because I thought it was worth trying to find somewhere to play regularly in front of a proper audience, because I've always loved the reaction. So, right, this funny little band; – I must get a regular pub. And I lived in Notting Hill and there was a place round the corner and I got to know the governor and said, look, can we use the pub? And it became a regular thing for a few months."

"He was wearing these little tinted oval Victorian glasses perched on his nose, a weird violet colour. He had a euphonium under his arm and was also wearing these horrible pink false ears."
NEIL INNES

They then established regular gigs at The Deuragon Arms in Hackney, East London on a Sunday lunch time and at The Tiger's Head in Catford, South London, on a Sunday evening. The Bonzo cocktail of jazz laced vaudeville found a ready audience as Neil Innes later declared. "What we played turned out to be wonderful drinking music, which astute landlords soon cottoned on to. As a result we ended up doing five pubs per week", which included a second gig each week at The Tiger's Head.

Sam Spoon's ingenuity and persistence paid off and the band had a regular place to play where they could bounce off an audience and gradually begin to hone their repertoire, which wasn't done in the normal way by booking a rehearsal studio and setting down to hard work in a professional manner. The world of the Bonzos was incredibly laissez faire and sometimes the results showed, but against all of the omens, slowly but surely the band began to emerge as a vehicle, which embodied at least some of the semblance of a coherent unit. Vivian Stanshall, with tongue firmly in cheek, billed the band as "The Mephisthophelean engines of pleasure." The line-up continued to change however and Vivian Stanshall later described one gig: "I was playing in a boozer, the Deuragon Arms, with sixteen banjo players, me mincing along the table, (I was always a terrible show-off and queen), and one piano." Neil Innes described the band as, "a little bit trad, but that was too rigid. We liked The Savoy Orpheans, Jack Hylton, novelty fox trots. We used to go to flea markets and buy up old seventy-eights like 'Jollity Farm', a send-up of a big 1930's hit, 'Misery Farm', 'Ali Baba's Camel' and 'By A Waterfall', and thus built up a repertoire."

The volume of their performances was certainly an issue as Neil Innes recalled. "In the early days I was a bit smothered. I just pounded away with chords on the piano while others went mad on saxes and tubas. At this time we couldn't afford any amplified instruments, and the whole music thing was just a laugh. We weren't trying. The Temperance Seven were, but the Bonzos were just men versus instruments."

17

But the band developed as Vivian Stanshall explained. "At first it was just a very reactionary orchestra at the art school, with reactionary music. After that we slowly started to improve and to perfect certain aspects of the chaos we created in that way. We started using newspapers, furniture etc on stage." In those days the outfit was sometimes 30 strong and included as many as 10 banjos and a couple of trumpets at one time. "We just sort of made the loudest discordant noise we could and held it for as long as possible."

As Neil Innes described the band, "they were more visual than musical, that's for sure. If you brought along an instrument, whether you could play it or not, it didn't really matter, all you needed to do is want to stamp your foot to a very fast temp, make a lot of noise, and get up and show off… it was a very young student kind of band; everybody should remember that."

ROGER RUSKIN SPEAR - TENOR SAX

Musically the band was making progress. There was still something missing on the visual side, but that void would soon be filled by the inimitable Roger Ruskin Spear. Once again Rodney Slater provides the missing information. "After that, when we had sorted ourselves out and got going a bit, we did a gig in the Kensington Arms and Roger came along. He'd sort of heard of this row going on in the back room and somehow it stimulated something inside him and he joined, with his mate Lenny Williams. Roger is immensely talented and has always played a huge role in the visual aspect of the Bonzos, what would now be termed "art terrorism", I suppose."

Roger Ruskin Spear too was keen to pursue a career as an artist, but the West London location of his own college meant he had hitherto been insulated from the unfolding world of the Bonzos who were mainly to be found in central London. "At that time I hadn't met Rod or Larry or anyone. Rodney and Larry started from one direction. I came in from a different route. We'd all experienced the Fifties and the trad boom. Rod and that gang came from that direction, because Rod was a great clarinetist and I'd heard Acker Bilk and I thought, 'Right, that sounds good to me', but pretty soon I thought,

One of the surprise additions to the Bonzo armoury was this vintage fire engine left behind after a charity fund raising event.
Photograph courtesy of Vernon Dudley Bowhay-Nowell.

'no, this is not right, you know, it's not authentic, so what's the real stuff?' I know, Duke Ellington! So we went back to our roots and formed a big band. So I had a big band running in Kingston, a Duke-Ellington type big band. And that went on for a couple of years, but it wasn't quite right, I felt there was something missing I was saying to myself, "I'd rather do more than this".

No discussion of the Bonzos can ever be complete without a touch of the cap to those who influenced the band. It seems that on every occasion that he was asked the question Vivian Stanshall was quick to pay tribute to the main source of inspiration for the Bonzos. John Platt was one of those who posed the question in 1979 and got the stock answer from Vivian, "If there was any influence at all it would be The Alberts or the Commedia del Arte."

The other Bonzos had all been touched in some form or other by the merry madness of the Temperance Seven and The Alberts. Although Roger Ruskin Spear had not moved in the same circles of the original Bonzos he too was an art student studying at Ealing. More importantly he shared the all consuming admiration for the same influences. "I think around the same time the Temperance Seven were playing locally. I'd heard they were brilliant. So we went along to the Palais de Dance to a jazz all-nighter and we sort of bought a couple of tickets off some girls who were coming out and got in just as the Temps were finishing their last couple of numbers. I couldn't believe it. I thought 'My God!

19

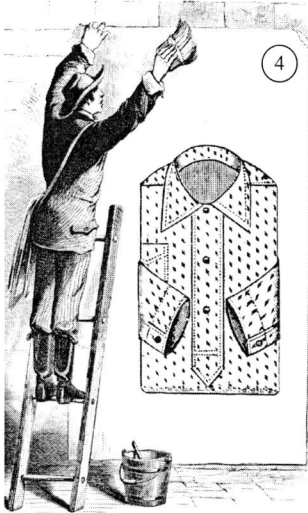

What was that?' But I had to persevere with Kenny Ball and Duke Ellington and all that. But it was clear to me that the Temps was wonderful stuff."

Even more important in the pantheon of Bonzo influences were the Alberts. This proto-Goons/Python outfit drew on a bewildering array of influences. The Alberts were Professor Bruce Lacey, Tony Gray and his brother Dougie Gray and together they had evolved a unique act, which revolved around dressing in Victorian clothes and playing a variety of strange instruments and incorporating a variety of peculiar and humourous props, which echoed the fast receding days of the Raj and the Empire. Previously Bruce Lacey had been one of the unseen faces behind the Goons. Bruce was to become something of a low budget props wizard and was the inventor of many of the strange special effects for the Goons films and live shows. He was inevitably asked to participate in Michael Bentine's "It's a Square World" and his influence can be clearly traced in the Bentine television shows.

On-line Bonzo archivist Ian Kitching recalls that a highlight of the stage experience from the Albert's was an exploding device, which ended "Goodbye Dolly Grey" with a jubilant shout of "Ladysmith has been relieved!" Bruce Lacey had been taught at the Royal College of Art by Roger Ruskin-Spear's father, who was the celebrated artist Ruskin Spear, and Roger and Bruce were to become friends. Subsequently the influence of the Alberts was always very much in evidence in Roger's work. It was in fact Bruce who originated the bubble blowing `I'm forever blowing bubbles' singing robot, which was later imitated by Roger and introduced into the Bonzos set to Bruce's great annoyance.

The Alberts played mainly music hall songs intermingled with some 1920's jazz. For larger, special concerts the Alberts would join forces with a variable cast of like-minded musicians and the Alberts would be transformed into a super group called The Massed Alberts. The Alberts had a variety of residences around London including the Fleet Street Jazz Club, a Friday lunchtime venue in Fetter Lane run by Ray Whittam, who also played tenor sax with The Temperance Seven.

The Alberts also appeared at Peter Cook's nightclub, 'The Establishment' in Soho, where they performed a DaDa-ist 'quiz show' in which Bruce assumed the role of question master. The Albert's approach to a quiz show was idiosyncratic and took a relatively simple format in which the competitor was asked a question. The competitor would then have a bucket of whitewash thrust over his head at which point the competitor would calmly say, "Could you repeat the question, please?" John Cleese and Eric Idle were also occasional performers at 'The Establishment' and it's not too hard to trace the possibility that the Monty

Another in the sequence of promotional photographs taken in late 1965 with Big Sid and Lenny Williams still in the ranks. In 1965 shortly before the band went professional Lenny Williams left for good, but the Bonzos retained its nine-piece status with the addition of Bob Kerr. Big Sid departed the scene in the summer of 1966 to be followed by Bob in November 1966. The remaining Bonzos soldiered on to record the "Gorilla" album.

Python team also may have drawn influences for the mock quiz shows that they presented such as "Blackmail" and "Summarise Proust", from the antics of Bruce Lacey and the Alberts.

The Alberts were the first of the anarchical music groups and were essentially a live phenomenon. According to Ian Kitching who ran a Bonzo web site for many years, Bruce Lacey has always maintained that The Temperance Seven were originally formed as an Alberts offshoot. Ironically, it was the members of the Alberts themselves who were later ejected for 'musical incompatibility'. In any event both bands were to create an unforgettable series of shows, which have not lost their lustre for Roger Ruskin Spear. "The Alberts came first though" says Roger enthusiastically. "The Alberts were the original Temperance Seven. I mean the Temps were from the art schools and out of tune clarinet playing, which I think Rodney has now perfected, but the Alberts were one step beyond. They were much more anarchic and there was a show called, "An Evening of British Rubbish" at one of the theatres in London and when I saw it, that was it. My God! It was all rubbish, but absolutely brilliant rubbish, anything played, explosions, the lot all going very anarchic and hugely entertaining. Back in Kingston I thought, 'Well, now this is it, this is more like it.' So then I began to take an interest in what you might call the scene. Bruce Lacey was at the hub of it all, Lacey was with the Alberts but they were a very independent group of guys, a bit like the Crazy Gang. Separate people doing a sort of communal act. A little bit like "Not Only But Also". Then

21

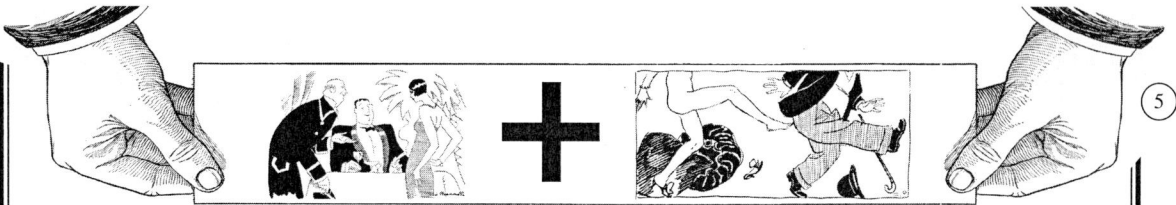

Peter Cook and Dudley Moore came on talking about teaching birds to sing underwater and we thought, 'This is it!' And it was! It all happened in the Sixties, it was a decade, which did sort of go 'boom!' like it suddenly all happened. For us though it wasn't about blues or guitar or Eric Clapton or any of that, it was the Alberts, Bruce Lacey, eccentric, explosions… – all this."

Roger Ruskin Spear still fondly recalls Professor Bruce Lacey, who was hugely influential in shaping Roger's thinking and his approach to the work, which would later bring so much to the look and feel of the Bonzos. "Bruce came out of the Army as an explosions expert and used to make robots. At Ealing College we were pushing the boundaries surrounding the ideas around sculpture and I thought this is kinetic sculpture, this is where I'm going, this is me. So I started building all props and things but I had nowhere to do anything with them in the fourteen-piece Jungle Orchestra that I was running. The Jungle Orchestra was a full-time job what with writing all the music out and some composing and all that. So I soon got frustrated and we gradually sort of split up."

For Roger Ruskin Spear things may well have rested there in the aftermath of his failed jazz band. The big band era was well and truly over and the renewed interest in the music of the jazz era was rapidly waning. Fortunately events were about to take a new and unexpected path as a result of a chance meeting with a new neighbour. "Around that time I moved into a flat and by chance living opposite was a chap called Chris Eadie who ran another band who'd been influenced by the Temperance Seven and he invited me to come along to this show somewhere up in London. So we came along and Ivor Cutler was there and there were the Massed Alberts in their sort of made up band, which was just people, all sorts of people including their girlfriends in fishnet tights banging cymbals just about anyone who wanted to be on stage could do. Amongst it all was Rodney and Neil, which was the first time we'd played together, so we all sort of sat and played these random funny noises and said 'goodbye, night' and all went off home, but I was impressed with what they were doing and I thought, 'who are those guys?'

Roger Ruskin Spear wouldn't have to wait too long for the answer to his own question because very shortly his musical path would again cross with those of Rodney Slater and Neil Innes. This time it was another friend, "Big Sid", who provided the impetus for the meeting. "In the Jungle Band I had Lenny Williams, a trumpeter from Kingston, who used to follow Bix Beiderbeck and in fact sounded exactly like Bix Beiderbeck. Of course, Bix Beiderbeck died when he was twenty-two or something, – so when Lenny got to

The Bonzo Dog Doo-Dah Band pose for a publicity still from late 1965. The group are wearing the thirties gangster style chic championed by Vivian. From left to right the line up in this photo is Big Sid, Roger Ruskin Spear, "Legs" Larry Smith, Vivian Stanshall, Sam Spoons, Leon "Larry" Williams, Rodney Slater, Vernon Dudley Bowhay Nowell and Neil Innes.

twenty-two he didn't know what to do because his hero had died. He thought, 'Well, where do I go from here?' But he played beautiful cornet in my orchestra. We also had a banjo player called Big Sid Nichols. Sid was a big guy so we all called him "Big Sid"…, we had a wonderful way with names in those days! Sid was a costermonger's son, (a rag and bone man), and he actually used to live in Shepherd's Bush, so he may well have been the basis for the fictional Steptoe. Anyway, one day Big Sid said, 'Oh, come down the Kensington Arms there's a house band down there, they're getting away with murder, you know playing rubbish and there's an out of tune clarinet player you would not believe!' And since I used to play slightly out of tune, I took up his invite. He said, "I know one of the guys there so bring Lenny and we'll go along'. So, of course, we go along to the Kensington Hotel and, of course, it's the Bonzos, the early Bonzos with Sam there with this pole, with all these spoons, and you could hardly get in, the place was bursting you know, and there was this racket. – I mean this terrible row. – I couldn't make out what the tune was or anything it was just going on. And then Sam would jump up and start playing the spoons… okay, so they came to a break and Sid

23

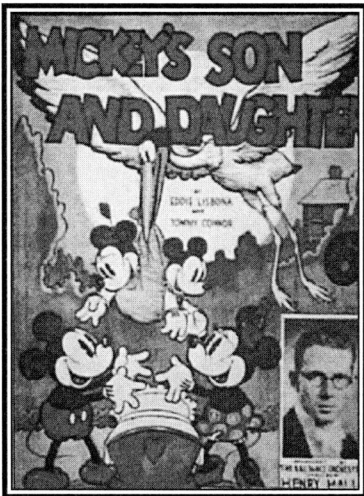

Mickey's Son And Daughter was a novelty song which made the transition from Tiger's Head stage favourite to fully-fledged recording on the "Gorilla" album. On stage the song was augmented by Roger's papier maché Mickey Mouse head which survived to be seen on the Astoria reunion and the subsequent tour.

introduced us so, - 'Can we sit in?' So Neil said, 'Yeah, yeah, yeah' you know and so we sort of muscled in and sort of pushed our way in on the chairs. Rod was there and a guy called Wally Wilkes on trumpet and I think Viv was there and Sam and Sid got up the back with his big banjo. Wally Wilkes was the original trumpet player. He was wonderful because he was the essence of the band. He'd be playing away and then he'd just stop playing and he'd sort of look round and say, 'It's good, innit? It's good stuff.' And Neil would have to say, "keep playing...', but eventually he didn't; and when Wally then gave up so Lenny came in. I mean Lenny was just as bad I think, but Lenny would at least play the entire tune. Anyway we sat in and played the evening and Neil turned round and said, 'Great solo.' He said, 'do you want to join the band?' At the time I said, 'No, I'm not joining any bands, I've had enough. I've had fourteen musicians on my hands and I'm sick of it you know, I'm not joining bands'.

Neil Innes obviously recognised a quality in Roger Ruskin Spear, which was in accord with his own vision for where he'd like to take the Bonzos and he was not about to be put off so easily. Neil kept the door open for Roger and the invitation to sit in was left open as Roger recalled. "Neil said, 'Tell you what, come along to the next gig'. I did and I kept saying to myself I'll do one then I won't come any more. "You don't want to get too involved." But there was clearly something there, I kept coming along, so it just kept on and on. In the end it was clear we were all in the band. The Bonzos at that stage became Neil, Vernon on the banjo, Sid Nichols also on the banjo, the two banjos gave it that big, thick driving sound, Rodney, myself, Lenny and Viv, and a guy called John Parry who went later on to form the Pasadena Roof Orchestra. (Lovely band, still going strong today.) John was on trombone and from the very first gig I think there was a furious row between Rod and Neil about the money or something, and this set the tone for the entire band really."

Of course it wasn't just added musical presence that Roger Ruskin Spear brought to the band. Roger has always been one of the leading exponents of adding visual art to music in the form of his wonderfully realised robots, gadgets and papier maché props. They have become

hallmarks of the Bonzos and supply the unique visual stamp, which separates the band from just about every other group on the planet. Vernon Dudley Bowhay-Nowell in particular has the highest praise for Roger's work. "They were fabulous. He was constantly surprising us with new inventions and new machines, and he wouldn't phone you up and say, "Hang on chaps, I've just been developing the new Acme rotivator moustache trimmer". He

Vivian loved fart jokes of all kinds...

would just turn up with these things and press a button and they'd work...hopefully. His stuff was just wonderful. He was an awfully good looking chap too, when we first started, and all the girls started screaming at him and so he grew this big, thick beard partially in the hope of hiding behind it, I think."

There is little question that Roger Ruskin Spear would indeed choose to hide behind a beard if it meant there was a better chance to express himself through his all consuming passion for music and art. "I was inspired by the visual side of things just as much as the musical side of things. I've always enjoyed pottering about in a workshop and tinkering with mechanisms. This was in some ways a route to bringing those discoveries to a wider audience. It was important to me that the band should have a visual presence but being perennially short-handed did mean a lot of rushing about".

Sam Spoons too was quick to recognise the huge contribution made by Roger Ruskin Spear and was impressed by how well his striking visual work added to the general feel of the Bonzos. "Well, we always tried to introduce props and nonsense into any number where possible. I recall on "My Brother Makes The Noises For The Talkies", Roger decided to actually make a flicker machine. Probably using something like an old 78 record player motor and just a cocoa tin with a series of slots round it, so that a powerful bulb inside the tin gave out these rays of light. When the number was being announced, he'd rush into the audience, turn on this machine... - 'click', - and hope that somebody would douse the lights at the same time, and there was this sort of flickering effect. It was simply realised but so convincing and so effective. In those days Viv would have a little mime prepared, and it would look terribly jerky and just look like a bit of old movie for about sixteen bars at the end of the tune, and as soon as it's finished the lights went up and everybody thought it was just something really quite fantastic. They would cheer like mad. Oh, wonderful stuff".

Over time various members drifted through the ranks of the Bonzos but by 1965 there was the beginnings of a settled line up, which comprised Rodney Slater on clarinet, Vivian Stanshall on

25

vocals and tuba, Roger Ruskin Spear on saxophones, Vernon Dudley Bowhay-Nowell on banjo and bass, Neil Innes on piano, guitar and vocals, Sam Spoons on drums and cutlery, Leon (Lenny) Williams on trumpet, John Parry on trombone and Raymond Lewitt also on tuba.

The early Bonzo sets were a pretty moveable feast but the surviving early examples raise a few intriguing questions such as what exactly was in "Military Medley"? A typical night with the Bonzos in 1965 included the following: "Ain't She Sweet", "I'm Forever Blowing Bubbles", "Abie", "Alexander's Rag-Time Band", "Whispering", "Yes Sir That's My Baby", "Ukulele Lady", "Sheik of Araby", "Bill Bailey" and, of course, "Tiger Rag", which was a featured show piece for the band who specialised in playing the familiar tune at dizzying speed.

"LEGS" LARRY SMITH - DRUMS

There was no doubt that the Bonzos were beginning to gel both in visual and in musical terms, however Rodney Slater and Vivian Stanshall were never content to allow the band to rest on its laurels and were always on the look out for new and interesting items, which would enhance what was an already dazzling show. Vivian in particular enjoyed the company of his friend Larry Smith, who shared Vivian's eccentric sense of humour and more importantly could stand the pace when it came to drinking marathons. Larry was on the fringes of the band for a long time before he made the leap from fan to artist as Rodney later recalled. "The next piece in the jigsaw happened maybe two years later when Larry finally came along to join us, because he had always been our greatest admirer and was a great friend of Viv's at Central."

Sometime during 1965 Vivian Stanshall managed to escape his duties on the hated tuba, which had fallen to Ray Lewitt. The tuba had always been something of a hot seat in the early Bonzos and the next change of personnel handling the duties on this most glamour-free of instruments finally produced the opening Larry Smith had been hoping for. On Ray's departure there was no danger of Vivian volunteering to resume tuba duties. Vivian was having too much fun in the limelight, so Larry's chance had come at last as Rodney Slater remembers. "When Ray Lewitt left, Larry was sort of brought in on tuba. He couldn't actually play bass or anything, in fact he could barely play the tuba, but he could tap dance like nobody else!"

Larry Smith had met Vivian Stanshall at Central and the two had quickly become firm friends. From the outset however Larry was aware of Vivian's capacity for dodging anything, which looked too much like hard work. "The master at avoiding his fair share of the physical toil

26

was Viv. Viv would take his ukulele in and out of the gig but that was enough for Vivian. Mind you, I had seen him work when he really had to. Before the band we were very close. I heard about him at college and he'd heard about me, and we were two cool dudes checking each other out. Thank God we were both at the same college because we met and he would come down to my house during the summer holidays and my dad would get us jobs on the building site. Believe it or not: Vivian Stanshall and "Legs" Larry Smith carrying bricks... – God it was so hateful. We'd sneak off to the pub at lunchtime and drink four or five pints of Guinness, which is quite a lot if you've got to go back and walk down a bloody plank carrying a wheelbarrow full of cement. I can't believe how we did it but it was enough for Vivian and he turned his back on physical toil from then onwards".

As the friendship between Larry Smith and Vivian Stanshall deepened the two were soon sharing digs together as well as enjoying as many japes and high jinks as possible. "I was still at art school with our Vivian and very much involved in a lot of scrapes together with him, we were good mates. We shared a little flat together up in Islington and we used to regularly eat poached eggs on toast and go to the Imperial Turkish Baths to get lathered up. We had huge laughs together and he always wanted me in the band, but I couldn't play a bloody thing! I had been playing the drums on my mother's coffee table with knitting needles and odd sort of things so I'd always felt I could handle the drums, but we already had a drummer, which was dear old Sam".

Larry Smith had previously been offered a chance to join the ranks of the band but the timing was unfortunate as Larry, then destined for a career in advertising, was away on an extended break in America. Many years later however he still recalled receiving the treasured offer from Vivian Stanshall. "There was some upheaval or other in the band and one day Viv wrote to me and said, "Well, why don't you play the tuba?" Quite why Vivian would choose to wait so long to draw his own flatmate and constant drinking companion into the ranks of the Bonzos is one of the many mysteries, which will never be resolved, but one thing for certain is that Larry was indeed formally invited to join the ranks of the Bonzos by letter in 1963 as Larry later remembered. "In fact, I've still got the letter that Viv wrote to me asking me to join the band, which is a beautiful piece of nonsense. I think he said, "We're now making regularly eight pounds a week and I would love to have you in the band". In his 1992 interview Vivian later explained to Phil McMullen in an interview why he had been so insistent that Larry Smith should be added to the ranks of the group." I loaned him that tuba and said, "Learn that and you get into the band". He learned two notes, none of them involving a valve... but "Legs" Larry had a charisma. He came out, waved, blew kisses... - people went mad! I recognised that and said, "keep him in the band". Rodney, who founded the band with me, hated him and I think he still does."

> "I grabbed his tuba, brought it back home to Mummy's house and blew my brains out for about a week trying to master this hateful bloody thing."
> "LEGS" LARRY SMITH

Larry Smith of course needed no second invitation or coaxing of any kind, here at last was his long awaited chance to become a Bonzo. Despite his complete absence of experience as a performer of any description, Vivian Stanshall sensed that Larry had a contribution to make to the band and for his part Larry was determined not to be thwarted in his quest for fame and stardom even if it presented itself in the unlikely guise of a gap for a tuba player. "So anyway, basically I got back and went up to London, grabbed his tuba, brought it back home to Mummy's house and blew my brains out for about a week trying to master this hateful bloody thing. So I did eventually get a kind of sound out of it and went back to London and auditioned for the boys, and after writing out a cheque to each of them for about four million pounds, they said 'yes'."

Despite the fact that he was a relative late comer this was still very much early days for the Bonzos and the group was still in its formative incarnation. At that stage Mr Smith was just plain old Larry Smith, a name that was just far too bland for the world of showbiz, especially with Vivian Stanshall in the ranks. Larry recalled looking around for a more noteworthy stage name. "I joined the band very early on, we were still playing in pubs at that stage and not taking it really seriously, it was just something to do twice a week. At the art school there was a film society and one night they showed "The Rise and Fall of Legs Diamond", who was this gangster that used to sort of dance around and then shoot half a dozen people, then go back dancing. I thought, that's kind of cool in a weird way, and I liked the legs bit so I nicked the name "Legs" from "Legs" Diamond and started to learn tap dancing."

Having mastered the tuba, "Legs" Larry Smith took to his new tap dancing mission with gusto, but once again arrived at mastering his new found skill by somewhat unorthodox means. "Central Art College is by Holborn tube station" says Larry, "and Viv and I used to busk in the Tube station, him on tuba and me tap dancing. We'd get enough money for beer and come back from the pub completely out of it. I liked to tap dance at Holborn tube station, because it had wonderful marble floors and a great sort of sound, some great reverb going on. But I did take a lesson or two in Notting Hill Gate with a guy called Leslie Clackett, would you believe? He had me running round the room on one leg, and then the other leg, and I just felt I can fake it better than this, mate, so I didn't

28

Undaunted by the unclement weather, the Bonzos soldier on for the benefit of the Great British holiday makers of 1965. This picture was taken shortly after the departure of Big Sid and the formal addition of Bob Kerr, the rest of the photos in this sequence appear on pages 32, 34 and 39. In the background can be seen the infamous Daimler ambulance purchased by Vernon on behalf of the band. Photos by kind courtesy of Bob Kerr.

carry on with it. I just got better by doing it more and more. If you do something every night you'll inevitably get better at it and that includes my other hobbies such as masturbation and the tuba."

Roger Ruskin Spear later recalled "Legs" Larry Smith's less than auspicious entry into the band and his struggle with his less than rock 'n' roll instrument of choice. The practical difficulties of playing the tuba were hugely at odds with Larry's highly developed sense of personal style, which always extended to looking his very best both on and off

29

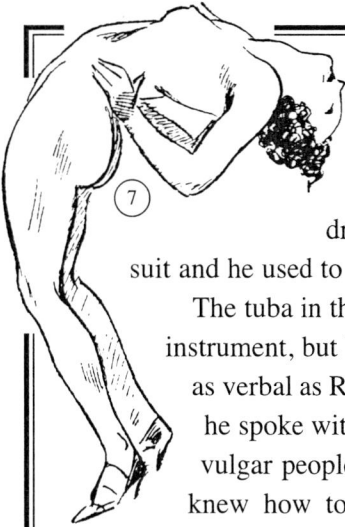

stage as Roger recalls. "Larry came in ostensibly on tuba to start with because Sam was on the drums, so Larry learnt the tuba and all right he couldn't wear his best suit because all the spit dribbled down and he used to complain he had stains on his best suit and he used to hate playing the thing."

The tuba in the eyes of "Legs" Larry Smith and Vivian Stanshall was a vulgar instrument, but Vivian was interested in all kinds of vulgarity. Physical as well as verbal as Rodney Slater recalls. "Vulgarity was a passion of Viv's, although he spoke with a plum in his mouth most of the time. He was one of the most vulgar people that you could imagine when he wanted to be, and by God he knew how to use it. But, and he frequently said as much, I was always considered the vulgar man in the band as far as he was concerned. I was working class and therefore the model for indiscreet behaviour and vulgarity and the source for new and unusual turns of phrases that he could use. I came from a different part of the country and some of our expressions were different. I never forget, we were on Maida Vale station waiting for the train, and that horrible notice comes up... - 'delays', - and in frustration I said, "Well, bugger my rags." And he'd never heard that phrase before and he laughed so much, – he did actually fall down on the floor, – literally frothing at the bloody mouth laughing at that. I mean he, in turn, had loads of things that I'd never heard before and that would set him off. He loved to use his own articulacy to project his rudeness onto other people and I was the recipient of that, because to him I was from the North you see, North Midlands actually, but to him it could have been a million miles away."

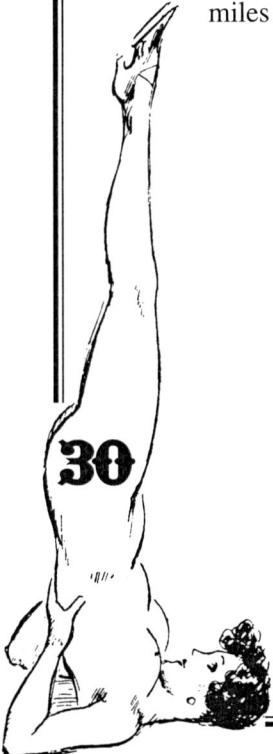

CHAPTER TWO
GORILLAS AND DOUGHNUTS

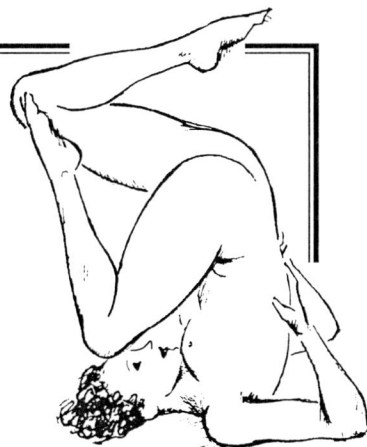

In the early days for the band there was an artistic agenda, which was to blend as much humour with the music and the Dada as humanly possible, but there was still no clear musical blue print, no Bonzo sound as such. Rodney Slater clearly recalls the fun of performing during this care free transitional stage. "We were just playing very loud, fast, joyous sort of acoustic music really. I mean we'd just come out of a terrible period of post-war austerity. We were all brought up in that. It was very grey and very restrictive and young people were looking for something to do to get out of it. And we just wanted to express ourselves. So as art students we didn't want the grey world and the doffing of caps to your parents and to authority. I mean the penny had dropped by then, that there were suddenly these things called teenagers and something called rock and roll had come along and it was horrible and disgusting. But there were bucks to be made out of it and so it was duly sanitised and you got people like Cliff Richard, and all the things that we didn't want to be."

The Bonzos were absolutely certain that they didn't want to become part of the sanitised British pop scene and in reality that was never likely to happen anyway. The Bonzos were just too different to be part of the herd as Rodney Slater recalled. "What made the Bonzos different was that we actually started saying something about our own culture and the things

31

Bob, Rodney and Roger form the front line brass section. Behind can be seen "Legs" Larry Smith on the detested tuba.

which affected us, rather than simply imitating the American style. And we just developed the visual side, through going round junk markets, and finding stuff that people were chucking out. There was an abundance of really good stuff on 78 rpms from the 1920's, - fun things, - and we started laughing at this. It wasn't straight jazz, but it was a kind of jazz and we loved it. It was very surreal in many ways. I mean, take something like 'Jollity Farm', 'All the little pigs they grunt and howl/The cats meow and dogs bow wow/Everybody makes a row down on Jollity Farm.' Well, I mean that's bloody absurd as far as I'm concerned. It's very funny and it fitted in. There was like a virus in the air from those years of these wonderful sort of visual pictures that people like Spike Milligan were creating. Now it was all in the imagination and it was up to you to interpret what a "flying NAAFI from Kuala Lumpur" looked like. And this is what we wanted to do, to create situations that would get a reaction and would make people think. And then we targeted the hypocrisy of show business, really, – that was our main sort of target."

The idea of the Bonzos as part of a movement, which was intelligent, articulate and satirical was beginning to coalesce in the minds of the band and the sheer number of gigs the band was

playing could only help to hone the musicianship of the performers who with the vigour of youth were able to tackle every tune at a pretty fierce tempo as Rodney Slater remembered. "The first gigs we played were on home ground, really. We did a lot of art schools and colleges, then in an unplanned way we just expanded into the pubs like The Tiger's Head, because that was regular work. People certainly seemed to love what we did because it drew the most amazing cross section of people. We were so undisciplined at that stage, though, that it was really like madness on stage. It was hyperactive. The music was always played much faster than is sensible to play music really. Nowadays it's impossible for someone like me."

Roger Ruskin Spear concurs with Rodney Slater on the subject of the up tempo performances. "The audience liked it though, or at least most of them. The show was always very visual and one of the great things that I remember someone said to me from that time was, "I can't stand the bloody music, but the crazy visuals you guys produce up there for two hours, doing what you do, is why I come here."

"Legs" Larry Smith too looks back fondly on the formative days of the pub gigs, which witnessed the emergence of the band's own unique character and did so much to enhance the confidence of the young performers. This was particularly helped by the increasingly warm reception which the band was receiving wherever it went. "They were great fun, the early days. We played mainly at The Tiger's Head, Catford, and it was a real East Enders' pub and the guys were so packed in they couldn't applaud because they all had great big foaming pints in their hands, so they sort of roared after each number. I used to wear thirties type gangster gear with a shoulder holster and a gun and, of course, all the geezers loved that. It seemed to strike a chord and suddenly I was one of them. And the shows were great. They would roar after each number and we were playing on stages the size of a sixpence. It made it even more manic and insane, because there was just no room and I'd be tap dancing on a table the size of a dart board and would frequently fall off and injure myself, but I didn't care. They really were fabulous times."

BOB KERR ON TEA POT

The fabulous times however were proving less than thrilling for trumpet player Lenny Williams who left the band and was replaced by Bob Kerr, a consummate player who brought his skills on cornet, trumpet and of course tea pot. Bob is a superb musician with a huge natural talent and he could see that this wild bunch of skilled and unskilled musicians possessed a unique quality, which meant he was happy to join the ranks of the Bonzos. "Well they already had a great act by the time of my first encounter, which was at The Tiger's Head. I used to go there on the odd occasion and sit in with the band because I thought they were absolutely wonderful, and I think there were about eight or nine in the band at the time.

33

Three years on from forming the band and the surroundings are still far from glamourous. Vivian entertains the great British holiday public at an outdoor seaside gig in the summer of 1966.

And then they asked me to join and I thought that was even more wonderful as it was a regular thing. We played there every week for a long, long time and, well, because it was so off-beat it was just so unusually fantastic that when I was eventually asked to join I was just really pleased, and that was long before the band went professional."

One thing that Bob Kerr particularly enjoyed was the contrast between the joyous world of the Bonzos and the straight laced serious world inhabited by the jazz musicians with whom Bob normally associated. "When I first started playing jazz, and I used to go to jazz clubs, everybody seemed so introverted. You know, not even announcing numbers or saying who wrote them or anything, they'd just get on and play them regardless of the audience. I thought, "How can they do that? You must talk to them or something, you must be able to communicate as well as playing". So then, you know, you tell the odd joke or something and then people laugh and you think, "Oh, that's good, I'll put a few more in",

34

and then it sort of evolves really."

What was evolving was a cult of popularity, which was to last the whole life of the band. By early 1966 it was obvious to gig-goers that there was something really special about the Bonzos and it was an infectious thing, as Roger Ruskin Spear later remembered. "It was a sort of fanatical following, it started off at the Kensington where I met the band. The Bonzos were also playing Sunday evenings at the Tiger's Head and also at the Bird in Hand in South London, which was a sort of bikers' pub then. We also

> "He couldn't actually play bass or anything, in fact he could barely play the tuba, but he could tap dance like nobody else!"
> RODNEY SLATER

had the occasional Sunday afternoon slot at the Tiger's Head and that built up the most incredible following, that's where Chris Welch got to hear of us because it was his local."

The Bonzos have never been an easy band to pigeon hole and things were no different in 1966 when even founder member and genuine musician Rodney Slater felt that the emphasis was on humour rather than music. "We weren't really about making music up till then. We were using it as a vehicle that we could use to express an idea which would be funny, which would make us laugh primarily, but we would also try to get a reaction out of people. We didn't know what that reaction was going to be, it was there to stimulate a reaction. I mean there was always a danger that they might throw things at you. If they did, we couldn't have complained because we just wanted people to notice us. And notice, hopefully, some of the points that we were making."

In his 1979 interview for Comstock Lode, Vivian Stanshall gave his own insight into life behind the scenes with the Bonzos, which completely reinforced the picture of unplanned chaos. "We never sat around the table and discussed what we were doing. Everyone was free to do what they liked. I don't know if we even liked each other, I'm not sure about that even now. It just seemed that we provided frames and opportunities. It meant that before I could make an even passable row on an instrument I had something bouncing along that I could do, mnemonic nonsense to screech to. I've always liked shouting and if it's aggressive titillating rubbish then all the better."

A great deal of what the Bonzos produced was rooted in the spontaneous nature of the act. There was little or no rehearsal and often the performers themselves didn't know what to expect, as Vernon Dudley Bowhay-Nowell recalls. "Roger used to do the explosions for the Bonzos and he used to keep an old wind-up

35

gramophone case that he kept the tins of flash powder in. It was a nice solid little wooden box and it had the gramophone mechanism removed from it. Roger was always rather amazing and would often arrive at the last minute and hadn't made up the explosions, and we would be playing and Roger would be fiddling about and poking flash powder in the thing. On one occasion somebody threw a fag-end into the box with the flash powder and the whole tin exploded and a mass of white smoke suddenly filled the room. Nobody seemed to mind, they just opened the exit doors and we went on with the show. We were extraordinarily fortunate on many occasions to get away with the most reckless behaviour".

Sam Spoons too was a great advocate of the spontaneous, humourous side of the band. "I used to really enjoy doing stuff like that. Yeah, I used to do some absurd illusion work with Vernon. I used to wear an orange suit and Vernon would say, "My man here will get in the trunk wearing, as you will observe; - an orange suit". And I'd get in the trunk and Vernon would say very slowly, "And I now wave the magic wand", and it used to take him ages to do anything. Now I've always been very agile, and during Vernon's pre-amble I was able to change inside this box. As I got into the box, I'd be making great play of the fact I was smoking a last cigarette. Naturally the box got fairly filled up with smoke, and I had to have a tube to breathe out of while I was changing. The illusion was that after a certain time the box would be open, there'd be a cloud of smoke and I'd get out wearing, - as Vernon would say, "A suit of an entirely different hue." - Blue rather than orange. Everybody was quite impressed with that bit of nonsense, because there clearly wasn't much room in the box. But one night the inevitable happened and the lid wouldn't operate properly. For some reason, it stayed down instead of releasing me. So I was trapped in a small box struggling to change suits in a cloud of smoke from a lit cigarette and it was only when Vernon finally realised that more and more smoke was emanating from the cracks that they came to my rescue and forced open the box. I was saved from the combined effects of asphyxiation and advanced nicotine poisoning, but it was all in the cause of art and the audience lapped it up… but it got me thinking and we developed the routine so that I actually got out of the trunk in a burnt suit. It had burn holes all over it. Those were the days before anybody dreamt that passive smoking could be harmful or anything. But I'm still here, folks!"

With crazy events like this taking place on a regular basis it was no surprise that the band continued to develop from strength to strength. It was inevitable that eventually the crowd began to ape the strangeness of the act, as Roger Ruskin Spear recalls. "The Tiger's Head gigs soon built up a fanatical following who would just come along and we'd see all the weird gear they were wearing, strange geezers appearing in the front row time and time again and they'd say, 'Oh, it's like a drug'. It became

almost like a workshop because we would play what we could play and the audience were so supportive and receptive that it didn't really matter. That inspired us to try and experiment with new things, if they went wrong it didn't matter. I think we did a version of "Singing in the Rain", which we tried with Viv and Larry doing a sort of Flanagan and Alan thing. It was dreadful but the audience went wild."

Running the back room department was the job which inevitably fell to Rodney Slater who was responsible for driving the band forward in commercial terms. "I was the driving force in getting them there and looking after the money. It was my role to collect the money from the promoters and doing all the nasty jobs, which nobody wanted to do, because otherwise the band would have collapsed

"It was my role to collect the money from the promoters and to do all the nasty jobs."
RODNEY SLATER

before it ever got to be a semi-pro band, let alone a pro band. Then as the band changed, because I'm not a great writer and I couldn't write for the Bonzos, I couldn't be responsible for putting the absurdity, the contradiction, the paradoxes, into actual subjects like Viv and Neil could. I knew exactly what Viv was doing all the time and I admired him tremendously because it was something I couldn't do and he admired some of the musical things that he couldn't do, in me, and that was our relationship, really."

With such popular acclaim and a developing creative chemistry, it was inevitable that the band would sooner or later turn professional and the time arrived in 1966. The Bonzos had enough members to fill the ranks of two or three regular rock bands, which was quite a financial burden to have to carry, but at the time it didn't seem to worry founder member Rodney Slater. "Well, actually, when we turned pro there were nine of us because Sid Nicholls, he also sort of drifted in. He was a mate of Roger's, and around that time Vernon buggered off somewhere and we replaced him with Sid, and then Vernon wanted to come back and we didn't want to get rid of Sid so we got rid of somebody else. But actually, when we turned pro there were nine of us, myself, Viv, Neil, Legs, Roger, Vernon, Sam, Bob and Sid."

The decision to turn professional did not present a huge risk to

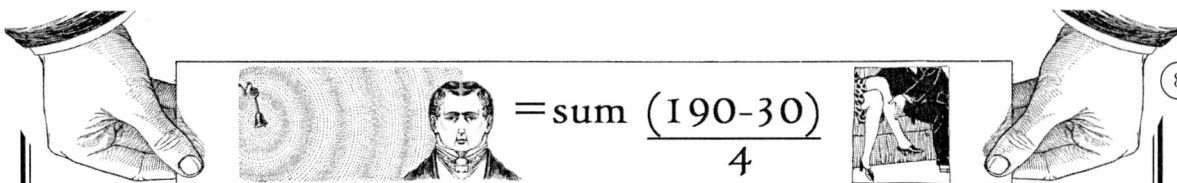

a group of young men who had no real commitments as Roger Ruskin Spear recalled. "When I joined the band most were all at college still. I think I'd just left and saved up enough out of my grant, (God I must have had frugal ways), to live for a year without doing anything to see if I could make it in the world of music. So I thought, 'Well, I might as well plonk away on this band'. Sam was finishing off his degree, a Masters, don't you know, at the Royal College and the rest of us thought, 'Oh, let's give it a bash,' so we sort of took on more and more gigs. We went from the Tiger's Head in Catford to pro status in 1966."

Not all of the decisions were as straightforward. Vivian Stanshall and "Legs" Larry Smith had received an attractive offer to run a design agency based in Italy but eventually after much discussion and a disastrous staff welcoming party the Bonzos won out.

REG TRACEY - MANAGER

The final catalyst that led the Bonzos to switch from amateur to professional status was the arrival on the scene of the band's first manager, an intriguing figure in the form of the late Reg Tracey. All of the surviving Bonzos have fond memories of Reg Tracey, and Rodney Slater is not alone in being able to vividly recall his first impressions from almost forty-five years ago. "Well the crowds rolling up to the pubs that we played in, eventually got bigger and bigger. I'm not quite sure how we ever got into The Tiger's Head, there were so many people there. Anyway it was there that we started to play regularly and really large crowds of people used to turn up, queue round the building to wait to get in and see us. Anyway, this Reg Tracey turned up once and offered to manage us. He came from somewhere in the East End and he was quite an amusing character. I can always remember him saying before gigs, "Okay, boys, on in two minutes. Be funny." I always remember that, "Be funny". He never understood what we were doing, but he did a pretty good job you know. He was as good as his word and in six months he got us what were then the biggest gigs in those days."

Roger Ruskin Spear takes up the story of the first meetings with Reg Tracey. "Then we played one gig in South London somewhere with the McGill Five who were sort of noted at the time for a particular sort of R&B, they did 'Mockingbird Hill'. One of them said, 'Ah, meet our manager; with him running the show you could go on the road, lads'. So that's how we met the manager who was Reg Tracey... the one and only Reg Tracey. His claim to fame was he was Kenny Ball's brother-in-law. God knows how many times we heard, 'Oh, I can get you with Kenny and the boys'. I don't think we ever did any gigs with Kenny Ball. If you listen to "The Bride Stripped Bare", at the

Vivian camps it up for the bemused seaside audience.

beginning you'll hear Viv say, 'And so the boys formed a band,' and – that's Reg, the very essence of Reg Tracey talking there on the record."

In 1966 Kenny Ball and his jazz men were still a huge name on the music scene and for a bunch of young art students this vicarious brush with the big time was something to be reckoned with, as Neil Innes recalls. "Kenny Ball did actually used to come and see the Bonzos at The Tiger's Head in Catford and Kenny Ball had a brother-in-law called Reg Tracey, who was smitten by the Bonzos and he wanted to become our manager. He had this wonderful nasal voice, which was distinctive in a plain kind of way, and we sort of thought, "Yes! That's our manager." It was wonderful. It was Reg Tracey who arranged for us to go to Newcastle and South Shields over the Easter holiday, and while we were there he gave us a contract. And the Bonzos had come into contact with Newcastle Brown Ale for the first time, and it was quite heady stuff. We remember looking at the contract, looking at Reg and sort of saying, "We'll sign it anyway, this is all part of the Dada, isn't it?" But is it? During that week Reg said to us in that very droll way of his, "Boys, I've got this great idea," he said, "for a television series. You'll be the band, I'll be the manager, and fate will play the straight man", and I swear we nearly wet ourselves."

39

"Legs" Larry Smith too recalled his early meetings with Reg Tracey and agrees with Neil Innes' recollection of the fateful moment when dazzled by the thought of the Northern club circuit and swimming in brown ale they signed their first management contract. "Reg Tracey came down from Epping and we actually turned professional really because Reg knew the club and ballroom circuits up North, so we went up and did the Northern clubs. We hadn't really even started and there we were doing the old dead people's circuit. So we got lost under there and Reg said, 'Well, boys, come on boys, be funny tonight boys'. I thought, 'Oh, God! This is terrible'. I think we signed our contracts completely blotto. I remember lying on couches in the digs you know and Reg saying, 'Sign'. In that condition it's pretty obvious we'll sign anything'. It was only later we realised just what we'd done, we'd signed up to this guy who really wasn't up to a whole lot beyond the Northern clubs circuit."

Vernon Dudley Bowhay-Nowell still has warm memories of Reg Tracey, of whom he was to grow very fond. In common with the other Bonzos, Vernon was impressed by Reg's ability to deliver on his promises.

"A nice little man called Reg Tracey rolled up, who declared he wanted to be our manager. He discovered us and decided that we should go on the road, but the chaps were still at art school so we had to stick to London initially. I had finished by then so I was doing some lecturing in South London but kept the band thing going, and then as soon as the rest of the guys had finished their courses the following year, off we went on the road and did these amazing North country working men's club circuits. And I suppose we were very much a student novelty to the workers up North, who found us very entertaining. And so I suppose that was it for me, really. At teaching you had to wait for your money, but if you played music you actually got paid immediately."

Unable to resist such promises the band signed with Reg Tracey and soon after they received their first Northern club booking, which arrived whilst the Bonzos were performing at the Blue Angel Club in Berkley Square. "We were playing at an incredibly small club in London for guard officers and their frumps when we had this offer for a trial run at a club in Sunderland, doubling Newcastle." So remembered Vivian Stanshall. "We went up in our Easter holidays and did it. Just went on and made an awful row and these people applauded. They all said: 'Great lads. We must 'ave you back at t'club.' And there it was. They gave us a six-week booking when we left school."

The lure of the Northern club circuit was the Holy Grail for working bands. Up North there were plenty of active clubs within striking distance of each other and it meant regular income for a band like the Bonzos. It may not have been the rock 'n' roll world of Cream,

'The Sheik Of Araby' was a very popular stage favourite to which the Bonzos added the refrain "with no pants on" and encouraged enthusiastic audiences to join in for added comic effect. The song was not recorded by the Bonzos but was revived for the Astoria show in 2006.

Hendrix and Pink Floyd, but with nine mouths to feed the Bonzos could not be choosers and they were sufficiently astute to realise that their show actually held wide appeal for ordinary working people every bit as much as art students, as "Legs" Larry Smith recalled. "I can still remember Reg declaring "Oh, hello boys. Yes, I'm going to take you up to the North of England now and you're going to do six weeks cabaret. I manage Kenny Ball by the way." He was a very sweet guy, just so bloody normal you know, he was lovely. Great bloke. He was always very clean, I remember. He always turned up smelling of Old Spice in the sixties, - (hateful stuff), - and he was always immaculate. But he certainly knew a thing or two about the Northern clubs."

The northern clubs were the first step for the Bonzos into the real world of earning a living as full time performers. They soon built a great reputation which was to stand them in good stead for a long time, as Vernon recalled. "So we got caught up with life on the cabaret circuit and spent much of our time touring up north for oh, it must have been the better part of three years. We were away weeks at a time. Sunday morning we would travel on to the new venue, find our Show Biz Digs, and present ourselves at the club or theatre in the afternoon. We often had to do a run through of our show for the management, and the lighting man could decide what was wanted.

One memorable early run through was for a gentleman called Joe Pullen who ran a celebrated club called The Talk of the North. We did the run through and were walking off when Joe who was sitting in the front row shouted out 'Well is that it then? We were somewhat surprised, and returning to the front of the stage Viv addressed him in his most superior tone, "What do you mean?" Where's ye're false tab then?" said Joe. "False tab! What's that?" replied Viv. "When you finish your act you run off t'stage, and then you run back and give them another one lad!" "We don't do anything false like that." said Viv with conviction. "You'll do a false tab or I'm paying you off now boys. Right! Who's next." That night we did the show which went down very well. At the end we left the stage and returned as instructed. Viv took the microphone and announced, "We are going to play you another number because Joe has told us if we don't do a false tab he's paying us off!" The audience loved it, and so did Joe who came backstage to invite us all round to the bar to

41

celebrate.

We played two clubs each night, our set was only thirty to forty minutes in each club. They didn't want you interfering with the time for gambling or other activities they had organised. It was essential that you played in two clubs each night to make it financially sensible. The difficulty was the clubs insisted that they were at least thirty miles apart so that you would not be drawing your audience from the same area. Our first set was usually around half past ten in the evening, and the second one about half past twelve. We would do our first set, and hump all the equipment into the vehicle, and rush off down the road thirty miles. In the winter driving over the Pennines on icy roads to our next venue could be pretty hairy going."

VERNON GETS SOME WHEELS

Being the Bonzos of course there was little prospect of the band choosing anything mundane to convey themselves. A transit van was the hard working fit for purpose work horse of the entertainment circuit and favoured vehicle for just about every other rock band on the circuit. The choice of vehicle was made by Vernon and it has left it's mark indelibly stamped on the Bonzos, as Sam Spoons recalled. "We travelled in an old Daimler ambulance that Vernon had, a wonderful old machine with a polished concrete floor. Driving up to Newcastle used to take two days. It had a soft and hard ride control lever which caused much comment. It was Vernon's pride and joy, but it used to gobble up the petrol, I remember.

On one of our long trips we pulled into a small garage and Vernon said to the elderly attendant, "Forty gallons, please." Many small filling stations at that time were not equipped with electric pumps that effortlessly fill your tank at great speed. Back then the old guy had to crank a handle. Each gallon was cranked up into a glass bowl, and released into your tank. We were there for some time. I remember the old man got so exhausted Big Sid jumped out and had to help him crank the handle."

Vernon has always had an interest in vintage vehicles and the prospect of the Daimler ambulance pressed into service as the official conveyance for the Bonzos appealed to his sense of the unconventional. There were other advantages which on occasion presented themselves. Being waved to the front of the queue when in a traffic holdup was one. He delighted in recalling the occasion when having been signaled to the front of a traffic jam the policeman

42

realising his mistake asked, 'Do you intend keeping this vehicle on the road in it's original livery? Vernon asked 'Why is it illegal? The policeman smiled and replied, 'No, so bugger off!'

"The Daimler ambulance had been designed for the new National Health Service, and supplied to London and Surrey County Councils. It weighed in at just under three tons empty. It was very large, and had a polished marble concrete floor which curved up to the side walls. The interior could be hosed out when more drastic valeting was desirable. The weight gave it a wonderfully smooth ride. There were of course no seats in the rear. We collected an assortment of sofas and arm chairs which were fortunately readily available from skips as we progressed. The sporting activities engaged in during long hours of travel stressed to destruction all but the stoutest furniture so we were constantly on the lookout for replacements. In the early days there were nine of us which was a squeeze, but eventually when there were seven it was easy to fit in. Three or sometimes four could sit across the front, because it was a very wide vehicle. I had control and so if the guys didn't behave very nicely, and I felt inclined to liven things up a little, I could dab my foot on the brake, and because the seating in the back was not secured in any way they would all slide on the marble floor and crunch up against the partition. As you can well imagine, the language on these occasions was extraordinarily interesting."

"We all travelled in an old Daimler ambulance, a wonderful old vehicle with a concrete floor that Vernon acquired."
SAM SPOONS

The desire to entertain was not restricted to the on-stage antics as Vernon remembers. "Legs" Larry always insisted on sitting in the front of the ambulance where he could orchestrate 'frights' to disturb the people in the back. He would suddenly shout out, 'Oh my God no! We're going to hit it!' Standing up he would throw his hands up to hold on to the bulkhead above. This would obscure the view for the guys in the back as forward vision was restricted to a narrow opening. This procedure in one form or another Legs Larry perfected for maximum effect. He usually chose a moment when we were about to negotiate a tight bend, a halt sign, or a hump back bridge when the seating in the back was probably already independently on the move. It was rather like an extended fairground ride with the advantage of no expense involved. Viv was reminded of his roustabout days in Southend. He enjoyed the displeasure and terror of his companions, but hated not being in control of the nightmare. Larry and I came in for a lot of stick!

43

After a series of appeals from Vivian, "Legs" Larry Smith finally joined the band in 1965 on tuba, and subsequently his tap dancing became a great hit with the Tiger's Head crowds. Following Sam Spoons exit "Legs" Larry became the drummer deftly handling the role much to the surprise of Gerry Bron who was managing the band at the time.

It was really great fun. I enjoyed the whole experience. To be on the road with such a mad bunch was an entertainment in itself. Being paid for it, and making people laugh, what could be better. Unfortunately driving the boys around presented a problem. Who was to be picked up or dropped off first or last caused endless argument. The driver of course had no choice. Leaving London could be a lengthy process. At each members address I would often have to wait while some essential mission was completed. The laundry collected, arrangements for the cat to be fed, all absolutely necessary

44

commissions. For this reason the afternoon could be well advanced before we cleared north London. The first section of the M1 had just been completed, but beyond you passed through the centre of all towns. Slow but much more interesting if you had the time. Our first trip to Newcastle

involved an overnight stop in Pontifract. Back in London I would have to do a similar very circuitous drive to drop the boys off. We'd often arrive back in the early hours when the only possible means of getting home would be a taxi, not a popular option. I was keen to get home myself, so moves were made eventually to get a roadie who would be more co-operative when put upon, and didn't complain!"

It was around this time that Leon Williams finally left for good and was formally replaced by Bob Kerr on cornet. Bob had played with the Bonzos occasionally but wasn't officially drafted into the ranks until 1966. Bob recalls the suddenness of the transformation. "When we went professional we were soon travelling all over the country, and doing these big clubs up north which were great. We used to be there for a week or two weeks and it was interesting to get away from London. We didn't really have any kind of a plan though - either career wise or musically."

Neil Innes is quick to endorse Bob's comments that the Bonzos still had no plan of any description. "I don't think the Bonzos ever had a kind of career move in their heads it was just fun you know. I mean we were all pretty impecunious, no money... well, only enough money for beer or paint, but not a lot of painting got done in any event. It was kind of a fun get together kind of thing and we didn't sort of see it any further down the line. We couldn't believe that we were suddenly going up north to the cabaret clubs. We travelled in Vernon's ambulance ~ and did this week in Newcastle and South Shields. Not Newcastle one night followed by South Shields the next. This was Newcastle and South Shields on the same night! We did 40 minutes in Newcastle, then straight after the show loaded all the gear up again - including the exploding grandfather clock - everything. We just shovelled it all back into the Daimler ambulance and we went charging over to South Shields and did it all again. We couldn't believe it, but people did it back then and that week was such a success that they said, "We've got another six weeks work for you" and then another six weeks and so we never planned anything. So you see we just found ourselves doing it and reacting to it."

Despite the fact that they had now joined the ranks of the professionals, there was very little which was professional about the way the Bonzos conducted themselves especially with regard to planning a show in a structured

45

manner. Roger Ruskin Spear remembers the laconic attitude towards developing an act. "Occasionally, we'd get to a gig early and set things up – it was nice if you got there in the afternoon and set up and you had plenty of time before you did the show, we'd say, "Oh, let's run through that number," or "Let's run through this". But a lot of the numbers just sort of came naturally. Somebody would have to say, "Let's do Ali Baba's Camel", and we'd say, "What? Never heard of that." And Neil or somebody would play it, and then everyone would start putting in ideas - "Oh, I could do that on the number", or "It would be nice if we played that instrument there." And then you'd do it that night and hope it worked. When you play in a pub, you try out ideas as you go along and if it works you think, "Oh, I'll do that next time", or "That was good". I'm sure everyone thought the same thing, although we never talked about it. It was just, "Let's keep doing that number until it's right."

It's clear from Roger's recollections that the Bonzos were not particularly keen on rehearsals. For his own part Neil despairingly recalled the almost total lack of preparation of any kind. "It was incredibly difficult to get the Bonzos to rehearse. It just evolved as it went along. I suppose a show is a rehearsal in a way, except there are people there and you've got to please them - although we didn't really worry about that too much as long as we pleased ourselves. But the thing about rehearsing is where do you rehearse and what do you do? Because when you're doing things like the Bonzos it's the audience reaction that makes you think, "Oh, that was good", or "That wasn't very good", and so you'd have to revamp things. But it was usually just talked through, it was never a case of, "Let's go and get a big studio and go and rehearse this number until we get it right". There was never any of that."

Rodney Slater is very much in accord with Roger and Neil on the subject of rehearsals. For Rodney, a great deal of the success of the band lay in the innate ability of the players and Vivian in particular to improvise brilliantly. Things had to change however when the band came under the stern glare of t'committee in the working men's clubs which imposed a new set of disciplines on the band which ultimately were to have a hugely beneficial impact. "There was an awful lot of improvisation but when we got into the northern clubs and proper theatre", remembers Rodney, "then we had to learn a whole new trade. You had to be able to keep the spontaneity and the absurdity within the rules, really, or you weren't going to get put on. You couldn't be too crazy. And really it's just about communicating. If you go too far over the top you'll lose, people won't understand you. You've got to stay within what can be accepted, whatever level you're at and wherever you are. There are always rules. If you go beyond them it may

backfire on you, i.e., you won't get employed… so what's the point? So we learnt pretty quickly and also it helped our show to actually put things in a presentable way."

There certainly was a degree of conformity but it is important that the reader does not get the impression that the Bonzos were ever polished in their approach to their act as Neil Innes was quick to stress. "Art students are, by nature, strangers to work and so once we'd worked out more or less the basics of what we did, we never went there again in any kind of formal way. It would be people sort of thinking of something and then surprising the others. Roger was particularly good at coming up with things, which were never announced. You'd be playing and thinking, "What on earth have you got now?" Or on other occasions I'd do something maybe Viv didn't expect, and he'd certainly do things that we didn't expect, and basically the rule was, if it got a laugh it stayed in. If you're with a bunch of people who are having a giggle in the same kind of prankster way, then something's going to bubble out of it."

It was not all fun and games for the Bonzos and the strain soon began to tell as "Legs" Larry Smith recalled. "We were playing night after night and at that time we didn't have any roadies, - we couldn't afford the roadies, - it was just insane. We'd do a show in Manchester, pile into the back of the ambulance, drive across Saddleworth Moors and jump into Yorkshire and do another gig. We'd be constantly packing it up again, going off to wherever it was, unloading it, doing the gig and packing… my hands were like kippers."

THE NORTHERN CLUBS

The rigours of life on the road were not made any easier by the Thirties fashion the Bonzos had adopted. As Vernon recalls, "We initially had the Thirties look with stiff starched collars. No slovenly casual dress for us. In those days before the domestic washing machine the steam laundry was easy to locate in each city centre. It was a first port of call when we arrived in town. Our attire required the professional attention desired by the fastidious gent. Collars in particular would be starched stiff and burnished with a beautiful sheen. Often though, two shows would be their limit, and so it was necessary to carry a substantial supply. This boring

47

duty did not preclude the opportunity for good practical jokes. The reception area of one laundry which we regularly used on our travels was rather grand, and featured a large goldfish pond. The raised edge made a good seat, and it was well stocked with fish. On our next visit whilst we were chatting to the young ladies behind the counter, Viv and Rodney sat on the edge of the pool, and plunging their hands into the water produced long slivers of carrot which wriggled in a very convincing way as they held them aloft, and with head held back devoured the morsels with obvious satisfaction. Their attention then returned to the water and after further plunging and splashing, more prey were caught and consumed. Finally one of the young ladies, alerted by the splashing, and despite our attempts to move into her line of vision to extend the performance, cried, "Ee! They're eating t'goldfish!" Her companion alerted, discontinued serving, and hurried off exclaiming "I'll get t'manager!" Explanations were not convincing, and further custom declined. Unfortunately the alternative laundry was at some distance."

Bizarre incidents like the carrot/goldfish stunt seemed to have been commonplace and Vernon still delights in describing the sight of Viv and Larry being chased out of a Chinese restaurant by a meat clever wielding restaurateur following yet another prank gone wrong.

"Our days in the northern clubs certainly felt like a different world. The variety, and absurd nature of some of the acts we worked with ranged from animal acts to genuine Hollywood icons," as Larry remembers. "During one of our tours the manager from a nearby club asked if the guys would like to come and see the Jane Mansfield Show. She was still a Hollywood big time glamour star. Her cabaret act consisted of a series of tableau's designed to show off her feminine allure. During one of these, Jane would step down from the stage and move around the tables singing a thwarted love song. She would sit on men's knees, muss up their hair, and press their faces between her ample bosoms. There was much ow and ah'ing and heavy breathing. For some, envy and disappointment at not being chosen, or embarrassment that they had. We had been invited and given tables at the front because as Show Biz professionals it was assumed we would be gentlemen and not take liberties with the lady when she availed us of her charms. It was quite an experience I can tell you."

There was a bewildering variety of acts on the north country circuit, as Larry recalls. "It was a very bizarre experience. Some of the people that were on the shows were just outrageous. Johnnie and Lynne doing her bird impressions or singing from The Merry Widow. A conjurer crossed with a ventriloquist, a singing strong man who did magic tricks, a comedian who did origami on a monocycle, singers on a high wire.

The sleeve for the "Gorilla" album was never destined to become a major design classic and was a disappointing effort by comparison to the groundbreaking music contained on the album.

And then some faggot tap dancing, called `Legs' Larry Smith. All overseen by t'committee who were like gods in that world. These guys took a liking to our act so we had a great time. It really was a great time. Great evenings. Wonderful girls. And we would drink pints of Special Brew, it was not on draught I seem to remember. Lethal, monstrous stuff, we'd just get them to open a couple in a pint pot. That was the life!"

It was not just the acts who were eccentric, there were also lots of colourful characters behind the scenes. Sam Spoons recalls, "Joe Pullen was a club owner, he always used to amuse us. I can remember him saying, "Ee boys, you're good box office now but don't go putting your prices up. A lot of bands

49

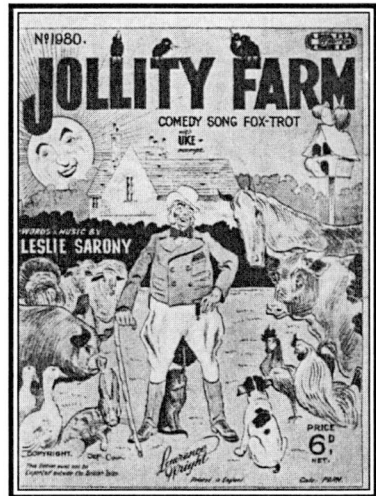

make that mistake. I'll tell you what I'll do, if you keep your price the same I'll do your laundry for you for free..." This was a concession which he thought might appeal to us, and could save him money as he owned a number of laundries. Joe Pullen was an amusing character, he was always very proud of the fact that Shirley Bassey had appeared in his club. I can still hear him saying "If it's good enough for Shirley Bassey, it's good enough for you lads". On one return visit to the club we arrived on Sunday afternoon to set up as usual. On entering we were almost overcome by the most awful stench. Joe was sitting several rows back from the front of the stage watching some of the other acts who were on the bill that week. He came over to greet us with a smile. "What in heavens name is the awful smell we asked?" "I ad't performing lions on stage here all last week. Bloody great it were. T'smell will soon go when club is full of people! They'll never notice it when you lads go on."

Bob Kerr was another of the Bonzos who was impressed by the scale and professionalism of the northern clubs. "The clubs were amazing. They were not at all what we expected. They were often huge places with big stages and excellent lighting. They were open till two in the morning. I suppose that was because they were clubs rather than pubs, everybody went there for the entertainment. They were packed, we would do a week or sometimes two weeks at a time. We used to stay in Show Biz digs in those days. The people who ran them were very nice people who loved having theatricals to stay. They did their best to provide for our unusual working hours. Breakfast was at midday. The dining room often kept shrouded in heavy curtains. Vernon attempted to draw the curtains on one occasion to the startled chorus, "The light the light! Oh the light! from a troop of dancing girls taking breakfast in their exotic negligées, and wished to draw attention to their feminine very delicate constitutions. We lived in a twilight world. Towards the end of one week we thought we'd reciprocate the hospitality to an elderly couple we'd been living with. We said, "Oh, you must come to the show as our guests." "Oh I'd love to come, but it's my husband." "Oh, he can come as well" we said. "No, he just won't come. He doesn't approve of dog acts." They must have thought we kept dogs in the ambulance."

The Swinging Sixties may have been in full swing in London, but some

The page submitted by Vivian for the booklet accompanying the release of "Gorilla". The cluttered interior of the room could almost be a metaphor for Vivian's mind overflowing with ideas for poetry, songs and works of art all vying for attention and their own place in the sun. In contrast to the bright breezy music of "Gorilla" the intense solemn face of the artist surrounded by a myriad of ideas both realised and unrealised hints at the tensions under the surface.

landladies were not so free and easy as Vernon remembers with amusement. On one tour to the north, Vernon, who had recently married, decided to take his wife along. "No unmarried women in the digs was a cast iron rule with some landladies. I had stopped doing the roadying and was driving just the two of us around. I'd arrived early at the showbiz digs that we thought we would stay in. We walked up the path to the door, and out came Mrs Ackroyd who said, "Oh hello love, are you one of the theatricals?" "Oh yes," I said, "I'm with the Bonzo Dogs". At this point I could sense a change in her attitude and noticed she was looking over my shoulder at my wife, who was slightly behind me. "And who's the fancy trollope with you then?" And before I had time to explain she launched straight into "I don't have any of that kind of thing going on in my house", so I had to explain to her that it definitely was my wife and that we had booked accommodation. I only take in men she

insisted. "Try next door." She said, "My neighbour's not so fussy.

Her neighbour was an amazing lady whose consuming interest was bull fighting. We had very fine accommodation but the décor was of southern Spain. All the rooms were decorated with artifacts and memorabilia from the bull ring, posters and pictures of famous matadors. It was like being in a bar next to the bull ring in Madrid. She kept her black hair swept up on to the back of her head behind a large tortoiseshell comb. When she swept into the dining room to serve you at meal times you felt she might snap her fingers, stamp her heels, and burst into a flamenco routine. Conversation inevitably returned to the beauty of the bull fight, and how soon she would have saved enough money for her to make a return visit. She was one of the extraordinary and unusual people we lived and worked with on tour that made life such fun.

The big working men's clubs were no less extraordinary. Two very famous one's we played were Batley and Greaseborough. I mean they could have Frank Sinatra over for a one night stand. It's quite amazing, and yes, it was quite an experience for us. It was a different world, really."

Roger Ruskin Spear also recognised some of the down sides of playing the clubs which demanded a deal more concentration. "It got even more difficult as the electronic instruments began to appear and we had to start plugging things in. In the early days it was easy, the chaotic feel was always there, initially it was a vintage vaudeville band that wore funny masks, hit each other with rubber clubs, and mucked around. That was fine, it was okay, seven blokes sitting there with an acoustic piano. It didn't matter if anyone stopped playing it was all bang, wallop, crash. Up north in Reg Tracey land of the clubs it had to be more controlled, and it was also very, very hard work. Unfortunately certain members of the band just couldn't hack it. Sid soon got fed up and left. Then Lenny left the band too."

Of course there was other work for the Bonzos beyond the clubs. In the south of England the band continued it's double life as the darlings of the college circuit. Surprisingly the act varied little between the two as Larry explains. "At the same time as playing the clubs we were also doing universities. We didn't particularly change our show, either. We didn't start to quote from Plato or

Vernon Dudley Bohay-Nowell: Bass guitar, banjo, baritone sax, bass sax, nightingale

The artwork produced by Vernon Dudley Bowhay Nowell for the Gorilla album. This is a particularly fine example of how adept the band members were at capturing and parodying the graphical styles which were then in vogue. Some forty years later Vernon reprised the style of his "Gorilla" contribution for the booklet which accompanied the release of "Pour L'Amour Des Chiens." See page xi of the colour section.

Greek philosophy, or intellectualise what we were doing for the university circuit. We just did the same wild bloody show. We had a structure to the show, but within that structure we just sort of did what we wanted, and literally there were times when we just couldn't play for laughing. We just had such a hoot on stage. I remember one evening, Sam came on with these silly red blocks, he'd have one clipped on, and he'd pretend to be juggling them ...anyway, he came out and he had a notice pinned to his shirt saying `We have been paid off', which means we've had the sack – that was the way the northern clubs put it - didn't matter

53

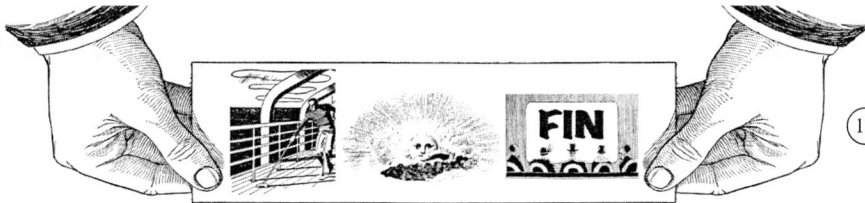

who the hell you were, if committee didn't like it, bugger off and you'd get given your money and thrown out the place. We hadn't really been sacked, but for some reason it just killed us, it was so funny. The wicked alcohol must have helped. Special Brew is filthy stuff. After the club and all't punters had gone 'ome the managers would sort of say, "Right lads, let's have a drink now", and the adrenaline was still coursing so you'd drink on another two or three hours. Every night you could be getting back pickled at three or four o'clock. It could turn you into a raving loony!"

Some northern clubs had a reputation for being rough and ready, but there were occasions when the band witnessed outbreaks of mass brawling at student gigs. Bob Kerr in particular has reason to remember the night in which an unruly mob precipitated his first sacking from the band. "We had a job one Saturday night, an Art School Ball in High Wycombe. It was in a fine old building, a Corn Exchange I think. We arrived early and set up our instruments and props, then made our way to the bar which was in a large room below the hall. The beer barrels were racked up behind the bar, and two old boys were serving rather slowly. We had been served and moved back to watch the pretty young things in their party dresses gathering there. Suddenly a party of rough Hells Angels poured into the bar. The slow service was obviously a target for their immediate attention. Three of them leapt over the bar and turning on the beer taps, proceeded to fill pint glasses, and hand them out. The barmen's remonstrations were ignored so they left to find help.

We hurried up to the backstage as we were concerned for the safety of our gear. It was at this point that Reg Tracy appeared. We could hear shouting and running about out front of the curtain. "Play!" shouted Reg, "I'm opening the curtain, it will calm them down!" We started playing a strident 'Rule Britannia'. Missiles hit the curtains as Reg wound them back. A couple of the Hells Angels launched themselves at the stage shouting "We can play!" As they scrambled to climb on stage I grabbed the nearest suitable object to ward them off which happened to be one of a pair of large empty barrels which decorated each end of the stage. I hurled it down knocking them off the stage. Things happened quickly at this point. Police poured in at the back of the hall, the Hells Angels made off through the Emergency Exits. Students lingered bewildered, Reg closed the curtains. The Ball was over. We packed our things back into the ambulance ready to travel on for our next engagement in Birmingham. A postmortem was held of the evening's events in the ambulance. Reg was furious with me. "Your actions were most unprofessional," he said. "You're fired for throwing that barrel at the audience, and not playing when instructed!" Anyway we had a great guy called Big Sid,

54

who was a banjo player in the band at the time, and he said, "Well, if he's going then I'm going," and Vernon said the same thing, so Reg had to retract it. So I was fired, but then I carried on in the band."

Carrying on in the band meant that Bob would at least record some vinyl with the Bonzos. Reg Tracey had concluded a deal with Parlophone which encompassed the first two singles recorded and released by the Bonzos. It's a rare thing in the music business for a manager to command lasting respect from his charges but Reg seems to have managed the trick as Sam recalls warmly, "I liked Reg. He got things done. As well as clubs we were playing universities - on a pretty regular basis - and he got us a recording contract and we were in the studios and in all sorts of publicity shoots."

April 1966 saw the release of the band's very first single, "My Brother Makes The Noises For The Talkies" on Parlophone and Roger Ruskin Spear too is quick to pay tribute to Reg Tracey for landing the deal. "Mind you, Reg got us into Abbey Road. He got us into Parlophone because he knew the people on the label and we followed the same route that the Temperance Seven had gone down and, of course, the Alberts. So we were following their recording route and we eventually did a couple of singles, which were "My Brother Makes The Noises For The Talkies" and "Alley Oop"."

Reg Tracey really had pulled off quite an impressive coup, which raised his own reputation in the eyes of the group. In 1966 The Beatles were at the peak of their fame, they were the royalty of the pop world and their name was currency throughout British society. The mere fact that they were recording in the same studio as the Beatles had used, and in fact were still using for the 'Revolver' album, was a source of huge interest. Even Roger Ruskin Spear who was not greatly enamoured of the pop world was impressed by the Beatles connection. "It was really impressive at the time because we were actually in the big studio you know where they recorded 'Sergeant Pepper', and thanks to Reg we did our first track there, "My Brother Makes The Noises For The Talkies", which is a bit of a contrast when you think about it!"

Despite its great sense of fun the Bonzos first single failed to chart. It is a great shame that a quintessential piece of British nonsense as "My Brother Makes The Noises For The Talkies", was allowed to wither on the vine. The "B" side of the first single, "I'm Going To Bring A Watermelon To My Gal Tonight", was a fun slice of innuendo from the Twenties, which completed a highly creditable first attempt at recording. As Vivian Stanshall much later recalled, "I don't know how it came about. I do remember going into the bigger of the Abbey Road studios and knocking out half a dozen tracks in three hours, which didn't surprise me in the slightest. I think they were all mixed and done the same afternoon. Not really chart-toppers were they? I heard them maybe six months ago and I didn't find them too embarrassing. Roger does a divine balls-up on 'Bring A

The Bonzos in a performance of "Look Out There's A Monster Coming" for the Do Not Adjust Your Set series. This was the vehicle for Vivian's satirical attack on the Black and White Minstrel show.

Watermelon To My Gal Tonight'. Starts off in the wrong key and saves himself brilliantly."

BOB DEPARTS

One Bonzo stalwart who did not stay long enough to record their first album was Bob Kerr. The popular myth is that Bob was poached from the ranks of the Bonzos by Geoff Stevens to front the New Vaudeville Band. This is something that Bob strongly denies. "I definitely wasn't poached. I left the Bonzos long before I heard of The New Vaudeville Band." In any event in late 1966 Bob did indeed accept an offer from producer Geoff Stevens to front the New Vaudeville Band, a group that was thrown together to promote the success of "Winchester Cathedral", a single that had been recorded by a group of session men and which had amazingly crashed the British Top Ten rising to number four. Even more incredibly this slight number had gone to number one in the States. Stevens now urgently required a real group to fulfill television appearances and some live dates. He is reputed by many to have tried to lift the entire Bonzos lock stock and barrel to be his new equivalent of The Monkees. After all the New Vaudeville Band's sound was remarkably close to the Bonzos so the idea certainly made sense from Stevens' point of view. Fortunately the idea was not acceptable to the remaining Bonzos.

As history records, the only Bonzo who took up the Geoff Stevens shilling was Bob Kerr. To be fair to Bob, the trumpeter had been the subject of a great deal of bullying by Vivian Stanshall who openly despised Bob partly on the grounds of what Vivian perceived to be his limited academic background and his apparent lack of artistic aspirations. Vernon Dudley Bowhay-Nowell confirms this fact and goes as far as to describe Vivian as a "terrible snob" who looked down upon people who were without the benefit of a tertiary education. In the end, Vivian began to refer to Bob as "the little pig" and Bob was finally driven from the band by Vivian's taunts and overt rudeness, which were both unnecessary and unfounded.

Despite the success of the Bonzos live performances and being one of the best paid bands without a hit single, there was a level of frustration and disappointment when they saw Bob Kerr with The New Vaudeville Band performing on BBC television on "Top Of The

Pops". What annoyed them the most was the look of the newly-formed band on television, as Neil Innes recalled, "The next thing we see is, on Top of the Pops, the New Vaudeville Band, looking exactly like the Bonzos with their suits and shoes and the cut-out speaking balloons: - "Wow! I'm really expressing myself!", and all this. The singer was in the lamé suit, and of course, it was the image of Vivian. Viv and "Legs" Larry Smith were the most outraged of the Bonzos because it was their idea that this Thirties stuff should be the look of the band. Most of us were never that interested in how we looked and couldn't actually give a toss, you know, what we looked like. Viv and Larry never forgave him for that. Partly because people kept saying, "hey, you're just like the New Vaudeville Band'!"

It has to be said however, that there was some poetic justice at work in all of this, as many of the hallmarks of the Bonzo set had been lifted straight from the Alberts who in turn drew on Spike Jones

"It was the first time Vivian had ever played a trumpet and he got got rather attached to it, much to everyone's mortification."

NEIL INNES

and his city slickers. However the gold lamé suit was pure Viv and he and "Legs" Larry Smith in particular felt that Bob Kerr had done a great disservice to the Bonzos by facilitating the emergence of their first direct competition.

Vivian Stanshall's anger grew ever stronger as the New Vaudeville Band continued to climb the charts and their fame, for a while at least, eclipsed the Bonzos. Not to be outdone, Vivian and "Legs" Larry Smith also took a juvenile form of visual revenge on Bob Kerr by incorporating into the "Gorilla" sleeve a picture of the top of Bob's head superimposed over a female crotch. In less dramatic fashion, inside the booklet on the Sam Spoons page, Sam is seen writing out various phrases quite visible among them is the phrase, "I Will Not Speak To The Vaudevilles!"

Eventually the others lost interest and the war against the Vaudevilles subsided into a humourous exchange of notes, which would be left with bemused club managers who had instructions to pass to them on to Vaudevilles who, on arriving at the club for their next gig, would be handed a note explaining "how to play the cymbals". Vivian Stanshall however

57

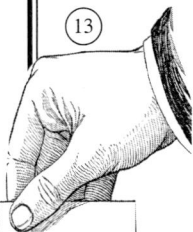

kept up the sniping long after everyone else had forgotten all about it and his last shots can be heard on the BBC recording of "The Craig Torso Show", in which the inept house band led by an appalling trumpet player are known as Bob Bent And The Boys.

After the Bonzos, Bob Kerr enjoyed only a nine month stint in the New Vaudeville Band who were managed by future Led Zeppelin manager, the infamous Peter Grant. Asking Peter Grant for a raise proved to be the undoing of Bob and he was soon ejected from The New Vaudeville Band. Having lost two great gigs in succession Bob realised that the only way forward was to have his own unit. In 1968 Bob formed Bob Kerr's Whoopee Band, which is still going strong today. The Whoopee Band has toured in the USA, Norway, Sweden, Denmark, Germany, Holland, Poland and Switzerland. The Whoopee Band also featured Vernon Dudley Bowhay-Nowell and Sam Spoons who joined the band after the unamicable split in the wake of "Gorilla".

Vivian Stanshall's obsession with the New Vaudevilles was to have a lasting effect on the Bonzo sound and seems to have been a major contributing factor behind the switch from jazz to rock, which ensured that the Bonzos would strive for the musical progression that would first show itself on "Gorilla".

ALLEY OOP

The band's second single was released on Parlophone in October, which was a version of "Alley Oop", with one of their old favourites, "Button Up Your Overcoat" on the B-side. "Alley Oop" had already been a hit in the UK in 1960 for the American band, The Hollywood Argyles, reaching number 24, and the Bonzos version was definitely a lack lustre affair, which relied upon Vivian rendering the original American song in a very mannered English accent. It was a slim joke to start with and it was no great surprise when that too failed to chart. Sam Spoons throws some light on this puzzling choice. "It was something that Larry and Viv were really keen to do and as no-one else had any strong views that became the second single." The reviews, although small and with the title miss-spelt both times, were reasonably positive. With a 3-star rating, and calling it "Allez Oop", the Record Mirror stated: "A novelty... but you really have to see this group to get the full message. Might just click and certainly amusing. Flip swings, trad-wise." Disc & Music Echo printed a much shorter review, which simply stated that the "Bonzo Dog Doo-Dah Band have never really been up my street. They do 'Aleez Oop' all right but I still prefer the original."

"Alley Oop" really was a surprising choice as a single, as included in the Bonzo's repertoire at that point were a host of more

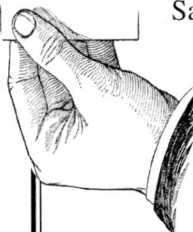

58

suitable numbers including many of the songs, which would later end up on 'Gorilla' plus a dazzling array of jazz standards and comic songs including originals and cover versions of "Tiger Rag", "Goodbye Dolly Grey", "When Yuba Played The Rumba On The Tuba Down In Cuba", "I'm Glad That I'm Bugs Bunny", "Crying In The Chapel", "Falling In Love Again", "The Craig Torso Show", "The Laughing Blues", "A Room With A View", "High School Hermit" and "Love Is A Cylindrical Piano", the last of which was later performed by the Bonzos on the Do Not Adjust Your Set television series.

Despite the lack of single success the Bonzo Dog Doo-Dah Band continued to get regular gigs following their success with the Northern clubs. "You'd do 45 minutes or whatever's required and then you drive 14 miles and do it again. We did it in the end for a whole year with no roadies, no nothing, and funnily enough they liked it." So recalled Vivian Stanshall but it was not as easy as the art school gigs where they had started. "Those places like Guisborough were terrifying. Clubs with racks and racks of people drinking Exhibition Ale who'd say, 'come on, make us laugh'." But make them laugh they did. "Ere, you lads. Come back. You're bloody marvellous like," as the manager of the Dolce Vita in Stockton declared in typical fashion, despite his misgivings about the bunch of ex-art students before their audience-winning performance.

Inevitably the blame for the Bonzos failure to conquer the world of recorded music overnight was laid on the shoulders of the long suffering Reg Tracey, which Sam Spoons in particular thought was a bit unfair to say the least. "I don't know how Reg could have worked it any quicker. But he never sounded quite right, he was too flat, too normal. He was never seen to be 'with it', so Viv decided he was not the one for us and I always thought this was desperately unfair."

Sam Spoons may have disagreed but the casting vote in the Bonzos now lay increasingly with the forceful figure of Vivian Stanshall and Reg Tracey's days were numbered. But it was to prove a costly withdrawal from the contract, which all of the Bonzos had signed as Sam later recalled. "I thought he was a very straight geezer. I didn't like the way we got rid of him. It actually ended up costing us and he probably deserved it. Anyway, it was then that Gerry Bron came along, and he was the right man to take us on to the next stage."

ENTER GERRY BRON

Roger Ruskin Spear was also aware of the legal difficulties that were presented by the putative move to the Gerry Bron agency. He too had a great deal of sympathy for his former manager and recalled the contractual mess, which inevitably followed. "Jack Bruce was in a band, which was signed to the Gerry Bron agency and Jack said, 'He'll be better'. But, of

course, we couldn't get out of Reg, so it was all argy bargy, and we ended up with Gerry Bron, and Reg had to get royalties for two or three years."

Gerry Bron picked up on the Bonzos thanks to the rock music grapevine and reports of established musicians who were impressed by this exciting new arrival on the live music scene. Gerry Bron's recollection accords with Roger Ruskin Spear's that Jack Bruce was the link to the Bron agency. "Well, I first got to know about the Bonzos because Jack Bruce was playing with Manfred Mann at that time and he said, "They're a fantastic band. You have to go and see them and they're looking for management." So I went up to Manchester, saw them in one of these working men's clubs, thought they were fantastic and went up to talk to Vivian. He said, "What did you think?" And I said, "I think you're absolutely fantastic!" He said, "No, what did you really think?" So that was my first meeting with Vivian Stanshall and I think that after that, nothing actually ever changed. I don't think he ever believed a word I said. But they were the funniest thing I've ever seen and I don't think they've ever been replaced. They weren't brilliantly musical, there was just nothing like them. The jokes that they had onstage were sensational; - absolutely fantastic. Today I wish I could go back in time to see the original Bonzos."

Gerry Bron was clearly won over by the artistry of the Bonzos, but he had underestimated the amount of effort, which would be required to manage this disparate bunch of lunatics and their odd leader. "Everything I ever did with the Bonzos was fraught with problems. They told me that their manager, Reg Tracey, was fed up with them and didn't want to manage them anymore, and like an idiot, I phoned up Reg Tracey and said, "I hear you don't want to manage the Bonzos anymore and I would be very interested in taking them over." And he hit the roof and said, "Where did you get this idea from?" And I said, "Well, they've just told me that." He said, "No, absolutely not!" There was a lot of acrimony but in the end we sorted out a deal."

The Reg Tracey contract, which had posed so many problems was just the first of many issues, which would require attention from Gerry Bron. The next issue was the disastrous recording contract that the band had signed with EMI's Parlophone label. "Then they also had a recording contract with EMI, which wasn't great and they came in to talk to me and I said, "Well, if we're going to get a new record deal we'd better sort out EMI." And they said, "Well, why?" And I said, "Well, you've obviously signed a recording contract with EMI." They all looked at me and said, "No, we've never signed a recording contract." I said, "Come on, EMI don't put records out without a recording contract." They said, "Well, we never signed a

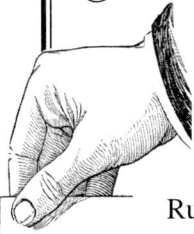

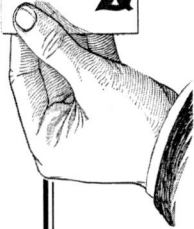

recording contract." So I pick up the phone and talk to Business Affairs and say, "I'm talking to a band called the Bonzo Dog Doo-Dah Band and they tell me they've never signed a contract with you." And there's a very frosty sort of response at the other end and they said, "Oh really. We'd like to send you a copy of the contract." So the contract arrives - and all seven have signed it! That's the sort of lunacy you were dealing with. Anyway that wasn't the real problem because that was only for two singles. But making records with them was not easy at all. There was only one person in the band that really played an instrument, Neil Innes. Rodney Slater was good too, the rest of them just pretended."

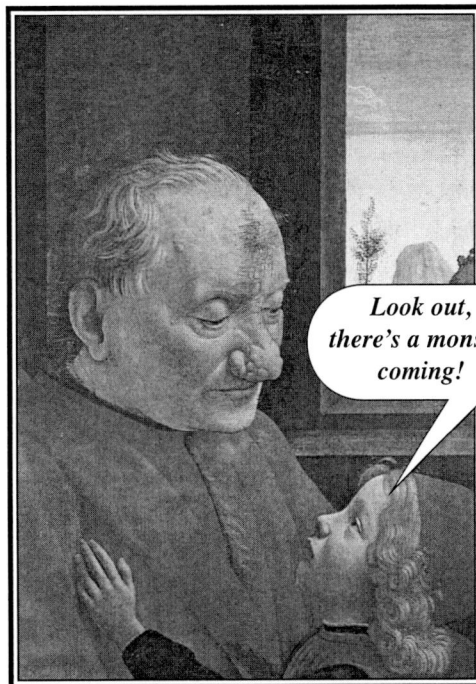

Look out, there's a monster coming!

The musicianship may not have been of the highest order but the Bonzos were never about virtuosity. What mattered to a large and increasingly fervent following was the ability to blend visual comedy with music and the obvious medium for the band was television. Rodney Slater takes up the story. "I mean we had this dreadful trio of trumpets. We thought we'd save great amounts of money on session men. None of us were very good, Grade III at the most was what we'd have got away with, – but things like that they work, – after about fifteen takes you sort of get it right!"

Fortunately for the Bonzos, Gerry Bron had the requisite connections and was able to take the band to the next level as Roger Ruskin Spear remembers. "Gerry came in to run the band and he certainly did the job, then it probably became a band as we know it now. The TV appearances on "Do Not Adjust Your Set" all came about really through the Bron agency and the later things, the "Urban Spaceman", which I think got us to Number 4, but that's about it."

Gerry Bron instantly recognised the unique potential in Vivian Stanshall as a front man. He was also impressed by the Bonzos ability to busk their way through just about any situation that was thrown at them. "I remember they once played University College in Holborn and they had all these big lights and whatever, and the PA system going. They were drawing so much power they blew the fuses so it all went dark and Vivian comes up to the front of the stage and tells a story, everyone laughs, tells another story, everybody laughs. They keep going,

61

they get the power back on again and they finish off the set. And I went round to the promoter and said, "I'm really sorry". He said, "what about?" I said, "Well, the breakdown of power." He said, "Oh, I thought that was part of the act" So nobody ever really knew what was going on."

The live work was providing an unspectacular but steady income but Gerry Bron knew that if the band was to reach its full potential they had to become recording stars. The first priority for Gerry Bron was to get the band into a recording studio. With this in mind Gerry organised the demos, which would eventually get the band to sign to Liberty Records, who would subsequently release the first Bonzo album, the legendary "Gorilla". Getting the band signed was to prove no easy task even for a skilled operator such as Gerry Bron, as Gerry himself later recalled. "On stage they were fine. They could be playing the banjo or whatever and getting a reasonable approximation of some kind of musical competence. It looked like they were playing brilliantly as they went so fast, but they weren't really playing well in musical terms. We couldn't get a record deal at that stage, so I took them into a studio and I said, "Okay, what we're going to do is we'll make three demos of the best songs that you're doing on stage at the moment and we'll take that round to the record companies." So we start off on song number one, get to the chorus and Vernon Dudley Bowhay-Nowell's playing the banjo and playing completely the wrong chords. So I stop them and I go in and I say, "Vernon, you're not playing the right chords in the chorus." He said, "I know, old boy, they won't tell me what they are." And that's the way they operated so you were up against it. Every single thing you did was a problem, musically. On stage they did a lot of improvising, so they got away with a great deal, but they really weren't very good at making records and it wasn't the sort of music, which was current. "Jollity Farm" wasn't exactly a hit parade type song so you had a number of problems. But nevertheless I finally got Liberty to sign them."

GORILLA

It didn't feel like it at the time, but "Gorilla", released in October 1967, was to prove the real turning point in the band's career. A brilliant record, the genius of which would be enough to guarantee the band lasting fame on the strength of this one marvellous recording. Forty years on it still stands the test of time as the funniest album ever produced in the UK. Rodney Slater recalls the significance of this landmark recording in the history of the band. "It was fun playing on stage. For us it was what it was all about. Up until "Gorilla", then suddenly we were working with a new

medium. It was a new challenge. I suppose it was very difficult to get the actual physicality of the stage act into recordings, so we had to go into a different area." According to Vivian's recollection for John Platt the band didn't even attempt to make the stage material translate to the recording environment. "We never did. They were treated entirely differently. I can remember it being a problem trying to transfer the other way. The number of people who asked us to play 'The Intro And The Outro', which took at least 50 overdubs so it was clearly impossible... though we did try."

Following the New Vaudeville Band episode there had been a change in musical direction, which can be clearly heard on 'Gorilla'. As Neil Innes remembered, "There was a sort of house meeting called before we recorded 'Gorilla'. I think it was "Legs" Larry Smith who said, 'Look, let's do anything. Let's do any style of music.' I mean we just loved this old Twenties and Thirties stuff but clearly we'd been outmanoeuvred. We were now getting on in show business suddenly, when the whole act had been lifted by someone else. We then decided to expand our style… 1950's rock and roll, flower-power, anything went… and start writing our own stuff. 'Gorilla' was a kind of benchmark album, because I think it was the first time we'd actually written our own stuff. We ended up writing our own stuff because of The New Vaudeville Band."

As Neil Innes stated, "Gorilla" was a sea change because the band had hitherto relied primarily on other writer's material and it was now that the song writing partnership of Neil Innes and Vivian Stanshall began to flourish. Rodney Slater quite rightly recognised this as a defining moment for the Bonzos. "This is where the writing really emerges. Neil and Viv just come into another dimension on "Gorilla". Viv had never stopped writing things ever since I first knew him, but suddenly there was this blossoming. It came out, just flowed out of him and he never stopped then for the rest of his life really. Likewise Neil went on writing Neil songs, which were as different as chalk and cheese from Viv's songs. They're totally different people but together they produced absolutely brilliant work."

In their own way Vivian Stanshall and Neil Innes were a great songwriting partnership in the mould of Lennon and McCartney. Rodney Slater is quick to pay tribute to the many skills which Neil brought to the band. "A lot of Viv's songs wouldn't have made it without Neil being there to write down the notes and give it some kind of format. That is a major contribution. And Neil was very quick at organising people like us who were just a great chaotic bunch really, to begin with. He could actually get some musical order into things very quickly whereas the rest of us would split hairs for bloody ages. So he did have an ear, which kind of resided outside the band, to things that might have opened up

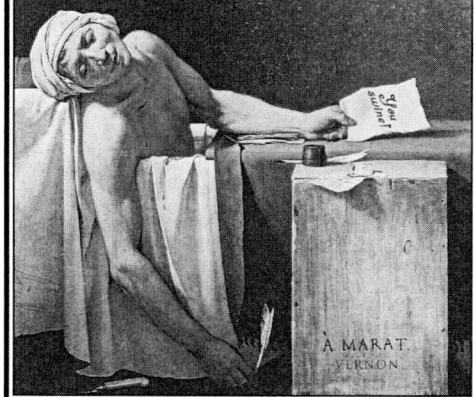

something else."

Vivian Stanshall was blossoming as one of the finest wordsmiths in popular music and Neil Innes could write great melodies with some very strong lyrics of his own. "The Equestrian Statue" was one such gem from Neil, which still delights today. Unfortunately all was not well in the Bonzo camp, Vernon Dudley Bowhay-Nowell was ill in the period leading up to the recording of "Gorilla" and a replacement bassist for much of the sessions had to be recruited by Gerry Bron. He arrived in the shape of Dave Clague, who contributed to the recording of many of the tracks on "Gorilla", including "Equestrian Statue", "Look Out There's A Monster Coming", "The Intro & The Outro" and "Piggy Bank Love". Dave also filled in for some of the early "Do Not Adjust Your Set" episodes.

By now Vivian Stanshall had got bored with Vernon Dudley Bowhay-Nowell, who he felt was rather too old school for the new forward looking world of the Bonzos. Shortly after the release of the album in December 1967, it was announced that Vernon was no longer part of the band. Vernon naturally took this rebuff rather hard. "I thought it was jolly unfair to fire me. I'd worked hard at it for four years and I was very upset about it at the time. I'd been stabbed in the back." The news didn't come as a complete surprise for Vernon. "I had of course the feeling that we were increasingly the backing band for Vivian as opposed to being equal partners in the project. It was quite disgraceful in many respects especially after all I'd done like buying the ambulance and so forth."

The departure of Vernon Dudley Bowhay-Nowell was very much as a result of the change in musical direction created by the New Vaudeville Band episode. Neil Innes is very much of the opinion that The New Vaudeville Band episode actually worked to the Bonzos advantage as it made the band determined to widen their musical horizons. "It actually did us a favour," says Neil, "because we started writing things and looking at all sorts of music and 'Gorilla' was probably so well received because it was the first album that had things like 'I'm Bored', and I think it's got to be a classic kind of album. One of my favourite tracks is 'Jazz, Delicious Hot, Disgusting Cold' and, regrettably, it was the first

64

time Vivian had ever played a trumpet and he got rather attached to it, much to everyone's mortification. He really couldn't play the thing, but became so enthusiastic about it, that track was the best example of Viv's technique, or lack of it. It was really loud and raucous and terrible, but I love the track for that."

The Bonzos conscious decision to widen the palate on "Gorilla" resulted in a magnificent record, which has its own unique quality that would never have worked so well had the material solely drawn upon jazz standards and novelty songs as Rodney Slater later recalled. "I think there really was something magic about "Gorilla" in the sense that it was released onto the unsuspecting public and there were one or two seminal Bonzo works on that, like "Jollity Farm". And obviously "The Intro and The Outro" was a sort of new conception in many ways. The absurdity of putting those people on those instruments, in that situation, is somehow wonderful. "Big Shot" is another one I personally enjoyed very much. "Equestrian Statue" was another favourite of mine and it was really disappointing that it didn't work as a single. It certainly deserved to and was obviously inspired by the release of "Strawberry Fields" and "Penny Lane", which had that lovely piccolo trumpet solo. Roger, of course, immediately gets out his home-made trumpet and makes this frightful sound, which you have to speed up to make it sound like the brilliant brass playing that the bloke on the Beatles record was actually playing. We loved the Beatles but we couldn't resist doing that, and fortunately they loved us."

Despite the brilliance of "Gorilla" the real cross over potential was lost on Liberty Records who initially pressed a mere two thousand copies, which was never going to be enough to put the album into the charts. Drawing on the wildlife theme Liberty did splash out on a fairly lavish party at the Paul Raymond's review bar in Soho, complete with a live Camel. Unfortunately the stress of being in a busy city centre caused the Camel to lash out and kick in the sides of a Mini. Vivian Stanshall in particular was beside himself with mirth over the possibility of some poor driver having to explain to his insurance company that a Camel had kicked in the side of his vehicle in Soho Square!

Despite their efforts on the press launch, Liberty did very little to capitalise on the huge cult following that the band enjoyed, as Gerry Bron remembered. "I don't think Liberty ever realised what was there. The Bonzos

65

(16)

were a cult band with a huge following and they had a tremendous audience… deservedly. I mean they were absolutely fantastic. And whatever happened on stage they always had a way out of it. I pushed for a pressing of fifty thousand records, which time has shown they could have sold ten times over, but Liberty only did two thousand. In retrospect I think the true reason that Liberty signed them was that they had just opened their operation in England and didn't have any acts and I talked them into the fact that the Bonzos were going to make a great record, which they did, actually. I mean "Gorilla", over the period of time, sold quite well and had some terrific tracks on it so I wasn't conning them. But they weren't really destined to become a musical act that sold in huge quantities. People loved them live and their records are so zany that initially at least the public bought it just as a memento, if you like, of what happened on stage."

The New Musical Express gave the album a good review, although the reference to the New Vaudeville Band must have grated enormously on Vivian's nerves. "Some quiet satire here to make you chuckle, specially at the 30's (Leslie Sarony's 'Jollity Farm'), calypsos ('Look Out There's A Monster Coming'), trad jazz and some crazy tracks like 'Big Shot', the world of the American paper back; 'Piggy Bank Love', a skit on high-pitched beat group singing; and a tear-down of 'Sound of Music'. But best of all is the Elvis impression on the 'Death-Cab For Cutie' track. Not unlike the Vaudeville Band at times, but much greater in its scope, vocalist Vivian Stanshall proves himself a most versatile singer and with Neil Innes, the musical director and pianist, has written most of the material, which is quite a giggle. There's a 16-page booklet inside the sleeve, which is amusing, too."

Another review of "Gorilla" declared: "A knockout! An hilarious, often brilliant first album from a group that combines some marvellous send-ups with switches to jazz and some attractive new songs. It's difficult to categorise them, and tell you what to expect, because they vary so much from track to track. But it's tremendously entertaining, excellently done all the way – especially the cool mickey-take of the ballad singers on San Francisco. A great sleeve, a very catchy 'Equestrian Statue' – in fact, a winner LP from start to end. Hear it at all costs!"

In terms of changing their style, Neil Innes remembers that, "It only took a year to develop. If it got a laugh, it stayed in the act. We became the darlings of the cabaret circuit and then colleges, and were earning as much as any group with a record in the charts."

The shift in style to include more rock and pop music had its benefits and

66

With "I'm The Urban Spaceman" the Bonzos at last had the chart hit which had eluded them for the previous three years. Another Neil Innes composition, this time produced by Paul McCartney the single justly spent fourteen weeks on the UK singles charts.

meant that the Bonzos started to secure more bookings with rock venues such as the UFO Club and the Marquee in London, both of which the Bonzos played in February 1967. They also started to be booked along with pop bands and performers such as the concert with Chris Farlowe plus Dave Dee, Dozy, Beaky, Mick & Tich, at the Barnsley Civic Hall in March. They were a hit at the Marquee and played there again in May, but still continued with the Northern clubs, playing La Dolce Vita club in Newcastle that same month. In June they played at the home of The Beatles, the famous Cavern in Liverpool, along with The Scaffold and The Escorts. They then began to make regular appearances at the Marquee as Alvin Lee of the band Ten Years After remembered. "Our first gig there was an interval spot for half an hour, and we had to follow the Bonzo Dog Band. The stage was literally smothered in blue smoke from their explosions, and we had to go on and play."

Despite the good reviews, "Gorilla" did not prove to be a chart hit. Gerry Bron however used the release to get the band more publicity with an appearance on the very popular BBC television programme "Dee Time" that October and also an appearance at London's Saville Theatre supporting headliners Cream. The performance of the Bonzos at the Saville was praised by the New Musical Express. "No group can take the Saville like the Cream, but for a while it looked as if they had been miss-billed. The reason: thirty, first half minutes of Bonzo doggery. A sort of Goon Show set to music, the Bonzo Dog Doo-Dah Band was making its Saville debut appearance but soon had the audience with them, their zany humour bringing them rapturous applause. Led by the alluring Vivian Stanshall in silver lurex jacket, lime green trousers, with matching low cut tee-shirt, the seven dogs, augmented by assorted masks, dummies, exploding lights, smoke, various instruments and everything but the kitchen sink, threw the Saville crowd into hysterics. In these days of miserable attendances for pop concerts, visually as well as audibly exciting groups like the Doo-Dah Band provide just the medicine for flagging box offices. And when an audience bred on the Cream calls you back for an encore it is high praise indeed."

67

Vivian, Sam, Rodney and Roger during the recording of Do Not Adjust Your Set. Vivian is wearing his trademark gold lamé jacket while the others are uncharacteristically smart in matching white.

MUSIC FOR THE HEAD BALLET

Gerry Bron did wield considerable influence in the media world and in addition to impressive gigs with the likes of Cream he was able to persuade the highly respected Pathé news reel company to make a film of the Bonzos featuring the "Equestrian Statue", which was released as a single. Although the track was performed live on stage by the Bonzos and was featured on New Faces, in later years Vivian Stanshall in particular revised his opinion of the song harshly describing it to Brian McMullen of Ptolemaic Telescope in 1992 as "Appalling rubbish!"

"The Equestrian Statue" was released as a single in November, with "The Intro And The Outro" on the B-side, but failed to make it into the charts. It was still common practice to release a single to promote an album, and the picture sleeve version of the single released in Germany carried an advertisement for "Gorilla" on the back cover, using a gorilla face as used for King Kong. The cover also pushed the Beatles connection with: "Aus der sensationellen Beatles' Magical Mystery Tour." And the originality of the Bonzos with "The Bonzo Dog Doo-Dah Band mit ihrer ersten Lanspielplatte."

Away from the recording studio the band continued to establish their pop credentials with further gigs in November at Burton's in Uxbridge and at the Saville, this time with the Bee Gees. They also made their first radio appearance on BBC's "Top Gear" and a further television appearance, this time on "Max Bygrave's New Faces". On the show they opened with the "End Of the Show"; "The Equestrian Statue" and "Little Sir Echo" with Sam Spoons doing his ventriloquist dummy routine.

"Gorilla was certainly helping to popularise the Bonzos and Vivian Stanshall acknowledged the impact of the album. "It's amazing how much difference the LP has made, and we are doing so much work now… it is astounding. Our single is selling well although there have been some distribution problems. I think the record company are swapping over to some new steam machines or something. Audience reaction to us is really extraordinary, even from people who might have come originally to see the Bee Gees."

In the December the Bonzos actually returned to the Royal College of Art for a gig, this time with Pink Floyd and Marmalade. And they made two further radio appearances in December, with another appearance on John Peel's "Top Gear" and also BBC Radio One's "Saturday Club".

In a typically warped piece of Bonzo logic a short harpsichord driven piece entitled "Music For The Head Ballet" occupied a slice of side two of "Gorilla". The album carried no notes and there was no indication as to the exact nature of the track, which made no sense on record but on film the whole truth could finally be revealed and the Bonzos leapt at the chance of

bringing the "Head Ballet" to the big screen. Rodney Slater later recalled the events surrounding the making of the film. "Around the time of "Gorilla" we also did the thing for Pathé Pictorial. "Equestrian Statue" was an obvious choice, but I was also pleased they used the "Head Ballet". It appears on the album but the "Head Ballet" was really something which was entirely visual; you had to see it or it made no sense, it was a completely visual thing. I mean, okay, Neil wrote the music and it comes across well on "Gorilla", but it had to be seen to be understood. It was all about the observation of just how limited movement of the head is compared to the rest of the body. So imagine, as Neil did, if you wrote a ballet confined entirely to movements, which are possible using the head, it would be a pretty strange, and rather limited experience. Compared to the rest of our bodies, heads just move around a bit. Neil seized on this and we developed this static dance featuring only head movements. In the film we get into the double take and it goes wrong and it ends up with Roger, who used to have this dummy's head on the end of the line and it all goes down and drops off. That's it, that's the "Head Ballet", it's not something for a record it has to be visual."

Not all of the Bonzos enjoyed their time working on "Gorilla". Vivian Stanshall had by now emerged as de facto leader of the band and had begun to form his own views on how the band should progress and which members would be involved. He had clearly marked the cards of both Vernon Dudley Bowhay-Nowell and Sam Spoons. Inevitably Sam picked up on the unhealthy atmosphere. "I think being in the studio, that's the most boring aspect of what you do. Being in a very small, claustrophobic room somewhere, doing things again and again and again and being told you're not keeping strict enough time, or you've got to keep the tempo stricter. When you've got six people who aren't quite fully competent, you're never going to get a take where all six are happy with what they're doing. So it's pretty tedious. Nonetheless I think we were all pretty pleased with what we were doing for things like the "Gorilla " album, for instance, which is obviously the one that I relate to most because I make a contribution on most of the tracks and of course, I wasn't included on a lot of the later material."

Sam Spoons in fact was not included on any more Bonzo recordings whatsoever. The press release gave the impression that Sam might have left the band, but it is a myth he is very quick to dispel. "I didn't step out, I was pushed. I was naive. I was a country boy, I didn't understand how things worked in London. I was always very loyal to the people I associated with. I never quite understood pressure groups or cliques and all this. It was all very new to me.

Neil Innes poses as a less than alluring Mona Lisa during the recording of the
Do Not Adjust Your Set shows.

People sort of scheming and developing things without you being there and all this sort of stuff, that was all very new to me. I became aware of the fact that I wasn't making as much of a contribution as I should be, but I wasn't given the opportunity. I realised that there was a scheme to actually push myself and Vernon out. There were personality clashes as the band began to take itself rather seriously. I think at that point I thought, 'we're too old to be pop stars anyway. What are we going into the pop market for, really? Surely we should stick with jazz-based albums.' But, no, it had to be a hit record and I always thought that would be a mistake. And sure enough, we started to get ballroom gigs and there was no point us trying to do a cabaret act in a ballroom situation. People standing in a

Vivian and Sam perform the famous dummy sequence on New Faces.

ballroom watching a show, it's not what they go to ballrooms for. It seemed bloody obvious to me. And one or two of the gigs were wrong and therefore things on the stage started to go wrong and personality clashes began to be more and more apparent."

For Sam Spoons, the end of the Bonzos was a big blow. Initially Sam resurfaced in Bob Kerr's Whoopee Band, and then in 1975 joined up with Roger Ruskin Spear in the band Tatty Ollity, who recorded what is now a very rare single, "Punktuation". Ultimately Sam left the full time music world and pursued a career in lecturing. Sam did however continue to practice jazz based comedy as a member of The Bill Posters Will Be Band, which toured extensively during the Eighties and has on occasion included other former Bonzos such as Rodney Slater and Roger Ruskin Spear in the ranks. At the time of writing (2008) the band still plays regularly at the Bull's Head pub in Barnes.

Gerry Bron agrees with Sam's analysis that back in the Sixties the real problems for the Bonzos stemmed from the switch from the road to the studio. "There was a huge culture shock involved for some of them when we got into the studio," says Gerry, "they always managed fine on the road. In fact, although it seemed they had lots of junk, their props inventory wasn't actually that extensive. There were seven of them and they all carried their own instruments. As far as I remember they fitted into the ambulance van and that was it. Not like a heavy band where you've got amps and all the rest of it, so I don't ever remember touring being a problem for them. And they did an awful lot of weeks in clubs up North and so on."

In contrast to the happy-go-lucky life of a band on the road where the individual performances are unlikely to come under intense scrutiny, the studio environment has a disconcerting habit of putting every performance under the microscope. In Vivian Stanshall's assessment, Sam Spoons' performances were less than satisfactory, as Gerry Bron recalled. "The problems really happened in the studio. Vivian in particular got very fed up with Sam Spoons' drumming and they decided they'd get rid of Sam Spoons and Larry would become the drummer, and

72

I thought "Oh God, what's this going to be like?" But I was surprised to find Larry was actually quite a good drummer, so that's one area, if you like, where there was a sort of noticeable improvement in one of the musical departments." When Sam Spoons departed and "Legs" Larry Smith stepped in as replacement, Gerry Bron was not the only one who was surprised by "Legs" Larry's unexpected transformation from tap dancing tuba player to drummer. Despite "Legs" limited experience and idiosyncratic style, Vivian was a keen supporter later telling Phil Mcmullen "I loved his drums... truly absurd."

Rodney Slater agrees that many of the personnel problems only really became apparent with the switch to the studio environment. "That was the other thing we had to get used to. I mean the first little records we made, they just stuck a mike basically in the middle of the room and we all played together, this hyper-manic stuff. But later it was like guitar and piano and they'd have to go on separate tracks because Neil played them both, then bass and whatever on drums. And then you have to keep time with the rhythm section... who's playing the wrong tempo anyway, so this was a different way of working. There was a lot of splitting off, saying "Oh, don't bother to come in because you won't have anything to do and you sit around getting pissed or whatever". If the band hadn't had a fairly strong identity I think people might have gone off and done something else."

With Vernon Dudley Bowhay-Nowell on the way out and now Sam Spoons, it was time to take stock. Gerry Bron did find it ironic that Vivian was making musical judgements in respect of the other players. "Neil was always fine. Neil is a good musician and could play everything and effectively wrote the songs for the others, but as far as learning their instruments, Rodney apart, well they just never bothered. We were in the studio in Rickmansworth and Vivian's playing the tuba and I say to Vivian, "Well, you should be playing a B flat there, what are you playing?" And he said, "I don't know". He literally tried every combination of valve settings until he found B-flat. Eventually I said, "That's it!" He said, "Okay, well thank you very much." He couldn't play the instrument. On stage you can play any old note you like, but once you get in the studio, you hear what's been played isn't what you should be playing."

73

CHAPTER THREE
URBAN SPACEMEN

As the band took stock of their achievements in their first year as professionals, it was clear that 1967 had been a good year for the Bonzos. The band had recorded and released a brilliant, ground breaking debut album that would stand the test of time. As the year drew to a close there was more good news when the band were invited to take part in the new Beatles produced film production, "The Magical Mystery Tour", which was to be broadcast to the nation by the BBC on 26th December 1967.

Everyone was aware that the film represented a massive opportunity to put the band on the map. There are various versions of the history as to how the Bonzo Dog Doo-Dah Band ended up appearing in "The Magical Mystery Tour", but one is that Mike McGear, their friend from The Scaffold, and brother of Paul McCartney, recommended them when John Lennon was considering using the New Vaudeville Band. Another was that Paul McCartney had recommended them after seeing the Bonzos perform at The Saville.

Rodney Slater has his own theory and is quick to pay credit to "Legs" Larry Smith and Vivian Stanshall who had made the co-operative effort possible through the relationships which were forged during epic drinking sessions in London club-land featuring the ever present Bonzo duo and the Fab Four. "All of the late drinking didn't appeal to me", says Rodney, "but it did lead to us meeting and working with the Beatles, which was a result of the heroic late night drinking and socialising that Viv and Larry specialised in. They were like Batman and Robin, totally inseparable, and they were always at the places where the stars went. They got to know John Lennon and the Beatles very well that way. I've never been one for staying up all night and buying shit liquor at expensive prices, so I wasn't with them." In his 1992 interview for Ptolemeic Telescope Vivian revealed the workings of the

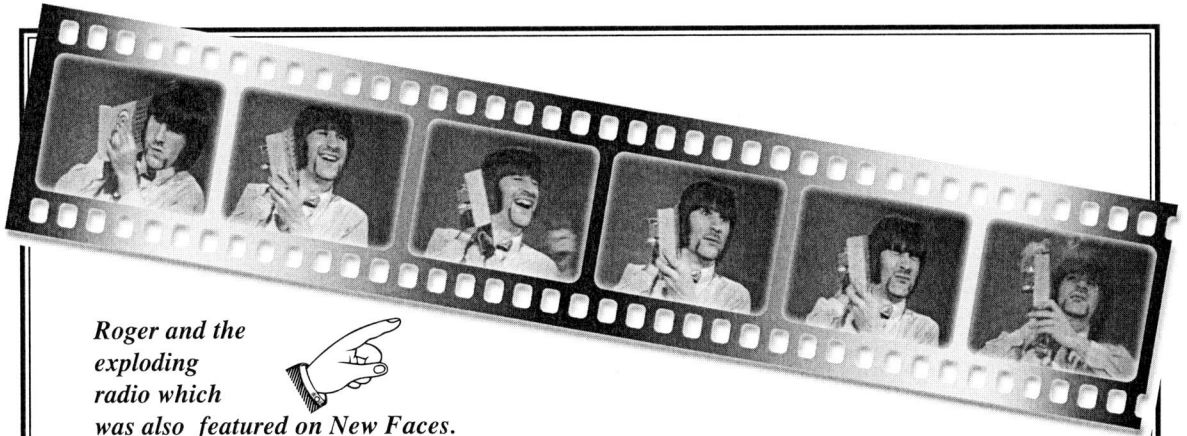

relationship between The Beatles and the Bonzos to Phil McMullen. "I got on with McCartney, and with Lennon particularly… And in that hideous Rolls Royce he conked out at my place or dropped me off. It depended on how drunk he was. And we had some terrible rows but we got on... Well, we just got on."

The opportunity to appear in the film was indeed very welcome news and had the potential to completely transform the world of the Bonzos, which certainly had its down sides by comparison with the rarefied world of the Beatles, as "Legs" Larry Smith recalled. "We were still doing the clubs when the Beatles rang up and asked us to do "The Magical Mystery Tour", which was rather good for our career, but we were working very hard then, too hard really, and the filming schedule was hardly Hollywood stuff. We ended up arriving at Paddington, on a train, about seven o'clock in the morning, having slept from Scunthorpe or somewhere to be woken up with a filthy cup of tea. It was all a bit quick that film, but it was always a thrill to be with the Beatles and we really did become big friends. It got quite relaxed in the end. I remember it was a fun relaxed atmosphere and John was wearing Viv's cap, which he took a real fancy to. I think we filmed it in about one take and even at the time you got the impression it really was a magical mystery tour where even they didn't know what the hell was going to happen next. But it got us involved in working with Paul rather than just drinking with him and he later agreed to produce 'Urban Spaceman', as we all know."

For the Beatles the chance to hang out with the Bonzos represented the opportunity to relax and have fun with like minded performers who understood the pressures of the business. "We were peer groups, the Beatles and the Bonzos were pretty much a shared experience. We'd all been guys in the van going to gigs and things like that," says Neil. "The difference was that we were still playing in clubs and could just get up there and play, which the Beatles could never do. I remember Eric Clapton used to say, "I wish I could muck about like you, guys. I've always wanted to come on stage with a stuffed parrot on my shoulder", but he couldn't, not with the posters out there saying,

75

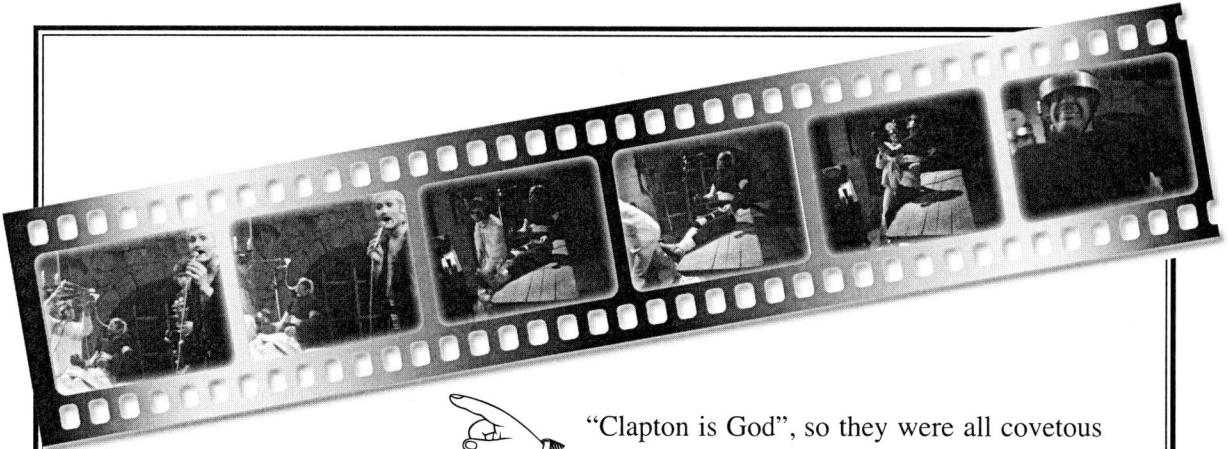

The Monster Mash sequence featured Sam Spoons and the UK debut of the electric spoons.

"Clapton is God", so they were all covetous of us mucking about. So it was a good exchange with the Beatles. We'd share a pint and have a laugh and George and I became very firm friends for years after. I don't know where the actual idea came from. I've heard that Mike McGear was asked to perform but he said to Paul, "You've seen the Bonzos, why don't you put the Bonzos in the film?" He said, "Oh, yeah, good idea." Viv and Larry also used to hang out with Paul and John. Viv didn't learn to drive so John used to have to drop Viv off at his flat, in the early hours of the morning. Viv would unfold himself from that ghastly floral Rolls Royce, and I suppose in The Beatles' case it was nice to meet somebody who had so much shared experience in common, and wasn't screaming at them, and probably knew a bit about where they were coming from in terms of the old art school background."

Vernon Dudley Bowhay-Nowell by this time was on his way out of the Bonzos and although he appeared in the first episode of 'Do Not Adjust Your Set', 'The Magical Mystery Tour' was to be his swan song and it was certainly a day with a difference. "We are the band that accompanies the Beatles when they arrive at the Raymond Revue Bar, and it was pretty exciting in those days not just because of working with the Beatles but because we actually had a naked lady fronting the band in that scene, so that was rather good and not something one saw very often in those days. Then there was the added thrill of all four of the Beatles at the time, sitting around while we were doing this stuff. I must confess I was quite envious at the time because I used to like shooting sixteen millimetre film and they all had the very latest Bolex, top of the range, doing their own little sort of private video bits."

The old saying is always to quit at the top - and if you are forced to bow out, then leaving a band following a cameo appearance with the Beatles is not a bad way to go! Vernon Dudley Bowhay-Nowell certainly knew how to do things in style. After the Bonzo's split up Vernon spent twenty years touring with Bob Kerr's Whoopee Band. He also met Alistair Bowtell and formed a special effects company who became famous for various television commercials such as Castrol Oil and for film special effects. This included

effects for many films such as the "Carry On…" series. Vernon particularly remembers the exploding violins he had to create in order for Barbara Windsor to hit Bob Todd over the head! During this time Vernon also met Steve Roberts, who produced the 'Sir Henry at Rawlinson's End' film and, indeed enjoyed a brief film career as Nigel Nice in the film. Latterly, Vernon has returned to his first love, the musical saw, which he plays in a band specialising in French music, going under the titles of Les Onions and Les Angles.

The one thing that puzzled everyone back in 1968 was why that particular song got chosen. Perhaps it had something to do with the stripper motif and the association with "cuties", but the reasons are lost on Neil Innes. "I don't know what made them choose "Death Cab For Cutie". Maybe it was the only thing at that time that would remotely fit the kind of groove of a Beatles' film because it had a kind of Elvis sort of tinge to it. Interestingly that's probably the only song Viv and I ever wrote together. We found this sort of true crime magazine and one of the stories was 'Death Cab for Cutie', so we just fantasised on that."

The relationship for Vivian Stanshall was with John Lennon and it did not progress into a working partnership, and although there was much discussion over the possibility of adding "Death Cab For Cutie" to the "Magical Mystery Tour soundtrack album, the Bonzos lacked the necessary clout and ultimately it was decided to leave the song off the album, which deprived the band of vital world wide publicity. In 1979 Vivian explained the circumstances surrounding the film and the failure to include the Bonzos on the soundtrack. "Paul McCartney came to some of our gigs, - (I know he was at the Lyceum and the Albert Hall), and I think he persuaded Lennon that it'd be a good idea to put us in that film. And that kind of put the Good Housekeeping seal of approval on us. The thing that pissed me off though was that they never put us on the record… - mean buggers." This still rankled with Vivian when he spoke about the 'Magical Mystery Tour' in the 1992 interview to Brian McMullen at Ptolemeic Telescope. "I think it was pretty blinking good. What really and profoundly pissed me off was that we didn't get on the LP. I thought it was mean, that. I think it was Paul McCartney! "

Stepping into the world of the Fab Four did have its advantages as Rodney Slater later recalled. "Working with the Beatles was also the only time I ever had a haircut in a salon as opposed to a barbers. Paul McCartney took me to a hairdresser, *his* hairdresser don't you know. I can't remember where it was and I could certainly never afford to go there again but he paid for it… - to have my hair cut in the style the Beatles wanted

77

That's a brand new scratch on that piano...

it for the film. And then all you see of me in the film, after that great expense, is my saxophone, legs and torso."

In his 1979 interview with John Platt, Vivian recalled the events of the recording. "That was fun to do. We had all our equipment stolen from outside the Raymond Revue Bar, so we had to hire everything. And we were persuaded by the management that we had to have haircuts. We all went off to Stanley Allwins and had these outrageous pooftah jobs done. It looked great; it was really stupid. I love having haircuts."

Despite the brevity of his on screen appearance Rodney Slater and the rest of the cast set about the launch party with gusto and the consequences for Vivian Stanshall were inevitable. Gerry Bron was obviously very sharp at exploiting publicity opportunities, but he had to be bullied by the band into allowing them to abandon a gig in Northern England to attend the party thrown by The Beatles at the end of filming.

"The party was fabulous, though," recalls Rodney Slater. "I've never seen so much drink laid out on tables. I mean, obviously one was bloody out of it very quickly, especially the Bonzo Dog Band who had some of the biggest drinkers anywhere at that time... Viv had to be carried out."

The transformation from beautiful swans back to ugly ducklings came all too quickly for the Bonzos. The tables were probably still being packed away from the party when the boys were back on the road as Rodney Slater remembers. "This really was getting back to earth with a bump. Worse still we had to get up the morning afterwards and get in that bloody ambulance and go back to a bloody cabaret in Darlington with heads thumping like drums."

Sadly for all concerned the finished film was less than engaging. Although the Bonzos acquitted themselves well they are one of the few highlights in a messy, self indulgent mess. The film was screened by the BBC in black and white to universal bemusement. After outraged calls to the BBC from Ringo Starr, the film was screened in colour two days later, but the public reaction was just as muted. The film was a turkey and even the Bonzos couldn't disagree with the public consensus as Rodney Slater recalled. "I mean,

78

surely the whole concept of the film, from the Beatles' point of view, was to let things develop. Their whole thing was get in the bus with these freaks and see what happens and film it as it developed. And, of course, we all know what did happen. It proved the point that films have to be carefully written, planned and executed!" Whilst The Beatles at this time were generally viewed by the media as the band who could do no wrong, "The Magical Mystery Tour" was not considered a success, although Neil Innes has subsequently defended it in the strongest terms. "I love it. The public reaction was a perfect example of people at their worst. People at their worst throw stones at things they don't understand. As the world gets colder it's one of the fires you'll want to be around."

Ultimately 'The Magical Mystery Tour' has to be viewed as a major missed opportunity but the Bonzos had done all they could and there would still be some lasting benefit from the project to come in the form of a highly successful single. With the band now slimmed down to a slightly more manageable six piece, the musical vision for the 1968 version of the Bonzos was becoming clearer. The band had dropped the 'Doo-Dah' tag and were now known simply as the Bonzo Dog Band. Old time jazz and novelty songs had only a very small part to play as the band worked hard to push back the boundaries in their quest to prove that there was more to the band than had been revealed on "Gorilla".

The spectre of The New Vaudeville Band continued to hang over the Bonzos and this running sore was one of the reasons that the Bonzos began to change musical direction and pursue a more rocky path. Their dalliances with the world of rock 'n' roll were also taking the Bonzos further and further away from their vaudeville roots although not everyone in the band welcomed the change of direction and personnel. Roger Ruskin Spear recalled there was a conscious movement to move away from the more traditional jazz based sound. "So Vernon couldn't handle the electric bass and that wasn't quite right so he was removed. Around this time Neil said, 'Piano, I'm getting fed up with this, I want to play more guitar!' So Neil got up, plugged his guitar in and that was it, piano gone. With Neil playing guitar it was obvious that there was no longer the need or even the room for banjos. Right, so we've got Larry on the drums, we've got Rog and Rodney on saxophones, we can all play trumpet but Viv bought a trumpet anyway although his playing was always terrible. With Vernon gone we needed a bass player and at that point the Bonzos were such an exclusive club that we just could not find a comedy bass player, so we got Dave Clague then Joel Druckman in. Bass was a real problem for the band. Either we had bass players who were frustrated and wanted to get up and do something or it wasn't in tune with what we were doing. Dennis Cowan though, was just quite happy to go 'dum dum dum' in the background and put a mask on or something and have a custard pie stuck in his face... – he was quite happy.

So we had Dennis in the background and we thought right that's the line up sorted. So it was a sort of fanatical following but obviously the money boys were trying to transfer to 'How can we get this onto record?' And we decided we couldn't really do things like that anymore and 'Urban Spaceman' had to go into the set on their own merit."

1967 was rounded off with an appearance on German television, appearing on "Beat Club" with the Small Faces, the Bee Gees and the Flowerpot Men, and then on New Year's Eve, they played at the Pink Flamingo club in London.

DO NOT ADJUST YOUR SET

The other big coup for the Bonzos arrived towards the end of 1967 when it was confirmed that the band had been invited to fulfil the role of house band in a new children's comedy series for ATV. The pilot programme was a Boxing Day special, which was due to be screened the same day as the Beatles 'Magical Mystery Tour'. The show was called "Do Not Adjust Your Set", and the pilot would lead to two series of the children's programme being broadcast in 1968 and 1969, creating thousands of new teenage fans for the Bonzos.

Neil Innes takes up the story. "Do Not Adjust Your Set' was the idea, I think, of producer Humphrey Barclay. He'd been given a remit to put it all together, so he picked us, the Bonzo Dog Doo-Dah Band, some various Oxbridge people like Eric Idle, Michael Palin, Terry Jones and somehow got hold of Terry Gilliam, who had just come over here from America. Of course, there was also the brilliant David Jason and Denise Coffey. I remember we started off doing a Boxing Day Special and we sort of eyed each other rather suspiciously at first, sort of wondering who did what. But over the period of two series we became very good friends. The Bonzos were, at that time, I think, probably more successful than any of the cast in terms of public recognition. We were up and down the country all the time and I think we were probably the highest paid band without a hit record at the time because we weren't really driven by having hit records, but we were heavily into having a good time and we had quite a following and a reputation."

On the first Thursday of 1968, "Do Not Adjust Your Set" was broadcast as the first of 13 shows, which would be shown each week. To coincide with the first episode, the Bonzo Dog Band were featured in Television Weekly. "Wild... Crazy... Hilarious... Great... These are just a few of the adjectives that have been used to describe The Bonzo Dog Doo-Dah Band, who appear each Thursday in 'Do Not Adjust Your Set'. They are complete entertainers because their comedy is natural. The Bonzos are seven separate entities who, on stage, merge into a funny and most original unit. The group is four years old, but only two members remain from that first line-up. They are Vivian Stanshall and Rodney Slater. The remainder of the cast have all been preceded

Scenes like this sparked Vivian to compose his own vulgar ditty which as Neil recalled went something like... "If skirts get any shorter, said the flapper with a sob, I'll have two more cheeks to powder... and a lot more hair to bob!"

81

19

Looks like they're enjoying their holiday

by many others. The group was started for the purely private enjoyment of the members who, at the time, were all attending art college. Although they finally turned professional in 1966, they have still retained to a large extent, the natural gaiety of an ad lib act."

The first series, which was broadcast from January until March 1968, worked very well indeed. The series soon drew a loyal and faithful audience, not all of them children, and collected the prestigious Prix De Jeunesse. "Legs" Larry Smith is just one of the Bonzos who remembers the series well and recalls how the series provided a platform, which was both visual and aural. "I think we really did our best work on 'Do Not Adjust Your Set". It was fun, but by that stage I'm afraid we were kind of knackered emotionally and, dare I say, spiritually. We were working so hard you've got to get a good night's sleep before, and it's hard work, television. We weren't disciplined enough by then to understand cameras and this sort of stuff. Dear old Daphne, the director, would go nuts because we'd never do the same thing twice. We'd run through these wonderful numbers but then... – camera two on Vivian, camera four on Roger... - oh, what's Roger doing now? I couldn't move too far because I was behind the drum kit and it's always the band that appears to come off badly, because if the angle is wrong and if we'd had more time to kind of focus on what we were doing I think the shows would have been even better. But they were great fun and a great team, and all the Python lot were just bubbling about. David Jason was a super bloke and the whole cast were magnificent really. It was a great little show too."

Despite the creative and commercial success of the series Gerry Bron, as always, had his fair share of troubles to contend with. Many of these problems arose from the anarchic nature of the Bonzos working ethos, which Gerry always considered to be unprofessional. Gerry knew that there were some fantastic visual gags, which could be captured with the full co-operation of the Bonzos, which was not always forthcoming. "Vivian in particular was difficult to work with," recalls Gerry in some frustration. "He was very difficult because he wasn't consistent and he was very erratic. That TV programme effectively generated Monty Python. The Bonzos did two spots in each of those shows but Vivian just didn't seem to grasp that the cameras need to see what your doing and that in a TV studio you need to favour the camera, which is going to record the gag. So I would go up to Vivian and say, "Vivian, when you get to this line camera three is on

82

you and the problem is that you're doing it with the wrong hand so you can't really see what's going on, but if you do it with the other hand camera three will pick it up." He'd say, "Got it, old man, don't worry". And they'd do the rehearsal and sure enough the correct hand was being used. Come to the transmission, back to the wrong hand and there's nothing you could ever do to sort it out. As I say, he was an enormously talented amateur but come to professionalism it just wasn't the way he worked. So he was difficult for somebody who, of necessity had to work in a professional way, but everyone revered him. And quite rightly so. He was a genius after all."

Rodney Slater looks back fondly on the making of the series, which had a hugely beneficial effect on the group. "We had to turn up every week at Wembley for the first series or Teddington for the second series, and there we met the future stars of Monty Python and David Jason, and all the things he became, and Denise Coffey. Oh, it was good. It gave us tremendous exposure. There were a few dangers. It was the first time I felt that my privacy was being invaded with people on the street recognising me because I was on the box every week without fail. And it was a successful show, one of these classics, which was taken up by adults, and became a cult thing. Absolute golden age example of British television. We did a number every week, and then we had little bit parts, – walk on parts, – and things like that occasionally."

Humphrey Barclay certainly got value for money as the Pythons proved that they were indeed one of the greatest comedy writing teams to emerge from the UK, added to this was the fact that the writing partnership between Neil Innes and Vivian Stanshall was also beginning to bear fruit as Neil recalls. "The Bonzos by then were writing their own material and obviously Eric and Mike and Terry were writing stuff. I don't know how much David and Denise wrote, but I think Denise wrote as well, so people would come up with ideas all the time and it became very popular for some reason."

In no time the series had managed to cross over from children to an adult audience. It was to become cult viewing and Neil Innes pinpoints the series as the beginnings of the vogue for intelligent writing and comedy, which was to achieve its zenith with Python. "Grown-ups were rushing home from work on a Thursday evening to tune in to this rather bizarre little programme, but it was clearly sort of trying to do things in a different way to how television was. There was this sort of thrusting new wave of fresh out of college kind of people, and they were pretty much allowed to do what they liked, and it was quite innovative in a way. It was a lot of fun to be asked to be sort of stool pigeon number three in a sketch, or something like that, and very enjoyable. And, of course, people tend to forget it was live and it's really good fun because if you do anything elaborate with a prop or something like that and it doesn't work, there's this wonderful panic in

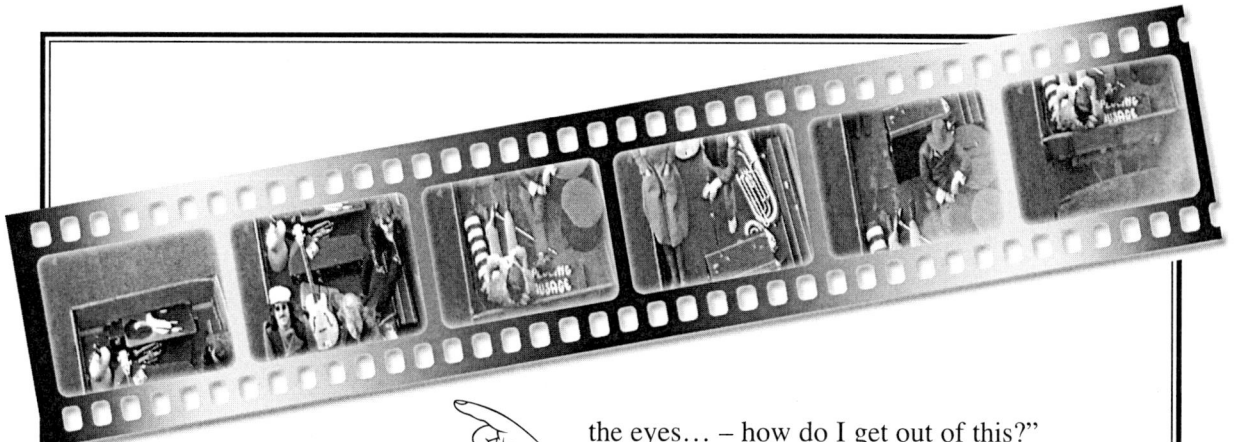

The Son of the Exploding sausage was another in a series of disappointing films featuring the Bonzos.

the eyes... – how do I get out of this?"

Despite the band's enthusiasm and the obvious success of the series, Gerry Bron still feels that "Do Not Adjust Your Set" represented yet another great opportunity missed for the band. "One of the problems was that I couldn't work out what the solution was, on television they just didn't come over they way they were on stage. I think you might have been able to film it but their show needs a multi camera perspective that you simply don't get on the average television show. I suppose you might get it on film. If you saw their show, it wasn't just Vivian doing something. There were all sorts of things going on on stage, you'd be watching Vivian and suddenly you'd realise that Neil's sitting there with a corncob pipe out of his mouth with thick, black smoke coming out of it, and you're sort of sitting there watching what's going on and suddenly there's Larry with the tuba, because he played all sorts of different things, and this used to happen at the Marquee a lot as it had a low ceiling. He'd be playing the tuba and suddenly the tuba would become stuck in the ceiling and then he stops playing the tuba and he is trying to pull the tuba out of the ceiling... just another average Bonzo gig."

Neil Innes also remembers the Bonzo's penchant for fooling around just for the sake of it. This was to prove great fun for the band, but it was infuriating for the people trying to make a television show. "Daphne Shadwell was the first director," remembers Neil, "and I thought she was amazing how she kept her cool and kept things going, because the whole day was a blur. But the Bonzos did their best to make things worse. We were sort of half way through the first series and somewhere in a hotel and the phone went and it was our management and they said, – "ATV want to know what props you need for next week's show." And "Legs" Larry Smith answered the phone and said, "Oh, three cardboard boxes, a petrol tanker and a springboard", and put the phone down. It was clearly a wind up, you know, but two days later the management ring up again, and I happen to pick up the phone and they said, "We've got the cardboard boxes and the springboard but we're having trouble with the petrol tanker. Would an oil drum do?"

The series was very progressive but some of the old attitudes of an older

Britain still apparently shone through unchallenged. One number that could not be performed in the same way today is "Look Out There's a Monster Coming". For this particular number all the band appeared blacked up with the exception of Neil Innes. It certainly would not happen in this millennium, but it was considered acceptable fare for main stream television in 1968. As the only member who refused to go along with the gag Neil attempts to unravel the conundrum. "I thought, isn't it a bit offensive to... maybe it was me on my high horse, but I said, "No, I'm not blacking up you know, I'm not doing this Black and White Minstrel nonsense". But there was a bit in the show where Roger used to wear a balaclava helmet and a hat and have a white rubber ring and he had white holes for his eyes and there used to be a moment when he burst into 'Swanee, how I love you, how I love you', a send up of the Black and White Minstrel Show. I dare say, at the back of Viv's feverish mind they were sort of monsters. These black and white minstrels with their strange garb, I mean why were they blacked up in the first place? I mean, they were monsters in a number of ways, mainly in their attitude, so it was kind of appropriate that "Look Out There's a Monster Coming" should have monsters, even if it's a Black and White Minstrel monster. So on another level you could say that it was an act of criticism."

Rodney Slater leaves the debate to one side and concentrates on the benefits of 'Do Not Adjust Your Set' to the Bonzos. "It did us a power of good. I mean it was wonderful free publicity and we got paid a small amount for doing it as well." Neil Innes certainly agrees with the commercial benefits and the lasting impact the series would have on the creative landscape of Britain. "It wasn't so much breaking the mould, it was probably inventing a new mould, in a way, because as I say, the art school influence on the toys of television had never been felt before. Terry Gilliam was there at the forefront and all of a sudden there's these other things you can do with pictures and fool around with images and things like that, so I think we were kind of in a workshop way of experimenting with the kind of things you could do. Of course, these things turned up in Python later. Eric Idle is on record as stating that - the influence of the Bonzos sort of persuaded them that the anarchy route was, in fact, quite useful, and especially if they had someone like Terry Gilliam there. Under the influence of the Bonzos I think quite a few people began to realise they didn't have to worry about a punch line, you could now say "And Now For Something Completely Different". Well, we haven't got to scratch our heads and come up with a really wicked punch line, we can just move on and it becomes more and more like real life, as it were."

While the television series was being made the Bonzos continued playing gigs. The set list at that time contained a strange mix, some of which was never destined to make it on to record. Regular stage

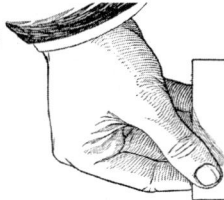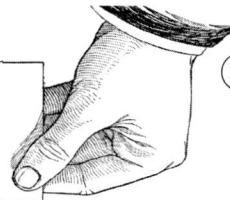

Fe

favourites at the time included "Little Sir Echo", which had somehow survived from the days when it was performed as a duet by Bob Kerr and Sam Spoons, "Mr Hyde In Me", "Monster Mash", "Shirt", "I Want To Be With You", "Give Booze A Chance", "We Were Wrong" and "Tragic Magic", which was later transformed into "Keynsham". "Give Booze A Chance" was performed on the John Peel radio programme. Interestingly, Rodney Slater around that time was seen wearing a shirt reading "Lump It John", which was his advice to John Lennon in response to the star's frequent grizzling in the press concerning the hardship of life in the Beatles.

The Bonzos still attempted to squeeze in as many shows as they could, resulting in a challenging and rather difficult schedule with the television recordings, as Neil Innes recalls. "Most of the time we were on the road, sometimes all week, and then we had to come to London and do the show and consequently we hadn't quite figured what we were going to do. I always used to think, "oh well, the cameras are never in the right place anyway. In retrospect it might just have been us." Despite the demands of recording the show the Bonzos continued in 1968 to constantly gig in venues such as at the Middle Earth in London with Alexis Korner in January, and during February at the Cardiff Sophia Gardens with The Move. They performed at the London School of Economics; Sheffield University with The Who; the Brighton Dome in support of Scaffold; and Leicester Granby Halls with Traffic, the Kinks and the Move. And despite their new audiences the Bonzos still appealed to students, playing at Barking College and Ewell Technical College in March.

Even when recording for "Do Not Adjust Your Set" had finished, the pressure of continuous work did begin to show. The band were due to go on a tour of 21 dates with Gene Pitney, Paul Jones, Don Partridge plus Simon Dupree and the Big Sound during April 1968, but it was reported that they had "withdrawn from the tour owing to pressure of other commitments." The Bonzos hadn't stopped performing altogether however, playing gigs during April such as the Marquee and Dunstable California Ballroom.

During May the Bonzos appeared once again on John Peel's radio show and played venues such as the Cooks Ferry Inn in Edmonton, North London, and in June they returned to Goldsmith's College where Neil Innes had formerly studied. The gig was reviewed by Beat Instrumental magazine. "Their stage act is largely built around the use of props – horror masks, explosions, weird instruments (constructed by the leaping Roger Ruskin Spear) – and Alma. She is a life-size rag doll who, in the words of Vivian, 'has blown her mind. I'm afraid there are bits of plaster and cloth hanging out of the poor dear's head.' Their stage dress could also be called eccentric. Vivian appeared in

86

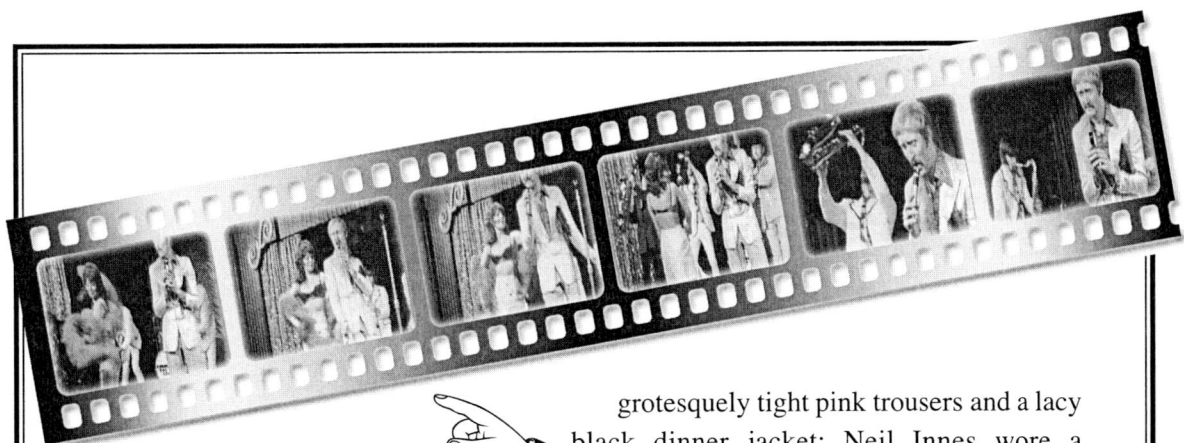

The Bonzos appearance in "The Magical Mystery Tour" was ultimately to prove a lost opportunity.

grotesquely tight pink trousers and a lacy black dinner jacket; Neil Innes wore a menacing Hell's Angels outfit; drummer Legs Larry Smith sported U.S. football padding; Rodney Slater had a voluminous powder-blue drape jacket, while Dave Clague just looked blinding. An awesome sight. The Bonzos' humour ranges from hopeless vulgarity to subtle whimsy, while their musical talents are indeed remarkable. Between the six of them they must play over 20 instruments, including a dressmaker's dummy with strings and pick-ups fitted!"

The Bonzos continued to play on the same bill as a whole variety of popular bands such as with Dave Dee, Dozy, Beaky Mick & Tich at Oxford University and The Nice at the Institute of Contemporary Art during June 1968. And by the time that they played with The Move, The Byrds, The Easybeats and Joe Cocker at the Albert Hall in London in July, David Clague had been replaced on bass guitar by an American musician called Joel Druckman.

There was yet another appearance on John Peel's "Top Gear" radio show during July 1968, and the Bonzos were now established as an essential feature in the rock and pop scene. During August they appeared both at a 2 day festival at the Middle Earth Club and also at the "Teespop" festival near Middlesborough. The Middle Earth line up included the Pretty Things, Terry Reid, Traffic, The Incredible String Band, Family and Fairport Convention, as well as a showing of "The Magical Mystery Tour". The Middlesborough festival once again included Traffic and Family, plus appearances from Ben E King and Joe Cocker.

Despite all this hip exposure, the band were still keen to keep their audience as wide as possible and continued to play at the Northern working clubs, completing a cabaret week at Guisborough Social Club in Rotherham in September. That month they also performed at Hampstead Country Club and a club called Mothers, in Birmingham, which was to become a favourite haunt.

GRANNY'S GREENHOUSE

Away from the constraints of the television studio Neil Innes was continuing to develop as a world class song writer

87

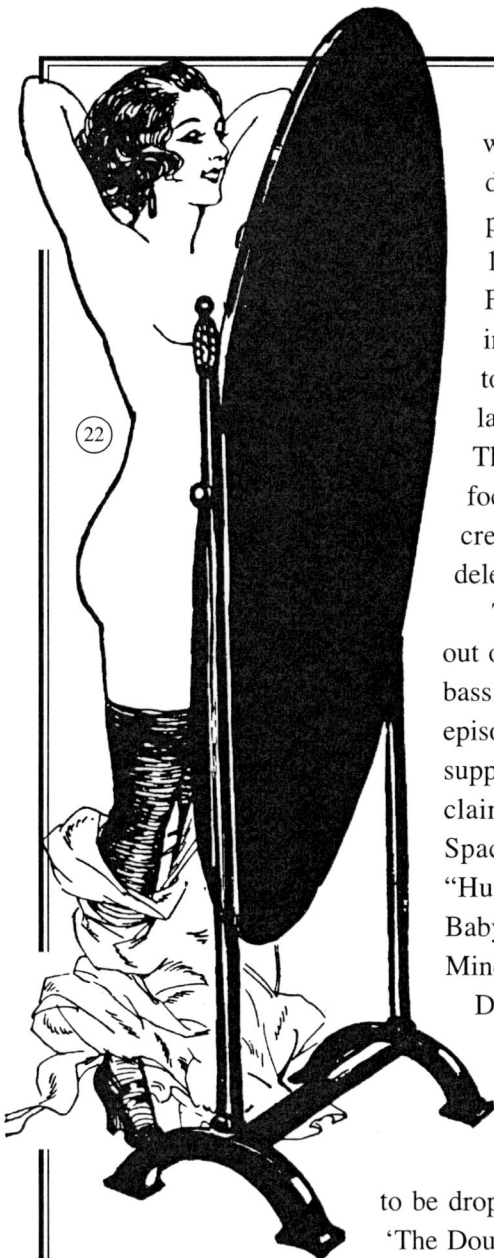

while Vivian Stanshall at last had the platform to demonstrate his extraordinary talent as a wordsmith par excellence. The album that the band recorded in 1968 was "The Doughnut In Granny's Greenhouse". For the record buyer expecting a record that carried on in the same groove as "Gorilla", this new album was to prove a radical departure. There were less belly laughs but there was some real depth and poignancy. The reduced ranks of the Bonzos had the effect of focusing the material. Neil and Viv were the main creative powerhouse and bass guitar duties were delegated to a succession of side men.

The first of these was Dave Clague who had helped out on the "Gorilla" sessions. Dave continued to supply bass guitar and is also to be seen on some of the surviving episodes of "Do Not Adjust Your Set". It was Dave who supplied "Fuzz Guitar" on "Humanoid Boogie" and claims to have played bass on "I'm The Urban Spaceman", "Beautiful Zelda", "Hello Mabel", "Humanoid Boogie", "Trouser Press", "Rockaliser Baby", "Shirt", "Monster Mash" and "Canyons of Your Mind". For the duration of his tenure with the Bonzos Dave Clague was still considered a session player rather than a full time member of the band despite the fact that he had by now effectively replaced Vernon Dudley Bowhay-Nowell on the road, in the studio and even on television. Dave Clague was to be dropped from the band after some of the recordings for 'The Doughnut In Granny's Greenhouse' were completed and was soon replaced by Joel Druckman.

The bass guitar duties in the second half of the album and for the rest of 1968 were handled by Joel Druckman who was an American spending time in the UK in order to avoid being drafted into the Vietnam war. "Well the thing about 'Doughnut' was that there were changes in the band," recalls Rodney Slater. "We had let Sam and Vernon go by that time and Dave Clague, who did a lot of the bass playing on 'Doughnut', was a kind of sessions man on loan to us from the agency because Vernon was gone and we didn't really have a bass player. To finish the 'Doughnut' sessions we had to get one of

The Doughnut in Granny's Greenhouse

*The weak art direction for **The Doughnut In Granny's Greenhouse** fails to make a coherent statement and leaves the viewer with a distinct feeling that the Bonzos are trying too hard to project a wacky persona. There are times when simply dressing up and taking some pictures is not enough.*

our own and we brought in the Red Baron, Joel Druckman, from America. He was a draft-dodger and a general vagabond, a lovable rogue really. Joel played bass with us for about a year, until we started going abroad and of course that meant problems because of his American passport. He left the band because he didn't want to end up in whatever the 1960s version of Guantanamo Bay was. So he was in there and he's not credited on 'Doughnut' either, but his picture is on the sleeve, the little bearded guy on the left. So we had him on there and he came up with these things, one or two other nice little one-liners and some truly dreadful harmonica playing."

Describe your function!

Joel contributed bass on a number of recordings at this time including "We Are Normal", "11 Mustachioed Daughters", and like Dave Clague, claims to have played bass on "Trouser Press", "My Pink Half Of The Drainpipe", "Rockaliser Baby", "I'm The Urban Spaceman" and "Canyons Of Your Mind". It is Joel Druckman that we hear in the role of interviewer on "We Are Normal". His is also the voice introducing "Trouser Press", and it is also Joel who calls out "Raw Meat!" just before "My Pink Half of The Drainpipe". He can also be heard saying, "I don't remember too well, but I think John

(23) Wayne was in it," on "11 Mustachioed Daughters". Joel is pictured on the album sleeve in the bottom left hand corner, holding a bell and wearing the distinctive purple stockings.

One rather strange duty Joel Druckman was required to perform on the 'The Doughnut In Granny's Greenhouse' sessions was that of the interviewer standing on a street corner and attempting to record the views of random members of the great British public for the track, which was to become "We Are Normal". The reason this particular interview segment drew so many weird responses from passing populace was the fact that the subject of the interview was Vivian Stanshall who had donned a giant papier maché rabbit head and stripped down to his underpants. "He's got a head on him like a rabbit," was one of the more useable responses from the bemused inhabitants of London that summer's day in 1968.

The title of this album has sparked much discussion over the years and is often credited to Michael Palin, however it was an honour he shared with Vivian Stanshall. Vivian delighted in all forms of bodily function, his humour was often lavatorial and would later reach it's apogee on "The Strain". Vivian also loved fart jokes of all kinds and unfortunately for those around him he also loved to practice the art of farting, the louder, the longer and the smellier the better as far as Vivian was concerned, which made life hell for the unfortunate inhabitants of the Bonzo ambulance. This was especially so as Vivian was a devotee of Indian food. He ate curries wherever possible and was a keen advocate of the mighty Vindaloo in particular. "Oh pooh! I smell Vindaloo," was a line written in honour of this unwholesome fascination. Vivian however was to meet his nemesis in the unlikely shape of Sam Spoons who in retribution one day unleashed his own potent offering of evil smelling marsh gas so foul that Vernon Dudley Bowhay-Nowell had to brake suddenly to allow the asphyxiated occupants of the ambulance to bale out of every available door and window. This earned Sam the lasting respect of Vivian who hailed the whole unsavoury incident as a great deed performed by a true master. Vivian loved crude humour and during the production of "Do Not Adjust Your

Set" he was struck by Michael Palin's reference to an outdoor toilet as "Granny's Greenhouse". This description delighted Vivian and he of course added his own inimitably vulgar twist with the image of the lavatory seat, which of course was the real "Doughnut" of the album title.

Let's take a taxi to my tent!

The mundane experiences of life on the road with the Bonzos continued to provide the inspiration for some fantastic material, which have passed into legend as Rodney Slater remembers. "The Trouser Press, that was Roger. We used to see these strange devices, which no one ever has at home. It's absolutely typical of the way his mind works. I mean who else would think of adding a pick up and actually trying to play the Trouser Press! All he really did was bang on it. It's just electrified banging through an amp, but he did used to take his trousers off when he did it, which was real music hall stuff, and put them in the thing in his horrible red and white spotty boxer shorts."

The conception of 'The Doughnut In Granny's Greenhouse' took an unusual form. The album was conceived in the same manner as a piece of architecture rather than a more traditional musical score as Neil Innes recalls. "Creatively we worked on a kind of graph, it was Vivian's idea. We thought we'd do a lateral graph of sort of waves breaking, and other things, and we drew a picture and did it like a score and so we sort of improvised in this kind of Stockhausen avant-garde, music-concrete way. We all basically had a good time but I think some of the writing on that was really quite good. I loved 'Can Blue Men Sing The Whites' and things like that."

Rodney Slater is very much of the opinion that by this stage the Bonzos on record no longer drew as much influence from what was being performed live on stage. Increasingly the albums were the product of the recording studio environment. "As regards the actual music there was less and less coming from the live act on that album," remembers Rodney, "because we couldn't do them on stage. The more we got into all this almost Beatle worship and using technology, we couldn't reproduce the songs on stage. We were a band. Music was part of it but a bigger part of what we were doing involved the band attempting to be lots of different bands each of which demanded different approaches to music and different

Is she still waiting for the wardrobe?...

approaches and styles. We loved the Twenties stuff but we did also attempt to be part of the musical landscape of the age we lived in. In some ways I think some of it was quite serious, actually. But always there had to be some other element, otherwise it fell flat on its arse. If there wasn't a funny thing that people could identify with, it wasn't Bonzo and it certainly helped otherwise we'd be just another band."

It was certainly true that "The Doughnut In Granny's Greenhouse" occupied an altogether different musical landscape from "Gorilla". There was at least one nod in the direction of what had gone before as Rodney Slater fondly recalls. "There was one endearing thing, which harked back to what we used to do, that was 'Hello, Mabel', which was a lovely song by Neil, which provided a great vehicle for Larry to do his tap dancing on. So that made it into the live set."

The popular music scene in 1968 was beginning to take itself very seriously indeed. The emergence of heavy duty outfits like Cream and Led Zeppelin posed thorny questions over the hijacking of the blues genre. The Bonzos played no part in the debate, but that did not mean it was beyond parody as Rodney Slater remembers. "Can Blue Men Sing the Whites" sort of parodied the great debate about white guitar players. The Bonzo Dogs' solution was to write something absurd while that whole debate raged."

The "The Doughnut In Granny's Greenhouse" album also offered the first positive proof that Vivian Stanshall had emerged as a wordsmith to be reckoned with. The essence of great poetry lies in the ability to take a complex idea and boil it down to a few perfectly chosen words so that a great deal more is conveyed to the audience than the relatively few words, which are actually spoken, or in Vivian's case sung. The title alone of "My Pink Half Of The Drainpipe" speaks volumes about the quiet suburban world, which was actually inhabited by Vivian who himself lived deep in suburbia at 221 East End Road in East Finchley. The seething mass of frustrations that lie just beneath the surface of these calm ordered and mundane worlds with their strictly demarcated boundaries are evoked brilliantly in the lyric of this little masterpiece. The song was also a rather desperate self portrait of an artist trapped in a world from which he longed to escape. Rodney Slater recognised that there was indeed a great deal of Vivian in the song, especially his longing to escape from the clutches of a conventional world.

As Rodney observed, "On My Pink Half of the Drainpipe" you see a sort of glimpse into the Stanshall stance on life, you know, "I will be completely bloody different, mate, and what you're doing is so normal and boring." I suppose that sentiment informed his work with the band and his reason for being in it."

Rodney Slater enjoyed the fact that from the outset "The Doughnut In Granny's Greenhouse" was different from previous Bonzo offerings. "We Are Normal", I think that's one of the first examples of me going into R&B madness at the end of it. I didn't often get a chance to do that. Interestingly, "Doughnut" is nearly all written and arranged by the band and some of it is more memorable than others, basically. "Postcard" I liked very much too. It's very unconventional and I've never heard anything quite like it anywhere else. It's certainly one of a kind. Some things like "11 Moustachioed Daughters" I enjoyed making enormously, but you really have to listen hard to hear anything I did in that because we were starting to develop this sort of a massive mix of things and the sound can be a bit muddy. Loads of tracks all bunged in and then mixing out little bits so you probably just get a little break here and there of a saxophone or something… – my Charlie Parker period… – so there's odd little licks at the beginning coming out through a lot of these heavy electronic numbers. You might get a few bars here and there emerge."

The Bonzos second album was released at the beginning of December 1968 and "The Doughnut In Granny's Greenhouse" was nominated as "Pop LP of the month" by loyal supporter Chris Welch in the Melody Maker, with a justifiably glowing review. "Anyone attempting the difficult task of analysing or even merely describing the Bonzo Dogs eventually ends up gasping vaguely about the Mothers of Invention, Goons, Temperance Seven, and a dozen more odious comparison. Easier and more truthful to say the Bonzos are – unique. Whether the humour and thought processes that went into 'Doughnut' can instantly communicate to the great mass of people is doubtful. The instant communication of their live performances was the main factor in their initial success and national acclaim. The band of Bonzo lovers has grown during the last two years, but the Bonzos themselves have raced on ahead in their ideas and attitudes. Fun is still the thing, – but on albums, which serve as stethoscopes to their erratic heart beats, the mystification count may increase to the point where 'normals' are baffled, and this is doubtless part of their intention. But anyone who responds to their anarchy, traditionalism, and romantic idiocy will find this an inventive, entertaining and often funny selection of diversions, a deep draught of the heady wine… inspired nonsense."

There was also a review in the New Musical Express. "On

The 1968 six-piece line up at the time of "The Doughnut In Granny's Greenhouse". The draft-dodging American bassist Joel Druckman is wearing the tweed cap. Rodney's T-shirt is a message to John Lennon to stop complaining about the pressures of life as a Beatle.

their latest album Bonzo Dog (who seem to have dropped the Doo-Dah bit from the title but still must be the zaniest group around) seem to be some-what exasperated by what they term 'Normals', who are all those people with closed-up minds condemning everything they don't understand, (which sometimes appears to be everything). I must admit that I didn't really understand everything Bonzos were trying to put across, but I will try to save some face by keeping an open mind. A cute trick on the first track, 'We Are Normal', is a bit of electronic fiddling, which had me looking for non-existent surface scratches on the disc and checking the turntable speed. The LP basically consists of the Bonzo Dog having a go

94

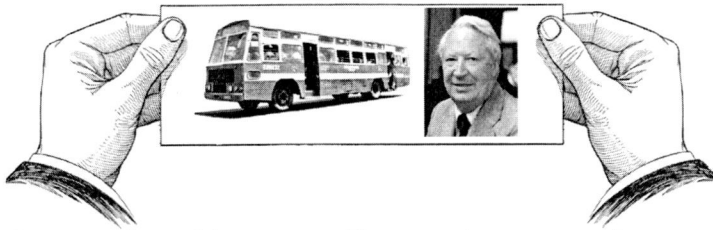

lyrically at the normals and instrumentally at various types of stereotyped, cliché-ridden music, including blues and soul. I thought some of the humour fell flat (as have some of their stage props recently), but the overall result is a very funny album. And, although done tongue-in-cheek, has some very good sounds. 'Trouser Press', a skit on square soul music, and 'My Pink Half Of The Drainpipe', a jibe at British semi-detached life, are particularly good. Most of the words are printed on the sleeve, which includes a weird booklet with pictures but offering no explanation to this good record."

For the record Neil Innes described "normals" as, "those people who don't understand other people and don't try to. They are people who laugh at others because they don't try to understand. Like if I walk in somewhere wearing this hat", (a rather becoming green felt masterpiece, tied round with a colourful scarf), "they will a laugh and point and say, 'yeh look… Geronimo'."

Also filmed at the same time as the front cover picture for the album, was a short promotional film. Sadly it consists of little more than the band larking around in the vague manner of unscripted music films everywhere. Further unplanned lunacy around this time was a film entitled "The Adventures of the Son of Exploding Sausage". This film was privately financed by a wealthy devotee and consists basically of the Bonzos setting up at a farmyard. In common with the rest of the Bonzos film oeuvre from 'The Magical Mystery Tour', to the Pathé promotional work, the "Sausage" was all filmed ad-lib. The film itself consists mostly of instrumental versions of a handful of Bonzo songs. Neil Innes fondly recalls a pony that would nod its head along to "Rockaliser Baby". Ultimately the film was consigned to obscurity but it is still shown occasionally by the British Film Institute in London.

I'M THE URBAN SPACEMAN

There is no doubt that by October 1968 the Bonzos were due a commercial break and to borrow a Reg Tracey phrase, for once fate actually played the straight man. It involved a little helping hand from their friends in the Beatles camp. In late 1968 the single "I'm The Urban Spaceman" was produced by Paul McCartney under the pseudonym "Apollo C.Vermouth". Paul, a keen follower of the Bonzos, wanted the experience of producing a record and this was his opportunity to dip his toe in the water with familiar company.

Neil Innes recalls the circumstances surrounding the decision to record the single with Paul. "By this time we were managed by Gerry Bron. Gerry was a proper gent, he really was. He really, really tried genuinely hard to get things right.

95

OK I'll try Radio
Luxemburg...

He was Manfred Mann's manager as well. He did, he really did try, but the Bonzos were simply unmanageable and I think it was so unfair, in hindsight, what we did to him over "Urban Spaceman". You see Gerry was a clock-watcher. He had set views and for him three hours was enough to make a track. I remember him saying, "I don't know what's got into Manfred Mann, it took him eight and a half hours to make "Ha Ha Said the Clown", and he wasn't joking! By that stage in our development we had all these ideas and we wanted to try different things. So we did feel somewhat constricted. Viv was moaning about it one day and Paul McCartney said, "Well, I'll come and produce the next one." So we said to poor Gerry, "We don't want you to produce this single."

The news came as something of a surprise to Gerry Bron who automatically assumed the band had been hoodwinked by some small time producer on the make, as Neil Innes recalls.

"So Gerry folded his arms and said, "Well, who do you think you're going to get to then?" After a suitable pause for dramatic effect Viv said, "Well… it's Paul McCartney actually." But then the cruellest thing we ever did to him as a serious businessman was to say, "Of course, we don't want Paul's name on the record." So the enormous commercial potential was cloaked by Paul's pseudonym Apollo C Vermouth. Poor Gerry, he was one of the best and he really could have built our careers, if we had given him proper co-operation but we were always doing nonsensical things like that."

Gerry Bron is the first to admit he was never in step with the Bonzos. Their thought processes were just too far apart as Gerry recalls from a visit, which Vivian Stanshall once paid to his office. "Viv walked into my office one day and he had this Mickey Mouse Walt Disney tie on, and I looked at it and I burst out laughing. And he said, "What's funny?" I said, "Well, the tie, it's the funniest tie I've ever seen". He said, "What do you mean? This is my best tie!" And he was dead serious. It really was his best tie, but the fact was that it had Mickey Mouse and Pluto and Donald Duck… - you wouldn't wear a tie like that to save your life! Vivian was in a different world, on a different planet as well."

It is interesting to note that the single that finally broke the charts for the band is one of the less overtly funny offerings from the Bonzo cannon. Neil Innes takes up the story. "Well, again, I don't ever set out to be funny. I just sort of try and observe and I think that's probably what we all had, as art students, been taught. We'd all sat and been trained to sit

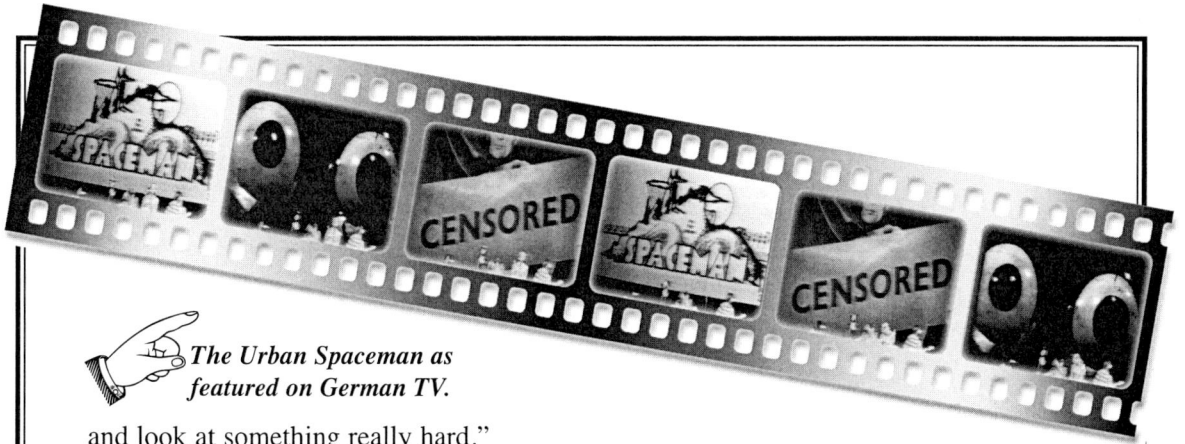

The Urban Spaceman as featured on German TV.

and look at something really hard."

The song actually has no connection with outer space. In fact the inspiration was the neglected inner space of post-war Manchester as Neil Innes explains. "I remember how the song came about because I was in Manchester, and a lot of Manchester in the Sixties was just being rebuilt after the war. It took ages as it was quite heavily hit in the war and in those days they called this kind of development site 'urban space'. They call them 'brownfield sites' nowadays. I just thought, "Well, if there's urban space why isn't there an urban spaceman?"

The song is also intended as a scathing comment on the rise of modern consumer advertising. "In those days we were seeing the embryonic beginnings of this awful one-way mass communication system. It was the time when for the first time the chains were really expanding into every town and the same shops were springing up everywhere.

The 'Urban Spaceman' idea somehow got coupled together with the idea that television is feeding you all these unhealthy images, the simulacra of shiny, smiley-faced people eating happy meals, and things like that, and so the 'Urban Spaceman' was really a kind of composite of the sort of ideal figure in an advert. He doesn't exist in real life."

"I'm The Urban Spaceman" was a serious attempt to convey a serious message in a humourous way. Many years later Neil Innes was to draw directly on the influence of French philosopher and social commentator Jean Baudrillard for the 2007 Bonzo reunion album "Pour L'amour Des Chiens." It is interesting to note that there is a direct link between the two works in the form of "Urban Spaceman". "I know this sounds all very pretentious, but the point was that I was, in my pompous little way, trying to sort of say, "Well, here's urban space. What about an urban spaceman? What would he be? He'd be the product of the advertising world, a glossy magazine or an advert on the tube. And an ambulance went by and went "nananananana" and so I thought, "Well, there's a tune."

"Legs" Larry Smith takes up the story of the recording. "We

97

were at Chappell's Studio in Bond Street and Paul arrived. We were all as nervous as hell and so he gathered us all round the piano and by way of an ice breaker he said, "I wrote this last night". He started playing "Hey Jude", so I guess we were the first people to hear it. It was great working with him, a producer that really knew what he was doing, not that Gerry Bron didn't know what he was doing, but we gave Paul the kind of respect that we didn't give anybody else, so we got on with it and we produced a great result."

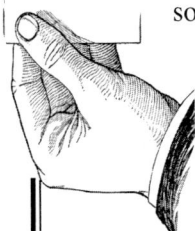

Paul McCartney was clearly a busy man and his idea of producing did not actually extend to mixing the sounds that he had recorded, as "Legs" Larry Smith recalls. "Gus Dudgeon actually did the final mix on Urban Spaceman. Gus had the multi-tracks and he mixed it at Decca's studios using some down time he pinched from the Moody Blues. He mixed it during one lunch hour when everybody had buggered off to the pub. Gus used to work there so he rushed into the mixing booth, put the multi-track on and mixed 'Urban Spaceman'. That's the final mix that you actually hear on the record. Gus was kind enough though to note all the fader positions and reset them afterwards so the Moody's weren't put out, or indeed any the wiser. Paul produced the thing and obviously got the sound out of band that he wanted, but Gus actually finally twiddled the knobs and mixed the actual track, that was it, our biggie. It was recorded on borrowed time as it were."

Neil Innes has a clear recall of the day when the single was recorded and how things actually came together. "Well, the day came when we had to go and record this 'Urban Spaceman' song and we were all waiting there and, of course, Paul turns up and he's sort of saying hello to everybody. Then he goes over to the grand piano and he says, "I've just written this", and he starts playing what turns out to be "Hey Jude". I think he was winding Gerry up a bit because he knows about Gerry's reputation for clock watching, so he's already gently wasting a bit of time, and this song goes on and on and on and I'm sort of looking at Gerry and wondering if he's squirming inside. In retrospect he probably wasn't in the least concerned. Even the Beatles hadn't heard the song and to have one of the Fab Four in your studio was to be part of musical history in a small way. Eventually we went on to record the track and he said to Larry, "You're doing this kind of thing, we'll track the drums." And so Larry tracked the drums, because it was a trad jazz thing. And then Paul got him to rock along with it and before you know where you are, this track is going somewhere different, the magic touch is there. Then Paul grabs Viv's ukulele and just comes in 'rinki dinki dinki ding' and there was a lovely moment when Lillian Bron came up to him and said, "What's that you've got there? A poor man's violin?", and Paul goes, "No, it's a rich man's ukulele". At the end we were all stumped when Viv had got out his garden

Vivian in sparkling form leads the band in a performance from the 1967 promotional shoot for Do Not Adjust Your Set. Just visible over Vivian's right shoulder is Sam Spoons who was shortly to depart the group.

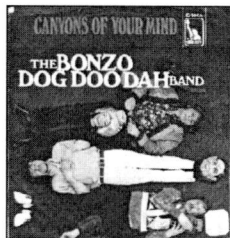

hose with the trumpet mouthpiece and the funnel and wanted to whirl it round his head. And it became part of the track, but it had to be whirled around his head to work. By now we're probably into the eighth or ninth hour and the engineer said, "What the hell's that? You can't record that!" And Paul said, "Yeah, you can. Just put a microphone in each corner." So that's another twenty minutes gone but Viv's whirling this thing around his head and Paul got it down perfectly, it was a great finish to the song!"

The Record Mirror reviewed the single. "These boys are so good visually but sometimes it is hard to get their particular sort of performance across on disc. If this doesn't make the charts, it'll get pretty near. A simple catchy little thing, with all those hoots and growls and booms and wah-dahs behind, and a wee surprise in the finale of the lyrics. Flip: Bonzonian comedy de luxe. Chart possibility."

All of the hard work on Paul McCartney's part paid off for the Bonzos, and the band at last made an impact on the singles chart at their fourth attempt. "I'm The Urban Spaceman" entered the UK charts at the beginning of November and rose to number 25 towards the end of the month prompting an article on the band in the New Musical Express, (although the publication got the name of the single wrong.) "The most pleasing sight my eyes have beheld for a long sock is that of those merry makers of mirth, the Bonzo Dog Doo-Dah Band, fair taking the NME Chart by storm with their 'I'm An Urban Spaceman'. As President of the Unofficial Bonzo Dog Doo-Dah Band Fan Club, I am mightily chuffed, as I am sure are the thousands of others who have been caught by the power of Bonzo Doggery. For those who enjoyed their album 'Gorilla' and who have been tickled by their hilarious stage antics, it seemed that the Bonzos would never succeed in capturing the essence of what is essentially a visual act and put it down on three minutes of circular black plastic. Happily they seem to have done it. Also, those that thrilled to 'Gorilla' will be pleased to note that the Bonzos' second album, titled 'The Doughnut In Granny's Greenhouse', is being released by Liberty on December 6, and should be in everyone's stocking. As singles success has been eluding them, I was beginning to fear that the Bonzos would never reap the vast audience they deserve. Now the 'Urban Spaceman' has made it for them, get ready for a Bonzo Dog blast off!"

No one knew it at the time, but when the single peaked at Number 5 in January 1968, 'I'm The Urban Spaceman' was destined to be the band's one and only hit single. To this day despite all that they went on to achieve the band can still, quite legitimately, be tagged with the unflattering epithet "one hit wonders". For a hard bitten commercial manager like Gerry Bron,

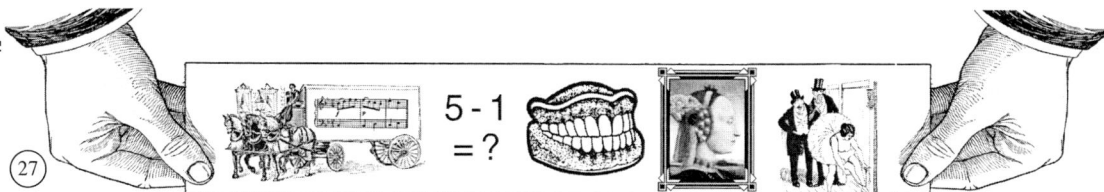

this was not necessarily a huge handicap, but even Gerry was beginning to come to the end of his tether with his infuriating clients. "In the end they had one big hit," says Gerry. "In fact 'I'm the Urban Spaceman' was a huge hit, which spent fourteen weeks in the charts. So they had that coveted hit song, which every band looks for. I mean loads of bands have existed on just one hit song. Most of what they did was quite tuneful and so they had an act and a following. It just wasn't run of the mill. It was completely different to anything else and, sadly, it's never been replaced. I'd love there to be another Bonzos. I thought they were fantastic, absolutely fantastic. Impossible, but fantastic."

The success of "I'm The Urban Spaceman" propelled the band even further into the public eye and with it came a spot on the BBC's weekly pop chart programme Top Of The Pops. Larry vividly remembers the recording of the programme. "I was in some crazy kind of long johns with stars stuck all over the place, but the rest of the guys were in… well some of them were in drag and some of the blokes were in black tie. For the first half of the song the camera panned round everybody, we all looked terribly normal and smart, and then the camera panned down and we didn't have trousers on! 'Ho ho ho, how very satirical, ho ho ho ho'. But it was just so stupid, I mean, it was just what that programme deserved."

Vivian Stanshall too noticed the change in audience reaction following the success of the single and his artistic sensibilities were disturbed by the inaccurate assumption that the song was in favour of the use of recreational drugs as he later explained to John Platt during the course of his 1979 interview for Comstock Lode, "It used to make me puke when it was obligatory to do Urban Spaceman, which I always hated… to tell you the truth. As soon as the first couple of tootles of that one came on, the place was in a riot. Not because I didn't like the song that much… - it was OK at first… - but I didn't like them picking up on things like 'I got speed', which never occurred to me. Suddenly it's something to do with methadrine, so that's all right. Absurd, stupid. That would piss me off." Strangely the successful conclusion of the long search for a hit single did not bring much comfort to Vivian who in 1979 expanded on his continuing unease over "I'm The Urban Spaceman" to John Platt. "I'm more interested in taking chances and sticking my neck out. I had a lot of worries. I didn't like it. It seemed to me an unacceptable gloss. There are and were other things that I'm more proud of, that justify that sort of attention rather than a well produced single. I didn't think it was particularly representative of the band really."

The bass player Joel Druckman eventually left the band after being required to perform as the dummy on "Little Sir Echo", which he felt was

"Here they are from England, the 'Baba Doopal Bondiogs' ...anyway here they are..."

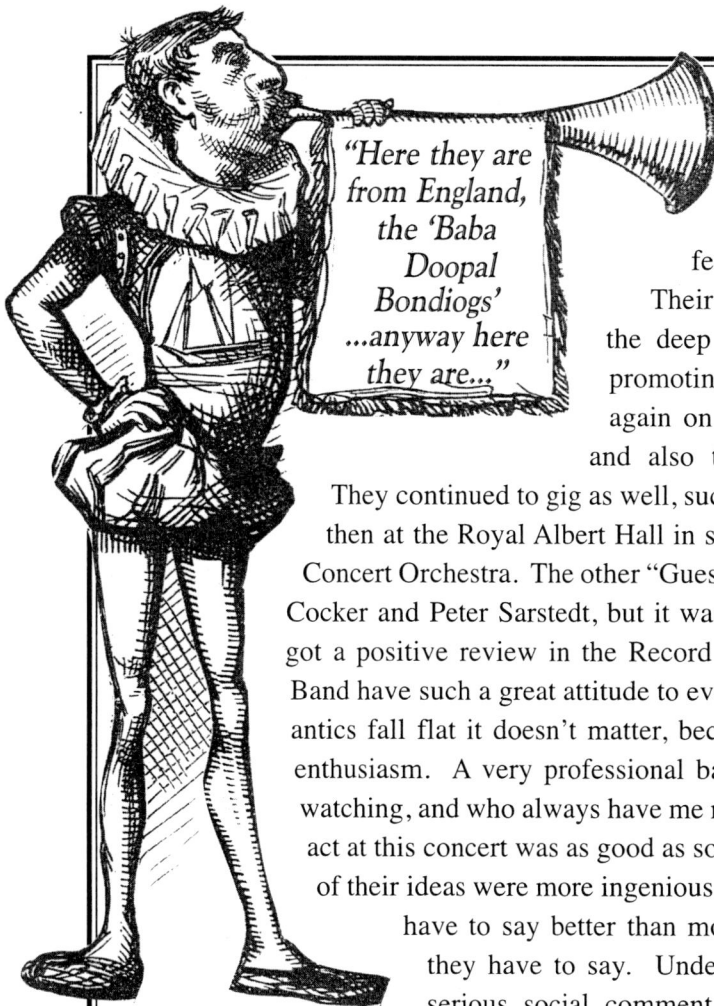

demeaning. He was eventually replaced by Dennis Cowan who could venture into America without fear of being drafted."

Their fourth bass player was thrown into the deep end during October with the band promoting their new single, appearing once again on John Peel's "Top Gear" radio show and also the "Radio One Club" programme. They continued to gig as well, such as at the Dreamland in Margate and then at the Royal Albert Hall in support of Tiny Tim and The National Concert Orchestra. The other "Guest Stars" supporting Tiny Tim were Joe Cocker and Peter Sarstedt, but it was the performance of the Bonzos that got a positive review in the Record Mirror. "The Bonzo Dog Doo-Dah Band have such a great attitude to everything that even when their jokes or antics fall flat it doesn't matter, because they do it all with such British enthusiasm. A very professional band of amateurs who I always enjoy watching, and who always have me rolling in the aisles. I don't think their act at this concert was as good as some of theirs I've seen… though some of their ideas were more ingenious than ever. The Bonzos sell what they have to say better than most… it's just that I'm not sure what they have to say. Underneath all their clowning, though, is serious social comment. (Still, that's what an art college education does for you.)"

Further gigs took place in November 1968 as "I'm The Urban Spaceman" continued to creep up the charts, including Queen Mary's College in London with Fairport Convention and Blossom Toes; the California Ballroom in Dunstable; the University of Kent; and the Marine Pavilion in Folkestone with The World Of Oz and Gasoline Alley. They also had further appearances that month on BBC radio on both "Saturday Club" and the "Radio One Club".

It is a moot point whether 'I'm The Urban Spaceman' is representative of the Bonzos or not. It is certainly a much loved and treasured piece of writing, which was brilliantly performed by the Bonzos and in many respects is the quintessence of sixties pop culture. The success of "I'm The Urban Spaceman" also opened a number of doors, which had previously been closed to them, as Rodney Slater remembers. "We toured Germany and Belgium and places like that where we had never appeared before and that was really on the back of the hit single. I sometimes think the Germans sort of got the idea behind the actual theatrical stagecraft, which Viv was

developing and the whole band was working towards, better than audiences in England. So the band were better received there than we could possibly have expected." The visits to Germany also provided an opportunity to appear before the German public on state television and the band were once again featured on the highly popular "Beat Club" series.

With both a single continuing to creep up the charts and a new album to promote, the Bonzos continued working up to the end of 1968. As well as gigs at the Walthamstow Assembly Hall with the Pretty Things; Brunel University in Uxbridge; and a "Christmas Carol Party" at the Royal Albert Hall with Family and Julie Driscoll & The Brian Auger Trinity, the Bonzos also performed at "The Save Rave" at the London Palladium, which was a charity event in aid of the Invalid Children's Aid Association. The show was performed in the presence of HRH Princess Margaret and included the DJ's Alan "Fluff" Freeman, Tony Blackburn and Emperor Rosko, as well as music from The Love Affair, The Hollies, Scott Walker, The Easybeats, Bobby Bennett, The Scaffold, Madeline Bell and The Paper Dolls.

Just before Christmas the Bonzos also performed once more on BBC Radio's "Saturday Club", plus they made an appearance on BBC2 television's new music programme, "Colour Me Pop". (So named because of the recent introduction of colour television.) On that same Saturday there was an announcement in the music press that the Bonzos had replaced their manager Gerry Bron with Tony Stratton-Smith and that they were planning to tour America the following April. There was also the denial in the music press that the band were thinking of breaking up. Vivian gave a little insight to this rumour when he stated, "I think the hit record was making us more business minded. We suddenly discovered that we could work 14 times a week and were doing so. But that kind of process dehumanises you and emasculates you musically. We got to the stage where we felt we would rather give up if we had no time to rehearse or improve our act. Changes were made and that was that."

Gerry Bron is still of the opinion that the success of 'I'm The Urban Spaceman' should have provided the band with a platform to really build a solid career in Britain, but

the band had its eyes on an altogether different prize. The Bonzos were in a big hurry to establish themselves in America and in April 1969, just at the point where they should have been building on the success of the single in the UK and European markets, the band headed off to America for their first American tour. Gerry Bron recognised the mistake at the time and it was to lead to the final parting of the ways. "They would have gone further than they did if they weren't so paranoid about The New Vaudeville Band," says Gerry. "They were absolutely beside themselves with jealousy, I suppose, that the Vaudeville Band had a number one hit in America with "Winchester Cathedral", and they hadn't had a hit there at all. So they wanted to get to America and make it big overnight, but the timing was all wrong and they needed to consolidate over here. They simply weren't ready for America and not enough work had been done so that America was ready for them, but they wouldn't be dissuaded. It grew into a huge issue, which is one of the final reasons I dropped them for management."

Quite understandably Gerry Bron was not at all bitter about handing on the Bonzo baton to a new manager. This time round it is telling that, despite the enhanced status of the group, there was none of the wrangling, which accompanied the end of Reg Tracey's tenure with the band. To a large extent it all appears to have been something of a relief to Gerry. "They were becoming quite painful to manage and Tony Stratton-Smith, who was the owner of Charisma, had obviously said to them that he could do something I couldn't do and crack America wide open for them. So I said, "fine, you're welcome to try". It gives me no satisfaction whatsoever but they never did make it in America. If they'd been more patient and not quite so neurotic about making it overnight in the States I think that they could have become one of the biggest acts of all time."

"For America you need planning, time and a strategy and you obviously need a certain level of stability that

Vivian in particular definitely didn't have. The band's stage act was all down to Vivian. Take Vivian out of it and you don't really have anything. Don't get me wrong, the others all contributed strongly, but he was the front man par excellence. He was fantastic as a front man. I mean his take-off of Elvis Presley was just unbelievable. – I mean it really was Elvis Presley. And he'd sing these bizarre lyrics to an Elvis Presley type song and it was just fantastic."

Years later Rodney Slater still recalls the arguments that raged over where the Bonzos should concentrate their efforts. "Gerry was a nice guy, basically, who had a very hard time. His ideas of promoting the band were great, he had good connections, but there was an age difference, a complete difference in our backgrounds. He came from a very established world, his father was Sid Bron, the music publisher with big offices in Tottenham Court Road, all that, he was brought up in that straight business tradition and we weren't. We were just crazy guys who didn't believe that everything couldn't be done our way. So he had a problem and we didn't fit in. In the end it got where we wouldn't do the venues he wanted. We got fed up with it but you'd have to admit that by this time, we were beginning to run dangerously close to being out of control. We were becoming disgruntled with what we were doing in the confines of the entertainment business and somehow it wasn't working, but I'm damned if I know what Gerry could have done. Where else could one have gone and still maintained the style of living we'd become used to? We were getting caught up in the thing that we're kicking against anyway and that's always the danger."

It was typical of the Bonzos luck that the announcement of the change in the camp precipitated a spate of rumours that the band was on the verge of splitting up. Vivian was quick to add flames to the fire with some fairly indiscreet pronouncements to the effect that the band was exhausted and burned out and that there was a real danger the band would break up if the management issues were not resolved. As a consequence the Bron Agency was forced to issue a very public denial, which stated that Bron would continue to act as publishers and in an agency capacity, but would relinquish their management role. The press release truthfully stated, "After long discussions with the band it has been decided to appoint Tony Stratton-Smith as the band's personal manager but Bron will of course continue to represent the group's publishing interests and act as agents". All of this was duly reported by Melody Maker under the distinctly unflattering bold headline:

"BONZO DOG BAND WILL NOT SPLIT".

The immediate crisis may have been averted by the appointment of Tony Stratton-Smith but there was still a great deal of unrest in the band as Rodney Slater recalled. "There was a lot of whinging and moaning about the fact that we wanted to, (some people more than others), go to America. It seemed the obvious answer because all these bands had

gone out there and got international fame; and big money too. We thought, "Oh the Bonzos should have some of that", and no one was giving us any of "that", so Gerry Bron was getting a lot in the neck over the fact that we weren't going out to America and coming back millionaires. In the UK people were falling down at our feet worshipping our artistic integrity and our craft or whatever, but we didn't have all the trappings of success, which normally go with it."

Fortunately the band did continue and on Christmas Day the band were back on television with a one-off 50 minute special of "Do Not Adjust Your Set", which was called "Do Not Adjust Your Stockings". The Bonzos also found time for two more gigs after Christmas, performing at a festival in Utrecht, The Netherlands with Pink Floyd, and then at the "New Year's Eve Gala Pop & Blues Party" at the Alexandra Palace in London, along with the Small Faces; Joe Cocker; John Mayall's Bluesbreakers and Amen Corner. Also on that last day of 1968 they appeared on German television's "Beat Club", along with Joe Cocker, Manfred Mann, the Bee Gees, Marmalade and Simon Dupree & The Big Sound.

CHAPTER FOUR
WRESTLE POODLES... AND WIN!

'I'm The Urban Spaceman' had continued to climb up the charts, reaching number 4 in the BBC chart at the beginning of the following year. This produced the opportunity for the Bonzos to perform on BBC television's 'Top Of The Pops', making a total of four appearances. However, the success of a hit single seemed to sit uneasily with the Bonzos, and the band found that there were difficulties with their audience. As Vivian Stanshall observed, "There was a difference in what was expected of you, what kind of motor you turned up in and what sort of roadies you had and whether you actually humped your own equipment around. One would assume that that would endear to your audience, but that doesn't appear to be so. I much preferred it when we'd turn up and see a couple of geezers who couldn't get in and say "wanna be a roadie?" and drop them a nicker and they'd help you hump the stuff in. Fine and healthy. At the same time, I like ostrich plumes and bags of swank. But only as long as they knew that I thought it was ridiculous. We acquired a different kind of admirer. I got the feeling they'd shout for anything, make a racket just because you're there. It used to make me puke when it was obligatory to do 'Urban Spaceman'."

Despite their obvious fatigue, and the frustration with the music industry as they often expressed in interviews at the time, the band continued to perform as frequently as ever in 1969, appearing on David Symonds BBC radio show and playing at venues such as Mothers in Birmingham; Rhodes Centre in Bishops Stortford; Liverpool

Philharmonic Hall with Scaffold; and Newcastle City Hall with Family and Gun during January.

The gigging continued in February with venues such as the "Disc Valentine Ball" at the Seymour Hall in London and the Dome in Brighton with Family and Free. The Bonzos also won further media coverage appearing on "Radio One Club" and again on the German music programme "Beat Club", with Canned Heat; Julie Driscoll & The Brian Auger Trinity; The Tremeloes and Billie Davis. More importantly, for their many teenage fans, a new series of "Do Not Adjust Your Set" began to be shown every Wednesday on ITV, the series running for 13 episodes through to May.

At the beginning of March the band were back on BBC radio on the "Symonds On Sunday" show and the Bonzos released their much anticipated follow-up single to "Urban Spaceman", which was the promising "Mr Apollo". Once again their luck deserted them and this fine effort failed to chart and Vivian Stanshall in particular took the disappointment very hard. "Mr Apollo" was a strong single, but was a little long for regular radio air play, and probably a little too quirky for the general record-buying public. As Neil Innes commented, "I was keen to do a follow-up that was sort of humourous but still catchy. 'Mr Apollo' was once like that. Most of it was mine but Viv got hold of it and it ended up well over acceptable single length because it wasn't until 'Hey Jude' that you could get away with over three minutes." Vivian Stanshall's view was somewhat different. "Our latest teen-style waxing 'Mr. Apollo', lasts four mins 21 secs. So what? Well, you'd scarcely believe the nuisance we've had in getting it put out at this length. Firstly we were told we ought to make a bastardised 'D.J.' version that would last the statutory two and a half minutes, (minimum de platter, maximum de plug plug), whilst the public could purchase the full-length copy. Or could we not re-record and shorten the whole thing anyway?"

The B-side, "Ready-Mades", whilst initially sounding like a regular pop song, was even more quirky when the lyrics were considered. In fact another song had been planned for the B-side. It was a song with the unlikely title of "It Was A Great Party 'till Somebody Found The Hammer", which Vivian Stanshall later confirmed had been recorded live at a gig. "It was done at the Marquee Club. There's an instrument makers in Manchester, Thomas Reynolds, who for the most part supply schools. And every time we were in Manchester, which was very often in the first year of our professional life, and see these chaps who'd repair a cornet or something for me, these old boys who were all in brass bands themselves. We had a great pile of musical rubbish on the stage and we issued everyone in the audience with whistles and then said 'help yourself to an instrument.' There was a mad rush and, as best as we could, we conducted them on the riff. So it was a wonderful cacophony. It was just a terrifically exciting row... but not very commercial!" And so the song was never officially released.

There was an amazingly inaccurate review of "Mr Apollo" in the New Musical Express; "With the latest Apollo space-shot having just completed its mission, this new one from the Bonzo Dogs couldn't have come at a more topical moment. It's not as good as 'Urban Spaceman', (which is always a danger with a follow-up in the same style as the original), largely because it doesn't have such a catchy chorus. But there's much more substance to it, including swirling Tornado-like organ, crashing symbols and various ethereal distortions. There's also much more humour, with lengthy spoken passages, simulating a tough-talking U.S. officer briefing the space crew."

It is some indication of the band's popularity at this time that they were voted sixth in the category of "Best Group On Stage" by readers of Beat Instrumental, beating bands like The Who, Ten Years After, and Pink Floyd. Throughout this period the Bonzos continued to play to live audiences in venues such as the Free Trade Hall in Manchester with their friends The Scaffold and again at Mothers club in Birmingham, during March.

In April the Bonzos completed gigs at The Royal Ballroom in Tottenham, the Locarno in Stevenage and the Boston Starlight Room, and also made radio appearances on the "Radio One Club" and John Peel's "Top Gear". In the days when compilation albums were not constantly churned out by the record companies and most record buyers had to be very selective about the few albums that they could afford to purchase, exposure through a budget priced sampler album was very effective. So the inclusion of "Can Blue Men Sing The Whites" on the sampler "Gutbucket: an underworld eruption", with bands like Captain Beefheart And His Magic Band; Canned Heat and the Groundhogs, brought them to the attention of more serious blues fans. As Vivian Stanshall commented, "Oh, by the way, we're now officially an 'underground' group. Liberty and United Artists records have brought out a new label called: 'Gutbucket, an underworld eruption' (referring to the artists' complexions, I imagine). Anyway we're in it."

In May 1969, with Tony Stratton-Smith now at the helm in the role of "personal manager", the Bonzos set off to conquer America their first visit to the other side of the pond. To coincide with the tour, at the beginning of June "The Doughnut In Granny's Greenhouse" was released in the USA, but under the title "I'm The Urban Spaceman", and it included their UK hit single in addition to all the other album tracks. Whilst the tour was not considered to be an overall success they did play some prestigious gigs such as the Hollywood Palladium, with The Who and Poco, and the Fillmore West in San Francisco with the Byrds, Pacific Gas & Electric, and Joe Cocker & The Grease Band, where they were received well. One gig where the audience did not appreciate them was in New Jersey where they performed in a vast sports arena with Sly & The Family Stone to an audience that was mostly comprised of 11 year old pop fans.

Vivian in a memorable pose for the Tadpoles shoot

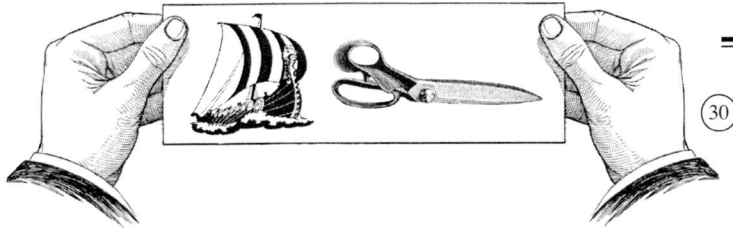

30

"Legs" Larry Smith remembers that the two tours of North America, which the band undertook proved to be less than auspicious occasions. "They were hard work those tours because we didn't have any money and the organisation was appalling," says Larry. "I did my bit to make things worse though. The first one we did was commenced just after I was up in Scotland for the week with my friend Duncan Urquhart. We were whisky tasting, or rather swallowing, so we were inebriated beyond reason for a whole week, and the band rang the police up and they were driving round this Highland village saying, "Has anybody seen "Legs" Larry Smith? He's wanted to go to America. If anybody's seen this man, phone me". I was still rather merry so I didn't even manage to get back home and pack, somebody had to do that for me, and I met everybody at Heathrow clutching this haggis in a brown bag, because in my advanced condition, I thought this'll be a fun talking point at our press reception. Unfortunately it proved otherwise because when I arrived at New York airport and we were going through customs and the immigration guy says, "What the hell's that?" And I said, "It's a haggis, it's a Scottish delicacy..." He picked it up and threw it in the bin. You're not allowed to take any food into America or bring any out, (thank God). Anyway the English press got hold of this and managed to get their wires spectacularly crossed and reported that I'd been busted for possession of hashish, when actually it was of course haggis. So it just shows you, folks, you can't always believe what you read in the paper."

The organisation was indeed appalling and the band had taken the stupid step of going to America in the hope that unconfirmed gigs would be confirmed and verbally agreed fees would be honoured. Fortunately there were some confirmed support slots and the audience reaction on the other side of the Atlantic was just as fervent as the UK, as "Legs" Larry Smith remembers. "The American tours were great from the performance point of view, I loved the crowds they were wonderfully welcoming to us. They didn't always start brilliantly as usually some guy would come out with a bit of paper on, which he'd written down the name of the band as he'd heard it gabbled out by Roger or whoever and go, "Here they are from England, the 'Baba Doopal Bondiogs'.... anyway here they are..." And we'd come out to the sound of tumbleweed rustling and cattle crossing the road, (as Mr Slater would say), because they didn't know who we were. There were one or two people who had obviously bought the albums on import or whatever, but generally they didn't know who on earth we were. Nevertheless, by the end of the show they'd be up on their chairs, on tables, screaming for little old Bonzo. It made it very frustrating because we weren't getting any back up from the

management, the label or the agency. The distribution was appalling, they got it all wrong. There were no records in the shops. We'd be appearing in Detroit and there'd be a window display in Chicago for the band. It just didn't hook up."

Unfortunately for the band Gerry Bron was to be proved right. The first American tour was badly organised and poorly promoted and was really limited to a few support slots at the Fillmore venues on the East and the West coasts intermixed with some minor gigs and a great deal of sitting around. For Rodney Slater it was to prove a less than rewarding experience. "When we got to America we were really in a constant haze of smelly chemicals, basically. Not that we were taking them, they were all around us and that's where that audience was... – which student is taking the mind expanding drug... – hence the joke and Roger's machines."

In the wake of the first American debacle the band parted company with Tony Stratton- Smith as "personal manager", although there would be a longer term role for Tony as label boss for many of the group's solo projects. In 1969 however, Tony Stratton–Smith was just one more skilled music business operator who just could not get to grips with the seething box of frogs, which was the collective Bonzo mentality. Eventually Vivian Stanshall came to the misguided conclusion that he had the necessary ability and decided that he could do the job as well as any regular manager. Given the unstable nature of the mercurial front man this was a huge mistake. In early 1969, Vivian summed up his views on rock management for "Friends" magazine. It certainly did not make for convincing reading from a man who was charged with making the Bonzos a roaring financial success; "First year after we left art school and decided to go professional we just went out to pasture on the club circuit and universities. As soon as it became apparent that we could earn money in those sort of places then we stayed there. It took supreme strivings to get out of that. Well it took 'Urban Spaceman', which was an incidental hit. Then we were put out to sniffle around in the arena of ballrooms and things. We were sent in directions that were completely unsuitable for us. They were decisions made on the basic premise that the idea of a band is to make money and as steadily as possible."

In contrast to Vivian Stanshall and his idealist approach to commerce, Gerry Bron was a man who understood the unbending rule that a professional rock group does indeed need to make money steadily otherwise it starves to death Gerry had already witnessed the unreliable nature of Mr Stanshall who was patently unsuited to life as a rock manager. "He wasn't barking mad" says Gerry. "I think, sadly, I never recognised that he was unstable and what his real problem was. He wasn't well-adjusted, he had some sort of problem. Maybe the fact he was so good on stage was the one way that he sorted himself out, but you couldn't really rely on him. I remember Vivian came to see me once and said, "You realise that we're driving ourselves into the

ground? There is no way that we can go on week after week doing exactly the same show. We're going to dry up and it's just going to fall to the ground and it's going to be the end of it." So I said, "Okay, well what do you want to do?" And he said, "...Well, we've got to take some time off, we've got to cancel some engagements and rehearse new material." I said, "Okay. Well, that's a really brave idea. Let's do that. You realise that it's going to cost you a lot of money, because every week that you don't play you're losing five or six hundred pounds." Which in those days was a substantial amount of money." He said, "Well, yes we do, but if you find me somewhere to rehearse we'll do it anyway. We're going to go there and we're going to rehearse a whole new show and you'll see it's going to be really worth it." So I find this rehearsal room in Ealing and off they go, we cancelled the dates, they started rehearsing".

Gerry Bron has always been a very hands-on type of manager, and he was definitely not the type to leave his protégés to muddle on in darkest Ealing without receiving a progress report, as Mr Bron recalls. 'So I phone up after a couple of days and say, "How's it going?" "Oh, it's going fine." "Anything I can listen to or see?" Viv said, "Oh no, no, no, no, it's much too early. We're just putting ideas together." So this goes on, and after about ten days I sort of get a bit shirty and say, "Well, look, I'm coming down." He said, "No, we'd really rather you didn't." I was having none of it, though, and I told him, "No, no, I'm coming down. I want to see what you're doing." So down I go and Vivian's there on his own and I said, "Okay, well, let's get the band together and go through some of the material." And he said, "Well, it's not really finished yet." And I said, "Well, okay, but let's go through it in the state that it's in." He said, "Well, there's only one of you, I mean we can't perform to one person." I said, "Vivian, I'm your manager, just get up there and play your new material." So he looks at me and he goes, "Well actually...there isn't any yet". I said, "But you've been here for ten days!" His response, "I know, but I've got these rabbits you see and I've got to build the hutches to keep them in, and that's what I've been doing. I've been building these rabbit hutches." I had no option but to believe him. Recently however I met his wife Monica, and I told her the story and she said, "We never had any rabbits". So I don't know what the true story is now. But that's what he told me at the time. He actually seems to have spent two weeks doing absolutely sod all. So that's the sort of person you're dealing with; not exactly Mr Reliable."

However, there is little doubt that Vivian Stanshall was most certainly the wrong man to try and manage the Bonzos especially as the band seemed able to take any promising situation and turn it to dust.

Back in the UK for the later part of June 1969, the Bonzos did continue performing at venues such as the Mothers club in Birmingham and then in July at the Lyceum in London with Idle Race, Velvet Opera and Peter Hammill. They played gigs at the Locarno in Bristol

and Van Dykes in Plymouth, and then embarked upon a tour of Ireland with The Nice and Yes. They managed to play in Belfast and Dublin, but the gig in Cork was cancelled due to "inadequate power supply and general disorganisation".

Following a performance at The Pavilion in Bath and yet another gig at Mothers in Birmingham, plus radio appearance on BBC's "Top Gear", the Bonzos appeared at the 10th National Jazz Blues & Pop Festival along with Pink Floyd; Yes; King Crimson and Soft Machine, in early August. As the Record Mirror reported: "The Bonzo Dog Band took most of the afternoon's awards in conditions that really work against them. At first, they didn't want the gig because their own unique comedy isn't usually effective to large crowds and loses power when seen from a distance. However, following Viv Stanshall's Presley routine on 'Blue Suede Shoes', his camp self-love antics and Legs Larry Smith's pseudo-star act, the set won the response tally for the afternoon."

August continued with gigs at the Locarno Sunderland and the California Ballroom in Dunstable; followed by yet another radio appearance on "Symonds On Sunday"; and then a performance at the Bilzen Jazz and Pop Festival in Bilzen, Belgium, with Taste, the Moody Blues, Soft Machine and Brian Auger and The Trinity. Then back home for a gig at the Eastbourne Winter Gardens.

The fact that the Bonzos were focussed on the great American adventure had not helped in the promotion of the 'Mr Apollo' single and by mid 1969 some real frustration was beginning to creep into the Bonzo camp. Nonetheless there were still a number of positive things happening for the band. The second series of "Do Not Adjust Your Set" had proved to be a success and had led directly to the "Tadpoles" album, which was originally conceived as a soundtrack recording. When contractual difficulties arose however, it metamorphosed into a fully flown Bonzo album featuring some of the tracks that had been recorded for the television series allied to some new recordings and a few fragments, which had been recorded at the same time as "The Doughnut In Granny's Greenhouse".

TADPOLES

ATV, the company behind "Do Not Adjust Your Set", suddenly took real notice of the Bonzos when "I'm The Urban Spaceman" became a hit single and it was quickly decided that a soundtrack album for the show should be released. ATV wanted the Bonzos to record more tracks for the album to make up a full album's worth of material. The problem remained that the Bonzos were touring extensively and there was no readily available new material, and what material there was had already been earmarked for the Bonzos own next album. Among

TADPOLES

Tackle the toons you tapped your tootsies to on Thames TV's "Do Not Adjust Your Set"

BONZO DOG BAND

LIBERTY

The Tadpoles sleeve exhibited the most care which had yet gone into a Bonzo album. The original release featured a series of cut out windows which moved as the record was withdrawn from its sleeve.

the stage favourites performed by The Bonzos at this time were "We're Going To Bring It On Home", "Tent", "Sofa Head", "Give Booze A Chance", "Busted", "National Beer", (later renamed "King of Scurf"), "Joke Shop Man", "Boiled Ham Rhumba", (later renamed "The Cat Meat Conga" when it finally appeared on Neil Innes's " Innes Book of Records"), "What Do You Do?", "Quiet Walks", "On A Wonderful Day", and "Look At Me I'm Wonderful". Much of this material would indeed end up on the "Keynsham" album and the band were not keen to delay work on their own full blown album so the compromise solution brokered by Vivian Stanshall was to re-master the recordings of the material, which had

115

already been used on the show, but which had not previously been released. The agreements with the Musicians Union at the time did not allow commercial phonographic recordings, ("records" to you and I), to be used and insisted instead on a new recording of each song being recorded. Accordingly, the Bonzos had already re-recorded many of the "Gorilla" era songs and there was also a wide selection of cover versions. Mostly these existed as backing tracks, which were permitted under union rules provided the band added a live vocal to them on the show itself. "Tadpoles" therefore represents a pretty disparate bunch of numbers of variable quality. This collection of unused material and items from "Do Not Adjust Your Set" was combined with "The Urban Spaceman" and the most recent Bonzo single in the shape of "Mr. Apollo".

In consequence of its unusual conception the album looks back toward the "Gorilla" era and has much more in common with the first album rather than "The Doughnut In Granny's Greenhouse". The choice of material therefore represents the demands of a children's television executive allied to some genuinely experimental recordings and a touch of expediency. Perhaps these are the reasons why the Bonzos themselves never considered this mixed bag of recordings a genuine Bonzo studio album.

"Tadpoles" starts with "Hunting Tigers Out In Indiah", a wonderfully harebrained piece of nonsense written in tribute to the men who manned the far flung outposts of the British Empire, England and the Raj. This new version of a Twenties recording set the tone for the album, much of which drew upon new recordings of vintage 78's.

In marked contrast to the opening track, "Shirt" features a more contemporary Bonzo idea. The track commences with Vivian Stanshall's classic interview on the subject of shirts, which segues into Roger Ruskin Spear's own composition, the son of "Trouser Press", featuring a solo by Roger on the electric shirt collar! Roger's trilogy of garment based material would later be completed by "Waiting for the Wardrobe". As Roger recalls, "Shirt" came from our experiences on the road with dry cleaners and laundry really. I mean trying to get your bloody shirts cleaned in Burnley or something like this was just a source of hilarity. "Shirt" was inspired by the sign reading "fifty-nine minute cleaners", where we rolled up enthusiastically only to be told, "Oh no, that's only the name of the shop dear, we don't actually do it in fifty-nine minutes". It wasn't three weeks, it was a bit shorter than that but it was certainly days rather than minutes, but that

kind of thing happened all the time and in those days we used to insist on wearing bloody starched collars. I mean we were all sado-masochists really. These horrible starched collars could be really painful. By the end of the performance they were completely limp anyway. We used to wear all this heavyweight clothing in the early days and be running around like maniacs. We used to reek afterwards, and we couldn't get them washed, it was terrible."

Neil Innes recalls how the more rabid offerings of the marketing trade were often the target for Bonzo humour. "The Bonzos laughed at the same things. We'd go into a Marks & Spencer or another kind of well-known chain store and you'd see signs up saying 'Shirt Event'. This gave Roger at least part of the inspiration for "Shirt". When you think about it in the cold light of day, I mean 'shirt event'! How stupid can you get? Clothing isn't an event. Somebody needs to get a grip and Roger picked up on that."

The next track on the album was in stark contrast to "Shirt". "Tubas In The Moonlight" is another piece written by Roger Ruskin Spear, which is evocative of the original Twenties tunes, which stimulated the Bonzos in the first place. "Dr Jazz" follows hard on its heels and is very much in the vein of the early Bonzo recordings with a superb humourous arrangement culled from a bewildering array of unexpected instruments. Next up is the "Monster Mash", a cover version of the song originally recorded in the 1950's by Bobby "Boris" Pickett. Vernon Dudley Bowhay-Nowell and Sam Spoons were both present for the original television version, which featured Sam Spoons as "the monster from the slab", only this one happens to be playing the electric spoons. This original vinyl side one of the album concludes with "I'm The Urban Spaceman".

Side two kicks off with "Ali Baba's Camel", a slight but fun comic song revived from the Twenties to great effect. Next up is "Laughing Blues", which even in 1969 was already a historical Bonzo artefact. It appears the track had been originally recorded during their 1966 Parlophone sessions, and despite the poor standard of recording it was shamelessly exhumed for "Tadpoles". However it is worth it for the unbelievable clarinet work from Rodney. Somewhat in the same vein is the next offering, "By A Waterfall", which had also been a hit for Jeannette MacDonald and Nelson Eddy. This number had proved to be a huge favourite on "Do Not Adjust Your Set" with the band designing their own water fall machine, with predictable results. In marked contrast to the acoustic noodlings of "Waterfall" the Bonzos then strike up the fuzz metal intro, which heralds "Mr Apollo". The glorious contrast between the hard rock intro and the acoustic chorus is still a highlight of the Bonzos work. Closing the album is "Canyons Of Your Mind", another Elvis powered classic. Despite the fact that it was only regarded strong enough for inclusions as a 'B' side it was to prove a hugely popular piece on stage

117

and was performed on numerous television shows. The toe curlingly awful guitar solo was brilliantly captured by Neil Innes and it remains a classic moment to this day.

On release, the album was found to be strangely devoid of credits. The reason may well be that no-one was entirely sure who had performed on which tracks. Some of the songs were recorded at a faster than usual pace to meet the unforgiving demands of a television schedule. The revolving door policy on band members and bass players also made it difficult to pin down who exactly had played on tracks such as "Laughing Blues" or "Monster Mash". Vernon Dudley-Bowhay Nowell is clearly seen playing bass on the broadcast version but the album appears to feature a different recording. To add to the confusion, both Dave Clague and Joel Druckman claim to remember playing bass on some of the songs, "Urban Spaceman" being the main point of contention. To complete the mystification however this is also the album that features the first contributions by Dennis Cowan on bass guitar. Dennis was to claim the bass player's slot for himself and was to last the distance with the Bonzos and many of the offshoots, which followed. At least there would be no further uncertainty with regard to bass on future recordings.

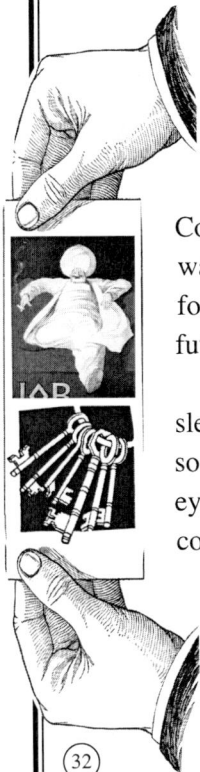

Of the four featured bass players it is Dennis Cowan who appears on the sleeve. The album sleeve seemed to have had more care lavished upon it than some of the recordings. The initial batch incorporated specially cut slots in the eyes of the band members revealing the inner sleeve and producing a pleasingly comic visual effect as the album was removed from its packaging. The album was to prove the Bonzos most successful album release rising to number 36 in the UK charts in the summer of 1969 and out performing the previous offering by four chart places.

There never has been an official explanation as to the name given to the album and no one is really sure how it came by the title. The name "Tadpoles" seems to have been chosen as a result of a chain of logic, which may have commenced with Vivian Stanshall reasoning that a tadpole is an independent entity, which is not a fully formed frog, and this collection of disparate songs were viewed by the band as "Tadpoles" because they were conceived independently and do not constitute a fully fledged album.

Neil Innes cannot throw any more light on the subject. "It was a strange time, we just seemed to say communally, "Let's go back to your childhood". Let's go back to the first love, you know. To this day I'm rather proud of some of the arrangements. I arranged "By A Waterfall" and I still love the way it works. Roger too contributed some great arrangements. His "Tubas in the Moonlight" is breathtaking. It's taken me years to realise where Rodney and Roger were coming from. They really admired Duke Ellington, I think it

118

In the aftermath of the Bonzo split, Roger Ruskin Spear released two solo albums, "Unusual" and "Electric Shocks" which are very much in the classic Bonzo style, and in some respects are more Bonzo than the Bonzos were themselves.

shows on that one."

In retrospect Rodney Slater too is slightly bewildered by the sheer variety on display but soon warms to his subject in the same manner as Bonzo aficionados everywhere. "Looking back on it that was bloody weird, what a collection of stuff! We've got the hit record, the B-side of which was also brilliant, one of my all time favourite things, "Canyons Of Your Mind". That was a cracker that was. Then you've got the failed single, which is "Mr Apollo". There are some brilliant lines in that too. I mean, "and now I'm two separate Gorillas", that was just a brilliant line. I still laugh at that and use it if I get the chance when people ask me how I feel. Ah, yes, there was a bloody classic on there: "Monster

Vivian's memorable opening sequence for "The Sound Of Music" in the first series of "Do Not Adjust Your Set".

Mash". I think that's a cracking track. It had already been a hit in the States; – number one with Bobby Pickett and the Crypt Kickers, I think. It's a brilliant track in its original form and I think Viv's input and all the other stuff made it even better. I'd have liked to have done more things like that, because it was a good track. We were brilliant on it, that demonic laughter at the end, it was just unbelievable. Then the other things I liked too, "Hunting Tigers", "Ali Baba's Camel" and "By A Waterfall", which are all kind of updates of old stuff, but we added stuff to them as well and made contemporary jokes in place. Roger wrote two things for that, "Tubas in the Moonlight" again absurd, violins and cellos are okay for romantic songs about moonlight, but bloody tubas? These great big lumps of metal and this great farting sound. How unromantic can you get? So Roger came up with that. What a hotchpotch of things, really. I begin to wonder why did we do that and why did we put them together? Probably because we were rushed off our feet and we had to produce an LP at that time. It's the only explanation I can think of, really. I suppose around this time we were working so hard writing time had sort of dried up, hadn't it? The Innes/Stanshall output is very low in that and Roger was writing good new stuff then. And then to fill it in we brought out five from the archive, really. It's all entertaining though."

"The album's finisher "Canyons" is particularly famous for Neil's awful guitar solo, which was a great counterpoint to all the axe hero-worship going on then. We played it live and sometimes the joke was being totally missed: – at Leeds University, as I was walking off someone said, "That guitarist's bloody crap". I thought, "You've missed the point, mate, haven't you?" Is this a university, for Christ's sake? Who let you in?"

The move back to novelty tunes, which was chiefly under the influence of Roger Ruskin Spear, was noted in the brief Record Mirror review of the album. "Songs range from vintage horror-rock – 'Monster Mash', through the camp Raj comedy number 'Tigers' to the cod Elvis – 'Canyons Of Your Mind'. Not as John Peel oriented as their last album and nearer to the fantastic 'Gorilla'." And a gushing review in the underground paper IT concluded: "One could go on at length about each of the numbers and still not capture the essence of the thing.

120

Everyone will discover bits on it that refer or relate to them; the Bonzos have sarcasm for everyone. Listen very carefully to the instrumental work and the arrangements though, because the group are incredibly good musicians, Neil Innes (guitar & piano) especially, and even without their unique and brilliant wit, they could probably stand up and play any band of straight rock musicians off the stage. Which reminds me of Zappa…."

A hit single was something every band aspired to have, but it did bring with it a series of obligations, which were sometimes quite onerous as Rodney Slater recalls. "I'm glad we did things like "Urban Spaceman" and 'Mr Apollo". For a while though it was a double edged sword, which condemned us to every Friday and Saturday night in a Mecca or Locarno, all over the country. We were there simply because we had a single in the charts, but we played to a lot of ordinary people there and the nice thing about that was that it went down okay. I think that is because all along, even when we were at our craziest, hippiest, smelliest performing the most way out sort of music, we kept the music hall tradition of warm, homely things that were funny and people could laugh at. That was always there. It was always with Viv, no matter how sophisticated he got he could turn and engage with people and he kept them involved with us. And there was Roger's slapstick. - I mean, all his clever machines and everything else but he was still a guy whose trousers came down in the act and all that, – and that engaged ordinary people too. There was something to laugh at. If you didn't understand what was going on you could laugh at Roger and what he was doing."

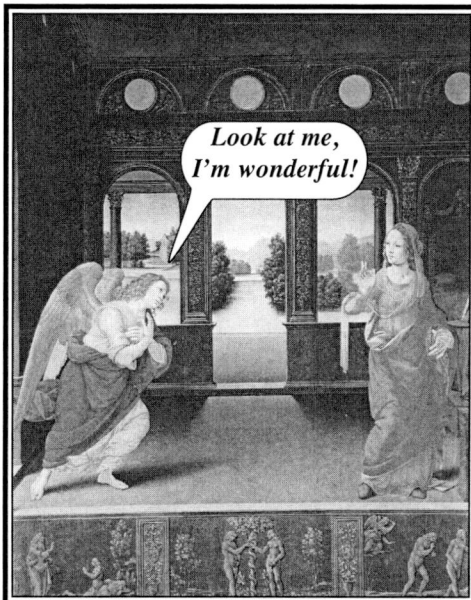

121

CHAPTER 5
TRAGIC MAGIC

As the summer of 1969 wore on the Bonzos were to be found playing on the first day of the Isle Of Wight Festival, the festival including performances from The Who, Joe Cocker, Free, The Moody Blues and Bob Dylan with The Band. In fact the set from the Bonzos started with a slightly different line-up, with Jim Capaldi of Traffic standing in for "Legs" Larry Smith on drums, who was off having fun in a helicopter with Keith Moon. During September the Bonzos continued to play gigs, visiting the Winter Gardens in Malvern; the Middlesborough Showboat; and, of course, Mothers in Birmingham.

One of the reasons why "Tadpoles" had been thrown together was the fact that the band still harboured ambitions to conquer America. Shortly after the album's release in August 1969 the Bonzos prepared for a second assault on the States. This time around they played the Boston Tea Party festival where "Legs" Larry Smith claims, "The Bonzos damn near blew the Grateful Dead off the stage." They also played at the Fillmore East in New York with Spirit and the Kinks, and over on the West Coast at The Winterland in San Francisco with Led Zeppelin and Roland Kirk. They also played at The Experience Club on Sunset Boulevard in Hollywood.

In addition to their desire for fame and fortune, one of the reasons why the band liked to tour America was the prevailing spirit of acceptance for artistic expression. Vivian Stanshall in particular responded to this sense of freedom as he later told John Platt. "I enjoyed the freedom. We were developing mammoth shows in so far as we were playing two to three hours, and some shows went on for four hours. It became freer and freer. We'd start off with some new melody, which would suggest a routine or mime or something else, there'd be people coming on and going off and doing stuff. It seemed that in America they gave you marks for the whole performance, rather than ticking you off, ("see me, should concentrate more"), after every song. It stretches you out a lot, America."

Despite the eventual warmth there was still a lot of work to do as Vivian Stanshall recalled one bizarre occasion. "The

122

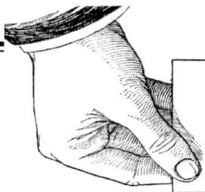

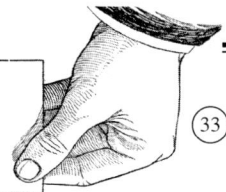

audience was comprised of stoned sheep, and they said, "You're the warm-up act," so we borrowed all these running shorts and things and came out and did some PE for about 15 minutes with beach balls and things and they were dumbfounded. Then the curtains closed and we went round the back and put on our glittery togs and did our set. And I don't think they ever asked, "Who were those guys?" They made no reference to it. Extraordinary. Bill Graham apparently loved the idea, and wanted them to do it at the Fillmore West."

However well the band might be received on stage, with Vivian Stanshall at the helm, the chances of a successful tour were even less favourable than on the first outing. Once again there was very little planning time and the Bonzos appear to have embarked on the unwise strategy of hoping to pick up gigs as the tour progressed. Not surprisingly the group soon grew very disillusioned with what they perceived as lack of support from their US record company and poured out the pent up vitriol to an unsuspecting American journalist who found himself on the receiving end of a two hour diatribe from Vivian and Neil Innes. This led to a rather unsavoury war of words in the press with the band criticising the label and the label fighting back on the grounds that it was merely "a distributor and not a babysitter". Vivian later recounted the scene at great length for Jonathon Green of "Friends" magazine, and if ever proof was needed of Vivian's unsuitability to manage the band then it has to be his own testimony. "We had an astonishing interview with a bloke in Cincinnati," recalled Vivian, "who came on a recording scene and he came along to say hello and he caught Neil and I in a particularly vicious and nasty mood. We were standing up on our hind legs and bleating. And we treated him to a two and a half hour harangue about the role of the artist and the sickness of the system and the persecution and all of the stuff and at the end of this incredible discourse he said 'We won't understand these people: - they're artists'. We were dumbfounded by that. It came as an incredible revelation to him that we had artistic ideals rather than financial ones. People who are creative, people who are the sacks of potatoes for these people to sell, are by nature lost before they have begun. You don't need to be a businessman. You have to be business-like about the way in which you're going to utilise what talents you have to get the best out of you and preserve you as a creator for later years. We just carried on through fiascos and ridiculous bookings and signing absurd bits of paper, - I'd just sign them to get them out of my life and never see them again. I'd sign anything and tear it up. And at the same time I was still trying to make things and masks and do this, that and the other."

The obvious fact that was preying on Vivian Stanshall's mind was the

123

parlous financial situation of the band. In one of his many unguarded moments Vivian shared the harsh truth with journalist Lorraine Altermann. "Being broke and in debt affects our work and the kind of people we are". Being broke and in a foreign country certainly helps to concentrate the mind. Despite all the factors ranged against the band the audience reactions were, as always, very strong indeed. Vivian too was touched by the strength of public reaction to the band's work as he later explained to Jonathon Green. "I'd never cut a gig even if it were totally unsuitable because I'd feel guilty about the people who come to see you. I really do. In the dressing room at Fillmore East about four or five blokes came in who'd come from Ohio to see us. If you start turning places down you think about the people like that that you'll be disappointing. Leaves me speechless how anyone could come that far to see anything. It would have to be Lourdes for me or a levitating poodle or something."

The continuing audience appreciation gave "Legs" Larry Smith an indication of how well the band could have done in the States. "I think we'd have done very well. There was at that time a guy called Chuck McCann, who was an actor, quite a well-known movie actor over there. Somehow we met this guy and he started to champion the band. He loved the band, and he sorted out a series of coast to coast national TV appearances for us on big high rating shows such as Ed Sullivan and The Smothers Brothers and we were all thinking, my God this is great, this could make the band. You know, break us over in the States. Unfortunately Roger just heard at that point from the agency that his wife had had a miscarriage some four or five days earlier and nobody had told him. So Roger, being completely pissed off with this, understandably just got on the next plane home."

With Roger Ruskin Spear gone the Bonzos had suffered a huge blow, but "Legs" Larry Smith felt the tour was still salvageable. "I tried to keep everybody together," says Larry, "I said look, it's tragedy that we ain't got Roger, but his machines are still here, they can still function. Some Redneck in Idaho is not going to lean forward into his television set and go "Oh no Mary Lou come and see... Roger Ruskin-Spear is missing from the Bunzee Doo Bohpal Brand". It was to be our first coast to coast appearance and it should have been a huge opportunity, but it wasn't to be."

US TOUR ABANDONED

It was now that the unsuitability of Vivian Stanshall for the candidate of band manager came to the fore. This was the moment more than ever when the Bonzos needed strong management to pull things together, but faced with the pressures of a strange continent Vivian's resolve seemed to crumble before "Legs" Larry Smith's eyes. "We could have done it but everybody started sulking over the lack of support from the record label and the distributors. Vivian, much to my surprise, suddenly said, "That's it. I'm going home.""

After the very public war of words, the cancellation of a string of gigs led the American press to turn on the band who were seen as the clear losers in the whole unsavoury episode. The Bonzos were obviously leaving the US with their tail firmly between their legs and Rolling Stone Magazine was quick to rub salt in the wounds with the dismissive headline: "Bonzo Dog Runs And Fucks Itself". Vivian Stanshall was under no illusions as to the seriousness of the situation and was publically quoted as stating, "we may

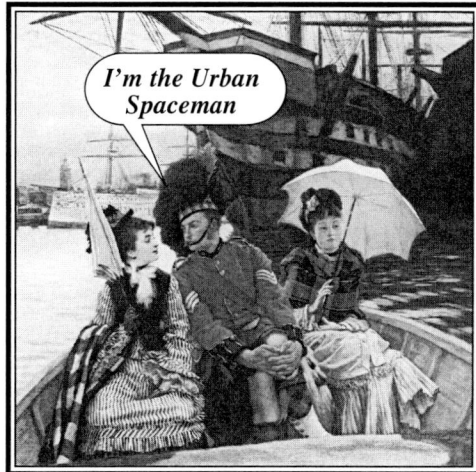

I'm the Urban Spaceman

never work in America again". The cancelled dates cost the Bonzos what was then a great deal of money, ($24,000), and it took three months of solid hard work back in England before the debts were paid off. Accordingly on their return to the UK in November the Bonzos were back on the road, playing venues including Lancaster University; Top Rank Cardiff; the Coatham Hotel in Redcar; the Free Trade Hall in Manchester and Queen Elizabeth College in London.

"It was a terrible time," recalls "Legs" Larry Smith, "and it only exacerbated Viv's condition. I was personally fed up with it all and I didn't go home immediately, I stayed because Keith Moon was coming in a couple of days who I had some great times with, so I stayed to boogie on with Keith for a while. The tour could have been great, but it was a kind of typical Bonzo luck that it didn't happen, in a way."

There has been a great deal of speculation with regard to Vivian Stanshall's abrupt change of personality in the wake of the second US tour, which a number of commentators have attributed to experiments with LSD. Rodney Slater is quick to dismiss. "Look we all drank and we all smoked cigarettes, apart from Roger, who did none of those things. Other drugs, sure there was the occasional joint passed round the bus by the roadies, that's where the drugs came from. I don't think anyone in the band ever spent a penny on them and certainly not Vivian. It was Valium, which wrecked him and it was his own bloody doctor who prescribed it for him! But, on the other hand, somebody had to do something to control his panic attacks. But was he partial to a secret indulgence in illegal drugs, which might account for some of his behaviour? I think not. There was no reason for him to have secrets. Drugs in that context are usually a shared experience and of course we were on a legal drug in one sense as most of us probably had several pints of beer in us when we went on. I personally couldn't drink more than two before the show because my lip

125

became relaxed and I couldn't play, which was a source of great disappointment to me. I had to wait until afterwards for my drugs."

There has also been speculation that Vivian Stanshall may have been spiked with LSD, but Neil Innes has no recollection of any such incident and simply maintains that the damage may have been caused by the effects of over work on Vivian's already frail psyche.

Neil Innes remembers how the band had to work incredibly hard to pay off their debts in the aftermath of the failed American tour. The band was exhausted by this stage and on the rare occasions when they still ventured into the Northern clubs they would actually attempt to get "paid off" without having to do the show. "Oh we definitely did that," says Neil. "As the years went by we didn't have a holiday. That was part of the problem, you know. We worked so hard in the early days, by 1969 we were exhausted, which is why we tried to get paid off wherever we could. We naively assumed this phrase indicated you got the money but were not allowed to perform the rest of the engagement, which in our tired condition suited us down to the ground. We heard that if you did something offensive to an audience, you'd get "paid off", and in our immature way it meant, "Oh, if you go in on a Monday night and offend the audience we get paid for the whole week anyway and we'll have the week off." Of course, it doesn't work like that. You only got the money for the work you'd actually done and we never managed to get paid off in any event. It ended up with Viv coming into the club, – (I think it might have been South Shields again), saying, "Good evening, ladies and gentlemen, the next time I say 'good evening' I'd like you to shout 'balls'." So he goes, "Good evening, ladies and gentlemen," and everyone goes "balls", and we think, "ha ha", you know. But at the end of the evening the management says, "Oh, got a terrific laugh, lads, you ought to keep that in." A few weeks later we met the same comic, – (we kept meeting the same people on the rounds), you know, and he said, "Hey, Vivian, that thing where you go 'Good evening' and they all shout 'Balls'?" Vivian said, "Yes." And the comic said, "I tried that in Jarrow and I got paid off." You see! Sometimes you just can't win!"

With the American fiasco behind them the chastened Bonzos set about the business of resurrecting their faltering UK career. The commercial fortunes of the group had taken a turn for the worse, but artistically the band continued to develop as musicians performing some fine idiosyncratic compositions. The next task was the completion and release of the "Keynsham" album, which was to be the true follow up to "The Doughnut In Granny's Greenhouse".

KEYNSHAM

This was a frustrating time musically for Rodney Slater, as he later recalled. "That was a time when we were maturing, and growing up as

Keynsham is one of the more successful Bonzo sleeves. Designed by Vivian the mythical Keynsham in the distance is the lunatic asylum surrounded by various demons of the mind.

musicians. I mean, for me personally I've always been an improviser so I like to be in there with people, reacting off them at the time and building on that. In a sense it wasn't my way of completely working, I'd rather be in with a load of jazz musicians who are turning me on. But I never ever got to that very much anywhere anyway. I always played in bands that insisted I played what they wanted rather than what I wanted. I think Neil just went off and wrote, but obviously he was influenced by what was going on around him in the world and music generally, in the same way that Viv was. But they had different focuses entirely. What also emerges from the recordings, looking back on them now, is their different ways of working. Viv is increasingly beginning to

127

"Keynsham is the ID."
VIVIAN STANSHALL

talk about the inner Viv, Neil is making observations on the world in general, and it was a classic Lennon and McCartney, actually. It was a classic one, just exactly mirroring it except they didn't make as much money!"

But the dynamics of the Bonzo writing partnership were pretty much the same as Rodney Slater recalls, especially when it came to artistic differences. "They fought like bloody cat and dog about it. As is emerging that Lennon and McCartney and the Beatles weren't that happy a group, nor were the Bonzos. But every band contains those dynamics. You just have to make it work together."

As regards the creative process in the Bonzos, Rodney Slater's main regret lay in the fact that there was little opportunity to improvise. "There was no jamming. You can't jam in rock music. It's very structured really, especially in the studio. It's all thought out and plotted. I mean, there might be a few suggestions, "Ah, but if I did this and I did that", and sometimes it would be listened to if the composer thought it was all right. But if it interfered with his idea, you know, "No, we won't do that". Basically, I mean it got to the stage where I had to learn to read music because I was always given parts to play that I couldn't bloody remember. People wanted me to play certain things, and I've got a terrible memory. You'll often see me in later clips I'm always there with a bloody stand in front of me because I have to write the dots down so I can get that bloody melody line right."

Following hard on the heels of "Tadpoles", with a gap of only three months, was "Keynsham", a full blown studio album of brand new material. Although this was indeed a completely new album, most of the material had already been performed on stage in live appearances and also radio recordings the year before. Many of the songs from the album were therefore already familiar to Bonzo audiences. The songs that were regularly performed on stage were "Tent", "Busted", "Joke Shop Man", "What Do You Do?", "Quiet Talks and Summer Walks", "Look At Me I'm Wonderful", "Keynsham", "Mr Slater's Parrot" and "We Were Wrong". These recognisable tracks were later joined by "You Done My Brain In", "The Bride Stripped Bare by Bachelors", "Sport (The Odd Boy)","I Want To Be With You" and "Noises For The Leg", in order to complete the album.

As the band soldiered on into the electric era, things were

128

increasingly frustrating on stage for the acoustic instrument players and Rodney Slater's solution was to equip himself with a synthesiser. "I got a synthesiser and on "Keynsham" I think there's only one straight sax track on it, that's "Tent". The rest of the time I was playing synthesiser. I had a tremendous range with this thing of mixing up all kinds of sounds or either imitating the instruments I no longer had to carry about with me and coming across on the same levels as everybody else. On stage around this time Roger just retired. He couldn't cope with the volume. It hurt his head, the bloody noise. So he just retired into the world of his machines. He didn't attempt to play much sax. I was pissed off with it too because the on stage sound in those days was appalling, the levels of sound in live performance. They could never get it right. I gave up playing flute. It was impossible. You couldn't hear yourself. You just had a mike and it came out the PA, which was miles away. I just couldn't cope with it."

There was a great deal more harmony and contentment in the studio environment. Released in November 1969, "Keynsham" went a long way towards putting the band back on the musical track, which proceeded directly from "The Doughnut In Granny's Greenhouse" album. Both the title and the words printed on the inside of the original gatefold sleeve of the album suggest this is another of the "concept" albums, which were then so heavily in vogue, but the listener would have to search pretty hard to find a common link or even a thread of any kind in the weird and wonderful collection of tracks, which make up this intriguing record.

The title of the album and a few of the vocal links are references to the notorious Horace Batchelor who clogged the airwaves of Radio Luxembourg with adverts for his infra-draw method of predicting the football pools, much to the annoyance of regular listeners, as Neil Innes recalls. "We'd all been brought up with this Radio Luxembourg thing and there was a character called Horace Batchelor who used to advertise his personalised infra-draw method of winning the football pools. He'd say very slowly in a west country accent, "I have personally won over one hundred first dividends", and he used to end it up, "So write to me, Horace Batchelor, that's Horace Batchelor, at Keynsham... K-E–Y-N-S-H-A-M". It felt like an eternity, but then he'd say, "I'll repeat that…", and it kind of clicked in the kind of peer group thing because everybody had heard that incredibly annoying advert with Horace Batchelor and his blasted infra-draw method."

There was a darker side to the creation of the "Keynsham" album, which in it's own oblique way also deals with the subject of insanity. Neil Innes recalls the moment when the album's theme emerged. "I think we started to look in on ourselves there and I said to everybody once in the dressing room, "Do you think this is actually happening or do you think we're in some kind of mental institution and we're sort of being led to believe this is happening?" Everybody picked up on the idea and said,

The Bonzos gathered together for one of the last promotional photographs taken at the time of the release of the Keynsham album. It was material from this shoot which formed the basis of the highly effective Vivian Stanshall cover.

"Yes, it's getting too strange! So in one respect "Keynsham" could be described as the location for the Bonzo mental institution and that of course proved sadly prophetic with what later happened to Viv. Starting the album with "You Done My Brain In" could have been interpreted as a huge clue really."

Vivian Stanshall himself was also inadvertently to touch on the subject of lunacy and its close relationship to the record, which the band had just produced, particularly in his extended interview with Jonathon Green for "Friends" magazine. "Keynsham may not be interpreted as an attack on the system, on the surface it's just another happy little piece. In fact it's a particularly vitriolic condemnation of this maelstrom of hatred and greed. There is some Fifties music in it. When I feel particularly aggressive, as I have done for the past six months, I use the most aggressive part of my life, which I suppose was the Fifties when I was a Teddy Boy. We discover things about ourselves everyday folks. In real terms the really sordid level of Northern club that comes over on the LP is a better place to play and sort yourself out than the ones we did actually play, which were slightly smarter. Padded loony bins. Lots of red, cheap furnishings and muted lights."

Despite the disturbing echoes around some of the subject matter, it is interesting to note that "Keynsham" is a firm favourite with surviving band members today. Rodney Slater in particular is an evangelist for the album. "Yes I absolutely loved it. I loved the whole thing, you know, I really did and I still do. I thought some of our best stuff was on there and I was musically much happier on that album than a lot of other things, which found greater favour with the public."

The "Keynsham" album was produced by Neil Innes and Vivian Stanshall. The cover artwork for this album is by Vivian Stanshall and is one of the more successful Bonzo sleeves, featuring a montage of intriguing images and drawings from the pen of Vivian Stanshall, which link to the lyrical content of the album. Vivian was also responsible for the much loved introduction to "Shirt" and later provided Friends magazine with an insight into his own desire to expand upon similar themes in spoken word recordings. "We had some very interesting conversations on 'Shirt'," Vivian is quoted as saying. "Some of them went on and I thought they were valid. One can only put out a certain amount of talk on a two pound record but it would be nice if you could put out a ten bob talk record. Or something that you thought was interesting. What represents a bloke is what he creates, the only thing by which he can be judged. It really is perverted, some of it. I don't think it'll be discovered. The sleeve notes are here but most people will just take them as arbitrary dada spewings laced with a bit of fun. I don't care. We are fighting battles against irremovable forces."

"Keynsham" was to prove a radical departure in a number of ways, not all of them welcomed with open arms by the press or by the group's supporters. In his extensive interview on the subject of the "Keynsham"

album, which was printed in "Friends" magazine, Vivian expanded upon the darker side of the album, which took the band further and further from its comic roots. "Paranoia is one of the themes of the album", explained Vivian. "There is a track on that about hatred of the system, which did its best to put me off Shakespeare and any poetry, painting... stuffed down my throat things that were obviously unsuitable and made things that were exciting to me unpalatable by making reverent, dead things out of them. I mourn the loss to so many people of so much because of the way they were taught. The odd boy also inhabits "Keynsham" because he doesn't like algebra and woodwork and games. He's a freak because he doesn't like things that are normal."

Vivian Stanshall was in expansive mode for the Friends interview and embarked on a further monologue in relation to the themes behind the album. "Does Keynsham exist? I'd hate to see it; it would be just as disappointing as actually seeing the Taj Mahal. That and the Tate Gallery were some of my earliest disappointments, I'd prefer to think and dream about it for myself. I can imagine Horace, ensconced in his palace with jewels and slaves and nubians waving fronds and having his body perfumed everyday and with these infra-draw systems that constantly send in cornucopias and increase the wealth and the whole thing swells and explodes." Now firmly into his stride Vivian was not be deterred in his continuing exposition on the meaning of 'Keynsham', which had taken on a huge significance in his mind. "In some small way Keynsham has taken over today from Mecca, Valhalla and even Heaven. Anyway it seemed a good idea to make Keynsham the capital of madness. Normality is what each person considers to be normal things to do... whatever I do is what I think to be normal. It's normal to make some compromise to a general rightness. It's incredible that people like me are viewed as freakish. Illogical. Keynsham in general terms is the ID. Inhabited by all the things that I've told and led you to believe are not normal. Humm, that exhausts that boring thing... next one please... what's your favourite colour...?"

The debilitating effects of their heavy workload and the demands of a constant touring schedule were beginning to take their toll. Vivian Stanshall was becoming more and more difficult to deal with and the difference between what the band was producing as opposed to what their audience expected was also a source of frustration on both sides of the equation.

For the first time the album included two straight numbers, which were included merely as a result of the fact that the songs had strong merit in themselves. These two interlopers were "Quiet Walks" and "I Want To Be With You", both of which marked a new level of quality and maturity in Neil Innes' song writing ability, but they were devoid of any attempt at overt humour. For a band with many fans avidly buying records in search of the next belly laugh, this was to prove a perplexing move, which was not fully understood by the record company or the fans, but as producers, the casting vote lay with

34

Vivian Stanshall and Neil. Neil Innes is convinced the decision was correct. "Why not?", says Neil. "I think every song in the Bonzos oeuvre has a place because it wasn't contrived, in a way. It was the real thing. It happened because of one thing or another and the band grew and changed. You can't spend your whole life in fits of giggles, there comes a time when you want to be serious for a moment, by the time of our fourth album I think we'd earned that opportunity and our audience went with us."

Neil Innes subsequently revived and performed "Quiet Talks And Summer Walks" for his television series "The Innes Book of Records". The new version incorporated a string quartet and Neil sang the song dressed as a flower providing a visual clue as to the identity of the songs subject, the first rock song to be written from the point of view of an observant bloom. At the time the inclusion of the straight numbers however charming was a controversial issue for some followers who felt that the Bonzos had no mandate to move beyond the strict confines of musical comedy.

"The Bride Stripped Bare By 'Bachelors' is another of the many references to the works of the Dada school artist Marcel Duchamps, who had conceived of the art form known as "Ready-mades" and in the process supplied yet another Bonzo song title, which appeared on the "B" side of "Mr Apollo". The title of course also provides a subtle pun on Horace Batchelor and his revealing Infra Draw system, which stripped bare the mystery surrounding the winning of football pools. This link was clearly on Vivian Stanshall's mind as he explained to Friends magazine. "What else is there to break the barrier of red tape except for winning the pools and getting a lot of money. I like the idea of that immensely, I think pools and that sort of thing is super, the more stockings we can get at Christmas in this dreary pavement the better. The whole thing is boredom, my god the whole world worships boredom. All working towards it."

At another level "The Bride Stripped Bare" is an accurate and painful portrayal of what it meant to appear in the Northern clubs and remains an intriguing recording, which repays repeated listens with fresh insights.

Another intriguing song title, for those who were not familiar

133

with the Bonzos stage performances is the song "Noises For The Leg". Like the "Head Ballet" before it, this was essentially a visual gag. The 'Leg' is in fact a mannequin leg into which Roger Ruskin Spear had inserted a strange device known as a Theremin, which basically is a device that produces electrical current over a surface and with the correct pick up produces a sound. The sound changes pitch according to the proximity of nearby objects, allowing Roger to produce a semblance of a musical scale by the act of waving his arms around the leg. Roger became very attached to his instrument, which he still carries around in a leg shaped instrument case.

Pushed to give his opinion on the album as a whole, Rodney Slater gives a truthful insight into his favourite work. "Oh, Christ. They're all pretty good really. I like them all because you sort of start with Roger's things, - the Theramin Leg and things like that. It was worth doing. With "Joke Shop Man" I'm sort of imitating a bassoon on this synthesiser I bought. With "Sport" we also picked up on a similar theme, "Let's go back to your childhood, childhood, childhood, childhood", so it was a kind of introspective album, brought about by the fact that we were actually beginning to question what we were doing for the first time. I love "Busted". On stage, Roger made this ridiculous giant policeman head. It was just so funny, it was a work of art. It was lovely. He used to come on and the "Allo, allo" bit. It was a huge head with a little helmet, and of course he did the classic thing, he took his helmet off and there was this little lump, shaped like a helmet, pink... – you know.

As regards the track, "Keynsham" itself, that tune is one of my happiest because that was the only tune that I got allowed to play on, really, a free blowing thing. I'm blowing all the way through that. We recorded it in a funny little studio in Gerrard Street or somewhere and it was just me and Neil, you couldn't separate us. You couldn't lose the backing track and you couldn't lose the synthesiser bit I was doing through it so it came out and it's a very loose, free-flowing thing. That's one of my favourite moments, actually, doing that in the recording studio. It's a nice thing anyway. I just like the song. I just felt at one with it. "Quiet Walks" was another possible hit. I liked it tremendously, just as a straight thing but, again, I was doing something different on it. I know I enjoyed doing it and I always go into a sort of reverie... – the world starts slowing down and girls are wearing flowery dresses and walking through fields in slow motion with hair billowing behind them. Then there's the recorders, and there's that lovely thing that Viv and I do; - we're both playing recorders so we're swapping these things, and then there's a violin, which is me on the synthesiser in the background. I liked it musically. I think it's a nice thing and I think it was something that might have gone into the commercial market but how can you tell what people will buy or not?"

The inspiration for one of the most famous moments on the album came from real life as Rodney will confirm. "Oh, the

Hunting Tigers was a stage favourite which was recorded for the Tadpoles album in 1968 and revived for the Astoria show in 2006.

parrot, yes. The parrot actually existed. I did keep parrots. Noisy, shitty parrots, yeah. Viv was intrigued with parrots, it didn't swear though, but he heard this "Bugger off! Bugger off!" from somewhere inside his head and that was it. "We Were Wrong" I also liked, it was just Viv and Larry doing a sort of a hooray Henry couple in a bar falling over and just generally making arses of themselves, something about frightening the horses is one of the lyrics".

The "Keynsham" album was to mark the end of Rodney's recording career with the Bonzos in the vinyl era. "The other thing, the really symbolic one for me is "Look at Me, I'm Wonderful", which was Larry being Mr Cool, which was his speciality. In fact he was no different on stage than he was off. I think he actually believed he was a superstar. To be so convincing he must have believed it, but it ends up with this play-off and it's kind of symbolic because it's the last tune on that side of the album and it's the last time I recorded with them."

For Vivian Stanshall the album did not appear to represent the same happy accident, which Rodney Slater enjoyed making so much. Gripped by a series of increasingly black depressions, Vivian saw the album in a much gloomier light. For Vivian the varied nature of the album can be explained by the manner in which it was recorded as he explained to Friends magazine Jonathon Green. "We really did get very much near to breaking up. This album is an expression of our hatred for the system and it's also the most together thing we have done. All of it is separate projects. We only liaised on two pieces. Everyone was working separately. We stopped talking to each other. We were looking out of the window. I'm empty, we felt, why haven't I done anything? How dare I get on a stage and talk about things I don't know about any more. All I can do is talk about this rotten load of shit. Irrelevant in any case. We were really falling apart."

Rather surprisingly for someone in Vivian Stanshall's condition, the factor that actually saved the day for the Bonzos was the enormous amount of hard work, which had to be done to get the album finalised and released in the wake of the split from Tony Stratton-Smith and the US debacle. "We started managing ourselves," explained Vivian, "and began marshalling ourselves like an army. We worked incredibly hard. We did it cheaply and efficiently." It is a sad reflection of just how difficult the band were to

135

manage that no-one was prepared to take on the mantle. It is telling that for an artist of Vivian's temperament and his openly declared anti-business stance that his only real solace from such a brilliantly realised album achievement lay in the fact that "Keynsham" had been recorded reasonably economically in the face of a band on the brink of collapse.

Around the same time the band were also working incredibly hard doing numerous radio sessions as Vivian recalled in later years for John Platt. "John Peel gave us an incredible amount of airtime and also we did things like 'The Brain Opera'. I can't think of any other band that were doing playlets, things with a 'concept' at that time. We also did 'The Craig Torso Show'. It was awful muck with terrible gags, but at least we were trying to do something theatrical, rather than just going on and doing a series of songs."

The review of 'Keynsham' in the underground paper Friends concluded: "It's an album very far removed from 'Tadpoles', their previous offering. Albums have progressed from fourteen short tracks, to about five long ones to the 'opera' form. 'Keynsham' is an example of the last, with its story, so nearly like a morality play. It's probably the best Bonzo's offering to date. Once again people will start saying – they must have run out of ideas. Judging by 'Keynsham', there will be plenty more."

The album may well have been recorded cheaply and efficiently but at this point the band were still struggling hard to replicate the success of "I'm The Urban Spaceman" and in November 1969 "I Want To Be With You" was released as a single from the album. There was a short review of the single in the Record Mirror. "Eye-brows hurtle up. A straight ballad? Pleasantly harmonised. Gentle melody. No sting in the tail? Nope. Don't think so. Mind you, the 'B' side is restrainedly funny. A change which comes off. Chart Cert." Unfortunately even with such a positive review it failed to chart.

Without the support of a hit single the "Keynsham" album failed to chart even in the lowly number 36 slot enjoyed by "Tadpoles".

Rodney Slater attributes the lack of success to poor marketing on behalf of the record company. "We were marketed appallingly. But, on the other hand, to be fair, we were such difficult people to market. What were we about? Just random thoughts, really. There's no coherent structure as far as I'm concerned, there's no consistent thing to get hold of, other than, "Look at us". We're art students making points largely about absurd things and other ways of looking at situations, which, in any event dear viewer, is up to you to form your own view on what we produce."

Rather surprisingly Vivian Stanshall took a different view to Rodney Slater. Vivian did feel that there was a unifying factor behind the work, which was expressed in typically colourful terms to Jonathon Green. "Unity in desperation was behind the "Keynsham" album. I can hardly believe that we have done what we wanted. It's perfectly acceptable to be a star, I'd love

to be a star. I like to go on stage with fantastic snakes exploding from my head as long as both we and the audience are both aware of what's happening and they realise I know how ridiculous it is then we can both enjoy ourselves."

Vivian Stanshall's words were a typical over-reaction. He was still enjoying the satisfaction of what for him was, in artistic terms at least, a job well done. When the first sales figures were announced and it became obvious that this album too was not destined to be a success, at least on the business side of the equation, Vivian's inevitable downbeat reaction to the lack of commercial success for "Keynsham" brought more problems upon his sagging shoulders. The pressure of running the affairs of the Bonzos contributed to the nervous breakdown that he suffered in late 1969 when the distressed singer was admitted as a voluntary patient to Colney Hatch Mental Hospital. Rodney Slater had always been conscious of the fact that Vivian was unsuited to any form of managerial role and was all the time aware that while Vivian was nominally the leader, the real organisational force behind the band was always Neil Innes. "Neil had the ability to think outside the world of the band. That was another example of chalk and cheese between him and Viv. Neil could organise himself and his affairs, Viv simply couldn't. Viv was all over the place you know, needed a nanny permanently, he needed someone to take the top off his egg, he just did not concern himself with worldly things. And the business side of things, he didn't understand. That's why he got ripped off so much and then there would be this typical sort of impotent fury when he realised he'd been done. Whereas Neil didn't usually get caught by that. He coped better with show business and with everyone. But even he couldn't save us from the sort of nonsense that has gone on for thirty-five years now about royalties but he's done his bit for the Bonzos as far as that's concerned and helped fight our corner here and there, on things like royalty rates. He's a business man. The rest of us weren't really, especially Viv."

As if to divest himself of the baggage of the Sixties, on Christmas Day 1969 Vivian slipped away from the Christmas dinner table and shaved off his trademark auburn locks returning to the table completely bald but covered in fresh razor cuts, which obviously was distressing for the assembled family.

THE LYCEUM ANNOUNCEMENT

With their front man and ostensible manager in this kind of shape things were clearly taking a turn for the worse. Nonetheless the band soldiered on and in December 1969 the Bonzos did a gig at Harrogate Opera House with Hardin & York and made an appearance on the Dave Lee Travis radio show on Radio One. "Legs" Larry Smith was seen hanging out at the star-studded charity concert given by John Lennon at the Lyceum, and it was when the band returned to play at the Lyceum at the end of the year, Vivian Stanshall made his famous announcement that the Bonzos had decided

to disband.

Neil Innes remembers the depressing effect of the lack of overt commercial success and the increasingly gloomy atmosphere, which prevailed in late 1969. "I did ask the others if maybe it was time to give it all up while we were still respected". With sentiments like this being openly expressed it will come as no surprise that things must soon come to a head.

Rodney Slater too was aware that the stresses of the business side of the music industry were really becoming too much for the band. "Just because I enjoyed the music doesn't mean to say that I was enjoying the situation of working in show business. That was just getting depressing for a lot of people. I may have seen it from a different perspective because I was happy to be in work performing music, but I was acutely aware how unhappy my colleagues were and I kind of suspected the band would split because of that."

Over the Christmas break it was indeed decided by at least some of the band members that the days of The Bonzo Dog Band were over, which lead to the announcement by Vivian at the Lyceum show on 28th December 1969. The suddenness of this declaration came as a complete surprise to Rodney Slater who was one of the members who had not been consulted. "Suddenly it just happened. It wasn't discussed openly. I was bloody pissed off when it just evaporated overnight like that. We were all up there on stage at the Lyceum and Viv gets up and says, "That's it. This is the last show". "I said Eh? Nobody told me before I came on", you know... that was like a slap in the face with a bloody wet cod! After that though things cooled off and we had a nice three months, with no pressure fulfilling the gigs we had booked."

Rodney may have been surprised and disappointed, but the disarray in the ranks was there for all to see as the extended review in "Friends" magazine. It was clear that the Lyceum show had been a fiasco with the band teetering on the verge of implosion. Jonathon Green was given the job of reviewing the gig and already had an idea of the disarray in the ranks of the Bonzos from his extended interview with Vivian for Friends magazine. In consequence his candid assessment accurately summed up the picture of a group on its last legs performing a lacklustre show arranged around songs from the new album and billed as "The Outrage Show". Despite the slovenly performance the Lyceum audience were still stunned by the news that "Keynsham" was to be the group's swansong. "The Bonzos have split up just when it seemed that all the hassles that they had got into, (as epitomised by the cancellation of most of their recent American tour), were over, their whole scene has blown up. Half way through their Christmas Party, the premiere of "The

Outrage Show", in the last Sunday Lyceum of the Sixties, a completely bald Vivian Stanshall, looking deceptively like the Mekon in a lamé suit, told the audience that this was it. No more Bonzos. In some ways it wasn't all that surprising, looking back. The whole concert had something of a death wish about it. The Bonzos couldn't get anything together. Only Aynsley Dunbar, drumming throughout, while "Legs" Larry Smith cavorted, seemed to have the first idea of what they were trying to get into. Nothing even looked like going right. The machines freaked and so did the humans. A subdued Rodney Slater was almost decapitated by a manic 'Legs' Larry who threw hi-hats and drum stools with careless abandon. It was the only thing he did manage to do with any success. The Bonzos have been a great band at their best, there's little point in charting the sordid details of what was their last concert. They got their encore, but the fast departing audience had to be reminded to ask for it. 'Monster Mash' had them standing, but it was more duty than pleasure. Even a forty foot transparent imitation swizprick couldn't make up for an emasculated 'Keynsham', nor was clowning Keith Moon any help. They blew it and everyone knew."

The down beat and thoroughly negative tone of the "Friends" review was tempered by the fact that only a short time before it had looked very likely that the band might be saved from the collapse, which now engulfed it, as Jonathon Green emphasised in his well written article. "For the Bonzo Dog to collapse now, seems right out of time. Earlier in the year it had seemed almost inevitable; soured by their sufferings at the hands of the business and falling apart as a band and within themselves it seemed that they couldn't go on. But over the last two months things have changed. The positive step of rejecting to complete the major part of the American tour gave them new energy, intensified by "Keynsham" - the first of their albums with which they had been fully satisfied, and on which they felt they were truly doing 'their own thing'."

Again Mr Green had put his finger on the nub of the problem for the Bonzos. "Keynsham" was indeed an album, which the band were proud of, particularly Rodney Slater, but the Friends article had successfully diagnosed the true state of affairs within the Bonzos. The root of the problem lay primarily with Vivian and Mr Green was fortunate in having an extensive interview to draw upon. "Friends" talked to Vivian Stanshall earlier in the year, when this new period of optimism was at its height. "With newly cropped hair, to symbolise his movement from fun and laughter to hard work and all the problems entailed in managing the band alone, Stanshall talked with obvious bitterness about what had happened and how very bad things had become. Tempered with the bitterness was sadness. One could not help but sympathise. But then it seemed as if his overpowering optimism could help the Bonzos win through. Now the opposite has been seen. Despite everything that has been said and done, the band has fallen apart. What its unique and very individual talents will do

now is still unknown."

Vivian Stanshall later explained to John Platt in an interview for Comstock Lode that he was insecure over the real artistic value of what was being performed by the Bonzos at this time. "It only dawned on me about six months before I knocked the band on the head that this was actually going to be a living. None of us thought that it was for real. I wouldn't say that we didn't take it seriously, because we really worked hard at it, but I think that there was a delicious understanding between audience and band that we were being paid for a load of codswallop, and of course we shouldn't be enjoying ourselves. Work shouldn't be enjoyable. But I thought all along, "Well, this is going to stop." I'd be found out, and then I'd be a painter."

The Lyceum was not actually the last show for the Bonzos, a number of shows had been booked through to March and the Bonzos had to honour those commitments. The reasons for the band calling it a day were obviously many and various, but as Neil Innes stated, the Bonzos had agreed to only "disband after we'd honoured outstanding commitments. It was the only planned thing we ever did!" With the imminent demise of the band now public knowledge, every remaining gig was sold out and the band received a riotous reception wherever they went. In February the Bonzos played venues like the Top Rank in Leicester with Joe Cocker and Mott The Hoople, and Southampton University with Idle Race and Hardin & York. They then performed their final London appearance at the Polytechnic in Little Tichfield Street.

A further single was released from the 'Keynsham' album during February, with the track 'You Done My Brain' on the A-side and 'Mr. Slater's Parrot' on the B-side. This was presumably an attempt to cash in on the final fling by the band with the publicity they received as the band completed its final gigs. There was a brief review of the single in Record Mirror. "Addicts will probably have the album, but this is vintage Bonzo-ism, now regrettably dying. (3 stars.)" Needless to say the single was not a chart success.

Early in March the Bonzos played another gig at Reading University with Atomic Rooster and Arthur Brown and then they played their final commitment at Loughborough University on 14th March 1970. And so ended the days of the original Bonzo Dog Doo-Dah Band.

For a while things looked up and it even seemed to Rodney Slater that it all might be set to continue, as the broken hearted Saxophone player recalls. "Then rather abruptly, we were all of a sudden playing an official last show at Loughborough University. We played the show, got off the bus one night and it never happened again. Went on to other things." Rodney Slater nominated March 14th 1970 as the official end date. The Bonzos had been in operation for eight years and enough was enough for Rodney.

The reasons for the break-up of the band have been explained by various band members over the years. At the

time Vivian Stanshall stated; "We had so many individual ideas that we wanted to develop, and we were turning out so much material that we couldn't effectively perform it on stage. It would have meant working with other people, and that just wasn't on. The whole Bonzo concept turned sour on us because we were creating so much." But then in another interview he stated: "I couldn't possibly see how we could communicate if we no longer shared even halfway in the experiences of the people we were playing to. At the end we were losing contact with our audience. We were wandering around with sequinned-trousered pooves all the time, slugging down large ones. It just creeps up on you until you're devoting the whole of your time to it and it gets more and more artificial."

With Rodney Slater now departing the ranks it was time to look back and assess the inevitable question, which was, had the Bonzos failed to live up to their true potential? "I don't know," says Rodney. "Did it have a potential? I think it was exactly what it was, people of a like minded bunch of art students thrown together. It was an accidental meeting and we enjoyed sharing a particular view of the world, the world at that time was economically viable and for young people it was a very, very good time to be young. We were the generation that just escaped National Service. I went to college with people who fought in Korea and so it was of its time. And I don't think anything should be hoisted up and put on pedestals but hopefully it's got a bit of human scale in it."

Roger Ruskin Spear reflected after the break-up. "I think we all realised towards the end of the Bonzos that art is irrelevant. The guy who's putting on the show is only thinking in terms of money, what you are doing means nothing. This feeling is rife even among so-called art fields… they are just the same as concert promoters."

CHAPTER SIX
...AGAINST A
WALL

Given the air of gloominess that had descended on the Bonzos as the new decade rolled around, it was no surprise that the band needed a break. Vivian Stanshall was visibly falling apart before their eyes. Unlike many groups there had been no great falling out, no on-stage showdown or fisticuffs in the studio. Surprisingly given all that they had been through together the members of the band remained on good terms with each other. To some of the players and Vivian in particular, this was not a break up. It was more a sabbatical, a chance to take a break and recharge the creative batteries away from the strains of the Bonzo collective. In Vivian's mind there was no question that the band would be resurrected at some stage. This was certainly not the understanding of Rodney Slater. Rodney decided the break up of the Bonzos was permanent and resolved to leave the music business as a full time occupation and pursue a career as a psychiatric social worker.

This was not a course that Rodney Slater had chosen to embark upon as he was very much at home in the ranks of the Bonzos and had not advocated the split. "I enjoyed the Bonzos," says Rodney. "I felt completely at ease with what was going on musically on "Keynsham" and would have liked to have continued with the band doing things like that. But I never did. Looking back now the Bonzos probably went as far as it could. Someone would have been hurt if we'd have gone on, I think. Viv was going mad."

Vivian Stanshall himself was certainly mentally unstable at this stage but he was also embittered and thoroughly disillusioned with the business, which he now considered to be something, which according to his interview with "Friends" magazine that needed to be fought and vanquished. In the wake of the commercially disappointing performance of 'Keynsham', the

overt humour seemed to disappear from much of Vivian's post-Bonzo work. In discussion with Jonathon Green, even before the Bonzo split, Vivian was looking back wistfully to the days when he could enjoy fun and laughter with his friends and colleagues. "Until I became wrinkled and destroyed by this system that I shall now make it my purpose to destroy, I used to laugh a lot. We all did. Our reaction at first was turning everything into a joke and tried to topsy turvy everything. And we went through some changes and destroyed the free-wheeling Dada thing. We had been trying to recapture that and we became enmeshed in the system and almost became part of what we were attacking. On the last series we were becoming much more aware of what we all should do and what our artistic shape should be and were discovering ourselves and we were really locked in by contracts and so on. At first the worse it became the more we laughed. And we were in these surreal situations. We were doing absurd things that we didn't like and it was ridiculous. And then we realised what was happening and we stopped laughing. Six months ago I began to force myself to work as a machine... the worst thing anyone could do is to stop me thinking and working. I never felt so poignantly and desperately that I was being strangled. I now feel that it is vital if I could stop other people from being trapped and destroyed in the way I have been."

Rodney Slater was acutely aware of Vivian Stanshall's deteriorating condition but there was little he could do. By contrast to Vivian, Rodney admired Neil Innes' level-headed ability to get things done. "I think Neil preferred working in a different way. And look at him now. I mean he's got it perfect and it works for him. He does all sorts of different things, his 'Innes Book of Records', Python, he worked with Grimms, – and his Rutles project, his kid's TV stuff. He did what he wanted to do. He couldn't have done that and stayed a Bonzo, there wouldn't have been enough time. Roger was also sick of it all, heartily, utterly sick, I think, and wanted to be home with his family. He became a lecturer, which gave him a solid existence and he continued in a part-time way with his wardrobe and various things that he did. After the break up I went into bloody silly things like sociology, psychology and psychiatric social work and just got off altogether. You just couldn't mix the two and I had to make a decision and make a change in my life. I would have liked to have gone on developing musical ideas like that. I never really came to do it again and when eventually I did start playing again there wasn't anybody around doing what the Bonzos had done and maybe I was too old, - I don't know."

Other members of the band had also seen the break up on the horizon and had begun to look to the future. "Legs" Larry Smith was as close as anyone could possibly be with Vivian Stanshall and he had been all too aware of the deterioration in his friend's mental condition. "Legs" actually released a single, before the official announcement of the break-up, "Witch Tai To" was released on Charisma under the pseudonym 'Topo D. Bill'. Among the musicians on this single were Roger Ruskin Spear, members of Yes and

143

Uriah Heep vocalist David Byron, another Bron client. "I suppose I was beginning to sense trouble ahead", says Larry, "but thank God, by then Stratton-Smith had come into the picture and he was running his Charisma label. I'd been out in America and heard this song called "Witch Tai To", which is a kind of Red Indian rain chant and it was so bloody catchy. This thing it got into your head. I brought it back to England and Tony said, "Yeah, we'll do this one." Larry was given the studio time and the budget he needed. Never one to miss an opportunity to have fun with a tight budget Larry could not resist answering Tony Stratton-Smith's rhetorical question, "anything else you want?", with, "I'll tell you, old boy, if you could arrange for forty-four drumsticks of chicken and a dozen bottles of champagne, that would be wonderful". When Tony Stratton-Smith responded that he had to be joking, Larry quick as a flash responded, 'No, no, we've got to have a supper break.' Larry got his wish and the record got made. "So we released it as a single. It didn't do anything chartwise in the UK, but it should have done because Tony Blackburn made it his record of the week, he was just nuts about it. He would play it, then he'd take it off and play it again half way through. It was a hit in France, I think, but it didn't do anything over here. So by then I was obviously into the music in terms of production and stuff."

In the meantime Vivian Stanshall set about busying himself with various projects, which had been simmering away at the back of his brain. The most ambitious of these was the "Brain Opera", a project, which he had worked on with the Bonzos. Vivian was now attempting to put the project together with Arthur Brown. Apparently a complete libretto was written by Vivian and the music was composed by Arthur Brown. Basic tracks and ideas were discussed and some recordings were made but this grandiose project had already been abandoned by the Bonzos and was not destined to ever be fully realised. The subject matter was a strange tale of a deranged media landscape in which 'The Craig Torso Show' is the highest rated programme and German surgeons vying for cash prizes and the chance to work in America. It was envisaged by the creators that an album would be recorded first, then toured as a live stage production. There was clearly some substance to the project and "Excerpts From The Brain Opera", were indeed recorded for the John Peel radio show, but the recordings were not well received. Despite all the effort, which had gone into the project, proper backing failed to materialise all that saw the light of day were several lyrics, which Vivian would later adapt into his own songs, and two completed songs, which turned up on the Arthur Brown album "Kingdom Come".

THE SEAN HEAD SHOW BAND

Vivian Stanshall should definitely have taken a much needed break in the aftermath of the Bonzos, but he continued to work as hard as ever and had actually begun recording solo

material prior to the band's final gig. In 1970 the first official post-Bonzo release to see the light of day from any of the Bonzos was naturally from Vivian in the form of a single released by a side project known as the "Sean Head Show Band", with former Bonzo Dennis Cowan on bass and Rema Kabaka on percussion. In a reprise of his Paul McCartney/'Urban Spaceman' coup, Vivian had managed to snare a pretty special guitarist in the form of Eric Clapton. The band released only one single, which was "Labio-Dental Fricative", a slight number, which not even the presence of Eric Clapton could help to propel into the charts. The New Musical Express described the single as: "An interim single from the ex-Bonzo, while he's still in the process of getting his biG Grunt group together. Support comes from the so-called Sean Head Showband, which comprises several well-known names who have to remain anonymous. A novelty song with a nonsense lyric and a bouncy beat, it's like a modern nursery rhyme. Very danceable, too." Interestingly the musical arrangements for the single were by Neil Innes.

The follow up to the Sean Head Band for Vivian was biG Grunt, a new project, which was initially composed of three former Bonzos in the shape of Vivian Stanshall, Roger Ruskin Spear, Dennis Cowan and former Bonzo roadie Fred Munt. Rather confusingly this particular collaboration was also called "Viv Stanshall & His Gargantuan Chums", with the only obvious difference to biG Grunt being Rema Kabaka on percussion. A single was released in 1970, a pretty tame track called "Suspicion", which suspiciously came out on Fly Records. This label was owned by Vivian's great friend and drinking buddy Keith Moon, so the name change from biG Grunt may well have been necessary for contractual purposes, allowing the same group to record for two labels simultaneously. There was a review of the single in the Melody Maker. "Viv returns with an Elvis type rock ballad. Toe-tapping and easy on the ear he displays a curiously deep voice and lots of deep breathing. There is a nice guitar passage, and an even better bathroom passage. Suspicion torments his heart and he begs his darling to give some proof of loyalty. She doesn't. On the 'B' side, or alternatively the other 'A' side, is 'Blind Date', which is much funnier and deals with the adventures of a gorilla on a blind date. It has a country flavour, which suggests the gorilla was brought up in Bedfordshire. Produced by Keith Moon, it's all obviously the work of madmen."

biG Grunt also made some television performances, before the inevitable split and its not surprising that with Roger Ruskin Spear in the ranks of biG Grunt that they obviously drew heavily on their shared Bonzo heritage and their stage show included several Bonzo hallmarks such as grotesque papier maché heads, masks, ping pong eyeballs and robots. The band also performed a version of "11 Mustachioed Daughters" for television. As regards the choice of repertoire, this was a typically

obtuse choice and did not help the commercial potential of the band and was almost guaranteed to hinder any attempt to reach a wider audience.

In any event the activities of biG Grunt came to a shuddering halt after just a handful of live shows when Vivian suffered what appeared to be a second full blown nervous breakdown, at which point he again shaved off all of his hair and temporarily turned his back on performing.

In the wake of the collapse of biG Grunt the affable Dennis Cowan was lucky enough to find himself offered a place in Neil Innes's new band, The World. The World released the single "Angelina" in 1970 on Liberty Records and also a follow up album entitled "Lucky Planet" to general indifference by the music world. In addition to Neil Innes and Dennis Cowan, the band featured Roger McKew on guitar and Ian Wallace on drums. Unfortunately The World split up shortly after the album was released and by 1971 Neil Innes had drifted into the ranks of McGuiness Flint.

Roger Ruskin Spear had in fact been the first to present his own show, performing with his 'Giant Kinetic Wardrobe' in January 1970. In 1971 he also joined up with Dave Clague on bass and vintage former Bonzo Lenny Williams on trumpet, and with Tat Meager on drums they formed Roger Ruskin Spear & His Giant Orchestral Wardrobe and released an EP entitled "Rebel Trouser". It included the songs "Trouser Freak" and a live version of "Release Me", and it seemed that Roger's fashion inspired corpus would just not lie down. Sadly things were just not happening for Roger and he decided to look up an old face from the Bonzo past. "In the year after the Bonzo split I actually decided to go and see old Reg Tracey again as I was struggling with my own solo efforts. I actually went to see Reg and ask whether he could get me some gigs because by that time I thought, 'I'm going to have a go at real show biz' and had my own band and act "The Giant Kinetic Wardrobe" with the robots. Reg and I explored the idea of working together again - but it just didn't happen and then poor old Reg died a few years later."

Some consideration was given at this time to reforming the Bonzo Dog Band, in the hope that it might help Vivian Stanshall, but it was decided that it would not help. Whilst Roger Ruskin Spear continued with his "Giant Kinetic Wardrobe", "Legs" Larry Smith started to make personal appearances at events such as at the 10th National Jazz & Blues Festival; at the Lyceum for a Yes concert; and at the "Furry Freaks Festival" in Worthing. Roger Ruskin Spear also appeared at the festival and commented, "By the time I got to the festival it had degenerated into chaos. (Probably something to do with Larry.) The farmer had turned off the power supply so I did an "acoustic" set and worked the robots by hand!"

A year after the band had stormed out of the USA, Rolling Stone Magazine decided the time was ripe to revisit the various solo members to check on progress. The resulting piece did not make for terribly

146

MUSICIAN CLOSES COMEDY SHOW

TELEVISION CORRESPONDENT ED PIXELL

BONZO DOG DOO-DAH BAND SAXOPHONIST ROGER RUSKIN SPEAR WAS AT LAST ACCUSED OF SINGLE-HANDEDLY JEOPARDISING THE FUTURE OF A CHANNEL FOUR SHOW.

The *CUT PRICE COMEDY SHOW* was to be seen as the future of British musical comedy but had to be shelved early on in its life due to the appaling antics of the obscure ex-Bonzo.

Commissioning editor Boris Nivek puts the blame firmly at the door of writer and impresario Ken Gold-blume-Johnson who told our reporter today- "I had for many years harboured the desire to showcase the dubious talents of Mr Spear and produce the "worst comedy programme ever."

Unfortunately, I succeeded in ways I could not have foretold. In 1980 I went to see Roger and his Band at the "Cartoon" in Croydon and couldn't believe my ears - it was quite the worst sound I had ever heard, undisciplined and caco-phonic - far worse than the Bonzos - I booked them on the spot!"

A radiopilot was then commissioned and all went well until we unleashed his talents on a live Television Show Audience.

His antics and general disregard for studio safety quite terrified the members of the public who were cowering in fear at the sight of his dangerous-looking robots and mechanical wierdos. His musicians weren't much of an improve-ment either. They changed each week and one week was fine with a Spike Jones style outfit, but next week it was "Punk" and the band were disgusting, vomiting and insulting the audience - it more than they could take.

To avoid a union strike we had to cancel the follow-up pro-gramme - the *"CUT PRICE MUSIC SHOW"*.

NEW BAND SEEKS VENUE

ROGER RUSKIN SPEAR is forming a new band, the person-nel of which is hoped to be Gary Neuman, and 20,000 Arthur Mullard impersonators. A suitable venue is being sought to record their new single - "My Friend's Outside."

LEG STOLEN AT A RECENT CLUB engagement, Musical comic Roger Ruskin Spear suffered the loss of several stage props and unusual instruments. Mr Spear tells our crime reporter "One of the most serious items was the "Therein Leg" as it was cast from my own leg. I suppose I will now have to make an inferior copy. I know who stole it and they are well on their way back home. I know who it was because they confessed to me at the end of the Gig.*"Gee Rarger we've ripped you off!"* they said (being from America)..I didn't believe them until I came to pack up and it was then too late."

LEEDS MAN ARRESTED

A **"FRIEND OF A FRIEND"** was severely beaten last night as he looked the wrong way at a policeman. A witness said that it was unlikely that this happened to Smeaton as he was an old Leodiensian and quite beyond this sort of caper.

John Smeaton was a noted engineer and builder of the third Eddystone Lighthouse. The remains of his "Smeaton Tower" can still be seen fourteen miles off the coast of Cornwall at Plymouth.

SPEAR QUITS WARDROBE

AFTER THE DEMISE OF THE BONZO DOG BAND Prankster Roger Ruskin Spear took his robots on the road in his own solo show the "Giant Kinetic Ward-robe" scoring much success on records and TV, but as he tells our "heavy rock" reporter Cuff Welsh, it all started to wane in the late Eighties.

"I can't remember the year but I can remember the exact second! It was the time of the emerging alternative comedy and cabaret scene and I had been booked into "Crazy Larry's" in the Kings Road.

Although the young girl compere had been briefed she had no idea who I or the Bonzo's were - so her announcement went.... "here he is... I don't know his name but he was in the ...." (at this point she dried again and stalled). I was just about to leap on stage and put her out of her misery when a look of inspiration came over her face and she announced with pride "But he knows Neil lnnes!"

It was at this point as I kicked the start button of the lead robot I thought "Sod this for a game of soldiers - it's time to go!"

The wardrobe and the solo career went into the boxes at the end of the show and didn't re-emerge until 2006 when a lunatic from north of the border decided to subject the British public to one more blast of lunacy.

147

inspiring reading and there was a distinct air of deflation in the former Bonzo ranks even a year after the split. Rolling Stone ran the article on 2nd December 1970 under the headline "Bonzo Remnants Running Around". Written by Charles Alverson, this brief review of the works in progress is worth revisiting as it captures some of the mood of quiet frustration, which dogged the initial solo projects and which arguably came to be the dominating feature of the first forays into the world outside the Bonzo cocoon. "Last March", wrote Mr Alverson, "the Bonzo Dog Band, after eight years of insanity and anarchy disguised as music, called it quits and shot off in all directions at once. The members of the silly sextet were last seen in the States in December when they got disgusted and flew home in mid-tour."

Charles began his brief review with a look at what Vivian Stanshall, (still known to many of his friends and colleagues as Vic), had been up to in his first year outside the fold. "After the band exploded, Vivian (Vic) Stanshall, the red-haired front man and one of the original Bonzos, formed biG Grunt, but biG Grunt folded after only two gigs when Vic, pushing himself too hard as manager, lyricist and leader, had a nervous breakdown and had to go into hospital for a couple of months. Vic Stanshall gave the Bonzos all he had, too, and a little more. Out of the hospital since last summer, Vic stays mostly in his cluttered house in North London surrounded by tanks of fish and turtles, pots of cactus, manikins, musical instruments and his 25 month old son Rupert."

The Bonzos were well featured in the music press and it is articles such as this, which throw the best contemporary picture of the band, sadly this piece is reflective of at least some of the band when they were at a fairly low ebb, as Charles was quick to note. "Cracking up and going to the hospital was a shattering experience, and Vic, although fully recovered, hasn't quite sorted out his mind. "Vic always lived on the knife-edge," says a friend, "and the pressure just got to be too much for him." Now, with his light-red hair and mustache and huge, octagonal glasses with clear-plastic frames, Stanshall looks like a slightly-bewildered wizard."

Fortunately the Rolling Stone piece did not rely entirely on the impressions of "friends". Alverson also managed to track down his subject and obtain an interesting first hand perspective on Vivian Stanshall at work just before the Bonzos reformation. It does however make for rather depressing reading as Vivian was always a candid interviewee going as far as to publicly discuss his precarious financial situation, which cannot have helped the creative muse. "He spends his time sculpting, painting, tending his fish, turtles and cactus, writing songs and trying to decide what he wants to do next.

"After an experience like this," he says, "you're sort of empty of what you were, what you thought you were, and you've got a lot of things to sort out.

"Vic says he'll go back to performing, "but first I want to find out what is important about what I'm doing here and then

148

assemble it." He's been writing a lot of songs, doing the music as well as the words. He works out the tune on the ukulele, ("a much maligned instrument," he says), the euphonium, a sort of tuba, and the recorder."

The Rolling Stone interview also provided a number of clues to the relatively poor quality of Vivian Stanshall's output at this time. This was a factor, which Vivian attributed to the fact that he was no longer working in the creative Bonzo hothouse. "Working alone like this has problems, I haven't had any kind of criticism for ages, and my work tends to sprawl all over the place. That was the best thing about the Bonzos. Anything you suggested got ridiculed at least five times. I'd like to get some of my work out and see how it does."

At this point one of the other major influences bearing down on the struggling artist was his precarious financial position in the wake of his serious mental breakdown. This was made embarrassingly clear when it was broadcast to the entire world in the pages of Rolling Stone. "Another pressing reason for going back to work, Vic says, is that he's broke. But he has a few things working for him. One is a musical he's collaborating on called "Warm Steps", which he describes as a "fantasy on drug use in various cultures." He also did a pilot show for a programme on Scottish television and has done a few television commercials. As we're talking, Vic's face suddenly comes on the silent television screen in a commercial for cheese crisps. "There's another few quid in the bank," says Vic with satisfaction. And he's also been talking with BBC radio about doing a regular half-hour show featuring some of the weird records he's been collecting for years."

While Vivian Stanshall was wrestling with his financial problems in the wake of the collapse of biG Grunt, Neil Innes was busy getting his act together with The World. One criticism that has always plagued Neil's career is that his work is too derivative of The Beatles. As a self confessed fan, admirer and close friend of the late George Harrison, it is something that Neil is unconcerned by, but in December 1970 the only one prepared to voice these criticisms was Borneo Fred Munt who, in Neil's absence, was for some odd reason quoted as spokesman for The World in the Rolling Stone article. "The World is really just getting started, gigging around Britain and the Continent". A single, "Angelina", did not do much but there was more hope for its first LP. The sound of The World is hard-rocking and happy, but compared to the madness of the Bonzos it is pretty sedate stuff. "I think they sound like the Beatles used to sound", says Fred Munt, "but Neil would kill me if he heard me say so."

Fortunately the ever supportive Chris Welch was on hand to get Neil Innes' reaction, which was published in Melody Maker in October 1970. "Nobody's mourned the passing of the Bonzos more than the group. But its demise seemed inevitable when they did not get the recognition they felt

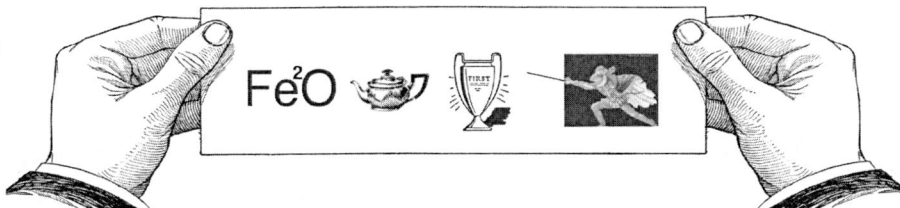

four years hard work deserved. It left high and dry a bunch of personalities with individual talents who were used to working together, in however loose a fashion. In some cases, their present whereabouts and activities are a bit of a mystery. Saxist Rodney Slater is believed to have given up the music business and has taken to social work. Legs Larry Smith produced a record, which flopped, and was last seen loudly hailing taxis in London's Wardour Street. Roger Spear, the ace explosions and machines man has gone out on the road with his own successful and hilarious one man show, The Giant Kinetic Wardrobe. One of the most positive steps for the future has been taken by Neil and bassist Dennis Cowan. They have formed a group simply called The World, have released a single called "Angelina" and plan an LP release called "Lucky Planet" on November 6th. All the material has been written by Neil and the music ranged from rock to pure pop. Naturally some of the Bonzos flavour has been retained, and humour has not been entirely abandoned from their "live" act. The line-up includes Neil (lead vocal, piano and guitar) Dennis Cowan (bass, guitar and vocals), Ian Wallace (drums, vocals), and Roger McKew (lead guitar).

Neil appeared in the Melody Maker's ale house, the Red Lion, this week, clutching a packet of Gold Flake "Honey Dew" cigarettes, and wearing an elderly sports jacket and a Volkswagen. "We've played a few gigs so far," he revealed, "and they went down really well." What led to the formation of The World? "When Vic (Viv Stanshall) got ill, I got a bit fed up. Dennis and Ian Wallace and myself were free, so we thought of forming our own group. It was all surprisingly easy. We got Roger McKew and we got together last May and started to rehearse. We're signed to Liberty, but we are also free to record with who we like. It's funny, we didn't know how it would turn out, but we are all pleased with the band, and I'm sure it will go from strength to strength, although it's early days yet. "I haven't really changed in my song-writing style. I write about the same sort of things really. Some of the songs have Bonzo titles like '9-5 Pollution Blues.' I was always interested in the things Vic did and I backed him up. I will still be dealing with images and outspoken ideas, but now I can get more into the music.

"The Bonzos were really individuals who were accidentally teamed up. It didn't break up through disagreements on policy, because we never had a policy. And it was not through personal reasons because we were closer friends at the end than we had been through the whole history of the band. We were just tired physically and mentally. We hadn't had a holiday in all the time the band was together. And we went through some heavy management scenes." Did Neil feel personal regret at their passing? "Oh, enormous... incredible feeling of nostalgia. When Vic got ill we

150

thought of reforming if it would have helped him in any way. "He was silly really in that he went on with the biG Grunt right after the Bonzos, without a rest."

What is the significance of the title of Neil's new group, - if any? "Nothing in particular except that it means a 'whole' and not being particularly dogmatic about anything. The name could either have been the 'Strawberry Armpit' type or joke names like 'The Thousand Guitars Of Vernon Motion.' Vernon Motion was the performing parlour snake of the Thirties you read about in the Sunday colour supplements. It's perfectly true! "We hope the band will sound fresh and our stage act isn't a heavy moody thing." What was the LP called? "Lucky Planet." Lucky hairnet? "Yes, that'll do! I've always been the quiet spoken member of the group. I got the title from the Evening Standard horoscope. Today - Jupiter is your Lucky Planet! "I'd like the group to be Overground rather than Underground. Nothing would please me more than to get into the chart. Not for the money - but to get the recognition. I just hope people accept The World as guys who can play their instruments and are trying to get something across."

Sadly despite many strong qualities The World album failed to capture the imagination of the British public and after a number of reasonably well received concerts it was decided to shelve the project.

Having dealt with the work of Vivian Stanshall and Neil Innes the next Bonzo to come under the Rolling Stone spotlight was Roger Ruskin-Spear, who had taken a typically idiosyncratic and difficult approach to constructing a solo career in the aftermath of the Bonzos. As Rolling Stone recorded it was proving to be every bit as difficult as it sounded to realise Roger's unique vision for a post-Bonzo solo act. "Next to Vic, perhaps the wildest of the Bonzos was Roger Spear, who specialised in robots, sound effects and diabolical machines. On the death of biG Grunt, Roger set off, surrounded by devices from the Bonzo Dog Band, to become a solo act. After starting with a gig at Birmingham University, he began to get a few more dates and tours with other groups." The article was not entirely accurate as Roger had performed with his "Giant Kinetic Wardrobe' prior to biG Grunt, but the effort required to perform on his own was certainly greater than with a group.

Of all the Bonzos Roger Ruskin Spear's work has lived closest to the edge and is not always necessarily accessible. Always chaotic with an air of unplanned mayhem topped by a rebellious subtext, Roger's act encapsulates the Dadaist heritage more than the others combined. Sometimes the show can go disastrously wrong leaving the audience bemused at best and sometimes openly hostile. This was a factor that Rolling Stone magazine quickly picked up on. "On stage, Roger is a dervish of action as he ricochets around the stage, playing duets with a robot with replaceable heads, a built-in tape recorder and an inflatable chest. In the course of his frantic act he tells jokes, plays a theremin shaped like a

human leg, acts as straight man for his robot, sings in blackface, juggles bricks and tries to fill the empty moments with corny razzle-dazzle."

"Sometimes it doesn't work. At the Hammersmith Palais the other night, the audience, restlessly waiting for The Who to play, greeted Rogers's frenzied efforts with barely polite tolerance. But with college audiences, the act often goes down like a bomb. Roger's getting enough work to make it, but it's a grind. He works without roadie or manager, so after the Hammersmith gig he had to drive 400 miles to Glasgow to appear the next night."

"Another scheme of Roger's is the creation of a band composed of 20 fat banjoists and one thin trumpet player. Or a great choir of people singing about frying pans, accompanied by taxi drivers brought in off the street to play instruments they'd never seen before. Spear admits that these projects are not likely to be vast commercial successes. "You'd have to prove they would work," he says, "and the only way to do that would be to find a rich loony to put them on.""

"While Roger beats his brains out and dreams of a rich loony sponsor, Rodney Slater, an original Bonzo who played swing saxophone among other things, works as a social worker in London and vows that he's through with professional music. "I saw the handwriting on the wall last Christmas," says Rodney, at 29 the oldest of the ex-Bonzos, "so when the group split I was already working days as a child-care officer." He now runs a youth club in London's Kentish Town. At his flat in West London, which is quite ordinary except for cages of birds and two racing bikes in the hall, Slater says that his years with the Bonzos were a "very, very valuable experience. I couldn't have spent the time better. But at the same time," he says, "I've no temptation to go back into music. There are too many 20-percenters hanging on to your neck." For him, Slater says, the Bonzo Dog Band wasn't exactly a financial bonanza. "I spent eight years of my life at it," he says, "and I came out dead even." But Rodney, stockily built with blond, moderately short hair and a flat-nosed friendly face, isn't bitter. "I set out to become a professional musician," he says, "and I did. I'm pleased about that." He still plays for his own pleasure. "It's always been for my own pleasure, really," Slater says. But he adds that next year he's returning to college to study social work and expects to make it his career. "Just like the Bonzo Dog," he says, "I give it all I've got."

At this point in his career "Legs" Larry Smith's output had come to a

BONZO DOG BAND

LET'S MAKE UP AND BE FRIENDLY

grinding halt. It would appear that there were no "Legs" Larry concerts, no recordings and no sightings of the great man, which left Rolling Stone somewhat at a loss. "The sixth Bonzo, Larry (Legs) Smith, drummer, tuba player and eccentric dancer, was last seen somewhere between Oxford and Brighton walking fast and smiling. If you see old Larry, tell him the other Bonzos are doing fine and would like to hear from him one of these days. Even a picture postcard will do."

LET'S MAKE UP AND BE FRIENDLY

The Rolling Stone article is a pretty accurate assessment of life for the ex-Bonzos in 1970. No-one was really thriving but there was no real reason why the band should not work together again. Vivian Stanshall and Neil Innes formed the Bonzo Dog Freaks in 1971, which included Dennis

153

Cowen and Bubs White, but this was not really the Bonzo Dog Band without Rodney Slater, Roger Ruskin Spear and "Legs" Larry Smith, and merely served to confuse the public. With the cumulative frustrations of life in the solo wilderness making life difficult, it is no surprise that most of the former Bonzos were quite willing to regroup in late 1971 in order to put together the one final record, which Liberty, now part of United Artists, felt they were owed as a result of the previous Bonzo recording contract. The label were in fact owed four tracks but it was soon agreed that the recording sessions would be prolonged in order to allow the band to create an entire album's worth of material.

That album would, of course be "Let's Make Up and Be Friendly". However the driving force behind the album was not artistic or even commercial, it was quite simply contractual as Neil Innes explains. "We suddenly found ourselves in this funny position of having said, "Right, let's call it a day." At that time we'd decided, "It's still pretty good, it would be much better to leave it while at least it's got some integrity". Then we started getting letters from the record company and we found we couldn't just split up and go and record on other labels because we ended up owing the record company four more tracks and we had been signed 'jointly and severally', which meant that even if we disbanded we were still liable so, "Let's Make Up and Be Friendly" became the name for the album, it was the original contractual obligation album, if you like."

For some Bonzos the return to the collective Bonzo fold was a welcome distraction from the unforgiving daily grind of life in the solo world. After all there was no bad blood between the members and here was a welcome opportunity to renew acquaintances as Larry Smith recalls. 'Yeah, it was kind of nice to get the call. I wasn't that involved with the intricacies of our dealings with record companies, but I think it was Liberty we were still with, although for some reason the records came out on United Artists. Liberty hadn't been bought out by EMI and we all got letters from Liberty saying, "Sorry to hear about the break up but, by the way, you're still under contract and you owe us a record", and all that sort of heavy stuff.'

"Let's Make Up And Be Friendly" marked "Legs" Larry Smith's emergence as a writer. "The Bonzos were a performing band," remembers Larry, "and I hadn't realised then the economic importance of actually writing the stuff! In fact, I've only got one track on any of the bloody Bonzo albums and that's "Rusty Champion Thrust", which was on the last album. By then my ears were perking up in terms of production, and I was then engaged for the first time in writing stuff and producing stuff and arranging stuff and I absolutely adored it. I could quite happily spend the rest of my life in a recording studio in some bunker, but up to that point then I wasn't that interested. So for the first time I contributed my own tracks, which I organised and put together, there's some big names on there. I mean Zoot Money's on organ, Stevie

Winwood's playing a little mandolin. There were two tracks we did actually, the other was "I've Got A Braun New Girl", a Hitler thing, because I was just about to launch into my Hitler period, but "Rusty" was the one which was chosen, it's about some gay lunatic and it was kind of a slow sort of shuffle. Tony Kaye was on organ, the guy was by then a good friend of mine and it was Viv's favourite track on the album, which was rather nice and it's something I'm still proud of."

The performers on "Let's Make Up and Be Friendly" are Vivian Stanshall on vocals and ukulele, Neil Innes on piano, organ and "heavenly squawking", Dennis Cowan contributes bass and slide guitar and voices, Roger Ruskin-Spear is credited with vocals, sax and xylophone, "Legs" Larry Smith contributed vocals and drums.

Additional contributions came from Tony Kaye on piano and organ, (this was solely on "Rusty Champion Thrust"), Hughie Flint on drums and percussion, Anthony `Bubs' White on electric "brainbiter" plus guitar and Spanish guitar, Dave Richards contributed bass, empyreal screeching, Dick Parry, (later to appear on Pink Floyd's "Dark Side Of The Moon"), was featured on saxophone and flutes; and Andy Roberts who provided fiddle, mandolin, rhythm and acoustic guitar and a further bout of "heavenly squawking". Rodney Slater is touchingly listed on the credits as being there "In Spirit". The truth is rather more prosaic. 'I wasn't there because I was concentrating on a young family and a new career at that time,' says Rodney. 'And I'm buggered if I'm going to get out there in some studio, which had nearly driven me mad for the last two years, breathing other people's bloody marijuana and alcoholic fumes at three o'clock in the morning. It didn't appeal to me at all so I wasn't there.'

It may have been a nice gesture to add Rodney as the Bonzos co-founder to the credits of the one and only Bonzo recording, which did not feature his input, but unfortunately nobody saw fit to follow through and actually send their erstwhile colleague a copy of the record. "Nobody sent me one' says Rodney, 'So I never got round to buying one or even listening to it. I had other things on my mind. I came across "The Strain" many years later when I worked with Viv towards the end of his life. He said, "It's irretrievably vulgar." Of course it is, it was meant to be irretrievably vulgar. That was pure Vivian."

Neil Innes also enjoyed his time making the album. "By the time of "Let's Make Up and Be Friendly" we had actually become more friends and stopped arguing about things so much." Friends they may have been, but not all of the Bonzos were happy at this point in their career to have their input dictated by the others. "Legs" Larry Smith now insisted on having artistic control of his own compositions and in consequence "Rusty" was recorded independently of the rest of the material. So was Roger Ruskin Spear's strange contribution, "Waiting For The Wardrobe", which explains the ever expanding collection of performers receiving credit on the album sleeve. Nonetheless, there were still a large

number of uncredited performances, among them Steve Winwood, as Larry recalls. "I think Viv and he were becoming big chums at that point and when we were out at the Manor, Branson's Manor, – where we did the album, Steve was only down the road in Wiltshire. He was hanging out at most of the sessions and there would be fun little contributions, which would frequently go uncredited."

The sessions were relaxed and fun. "Let's Make Up And Be Friendly" was the first recording to be undertaken at Richard Branson's Manor recording facility. The journey to darkest Oxfordshire was normally undertaken by car or in extreme cases in transport supplied by the studio. Vivian of course did not drive and was certainly most unimpressed by the clapped out ambulance fitted out with mattresses in the back, which was sent to collect him from Ealing. This was yet another example of the Bonzos as "funny men" being treated with a lack of respect bordering on disdain. Vivian had seen enough of ambulances and when the rickety machine broke down he merely hailed a taxi and on arrival sent the driver off to collect the hefty fare from Richard Branson.

At that stage Branson had other things on his mind. Manor studios was not yet the famous recording institution it would later become, as "Legs" Larry Smith recalls. "We seemed to be there a year, because when we got to the Manor the desk was in bits and Branson was hovering around, saying, "Oh, I'm terribly sorry, we're just not ready for you." The Manor was this wonderful old manor house in Oxfordshire and we stayed there for what seemed like six months, but I think it was probably two months, maybe three months at most. We just didn't think we'd ever leave the place and there was certainly no rush. It was bizarre. And every night we'd have these huge banquets. Fabulous! Great stuff!"

As regards the actual recordings Neil too has very positive memories of the making of the album. "It's different. There are some bits on there I really like, "Don't Get Me Wrong" is hilarious, it's Viv's narrative and it's just brilliant the way he sort of allows a whole solo to go by like the musical equivalent of a split infinitive, and all of a sudden we hear, "..against a wall", which was part of another sentence about five hours ago! I haven't heard it in a long time, but it was a lot of fun to make because it wasn't just the Bonzos. Andy Roberts is on there, Dick Parry on saxophone and Steve Winwood on organ. And I still remember the Hammond organ being in a kind of stone kitchen. It was recorded at the Manor, Richard Branson's place, and we were the first people to use it and Stevie was sort of sitting at the organ in this kind of place where the echo was good. I mean it was chilly

38

156

and Viv was sort of leaning over him trying to explain what he needed and saying, "I want balloons, I want balloon pigs, little pigs with balloons", and Stevie said, "Just tell me what you want, Viv, I'll play it". I have very fond memories of that time because that was the first time we heard the infamous Troggs' tape as well, and we were all rolling around the floor laughing together."

It will come as no surprise to the reader to discover that there was a distinct evolution in style by the time of these last recordings. With the refusal of Rodney Slater to return to the fold the wonderful saxophone lines, which had given the earlier recordings their own distinct flavour were noticeable by their complete absence. "Well, we had to lose the jazz," says Neil Innes, "when we'd made the decision to do any style of music, well, the jazz found itself edged out. I think I probably, shamelessly, sort of went more poppy, you know, because it was intriguing me and I'd always loved the Beatles' 'Penny Lane', and I thought that was like a movie in a pop song. I thought that was really, really a breakthrough and I thought, "Well, hell, if you can do that with images in pop songs..." And that was intriguing me that way. And musically I was also going in another way with things like "Turkeys", which you could probably describe as being Zappa-esque, but it wasn't actually influenced by Zappa because I was already writing that kind of "Rawlinson" music and "Rhinocratic Oaths", it wasn't jazz Zappa's kind of music can go this way and that can go this way, if anything I'd say the influence was Debussy."

Unfortunately the relationship between record company and the Bonzos was becoming strained by the excessive length of the recording sessions. With the album complete it was time to decide on a single. The track that was chosen by the band to promote the new album was "Slush". The label actually went as far as pressing up the first batch of singles before someone must have realised that this was yet another Bonzo wind up and the release was cancelled. The few singles that were made are now highly sought after by collectors, especially as the "B" side, "Music From Rawlinson End", consists of the backing track for "Rawlinson End" minus Vivian's vocal.

Given the breakdown in relations surrounding the album it was no surprise that there was no real promotion behind the release of the album and like "Keynsham" before it, this new record completely failed to make any kind of impact on the top forty. There were no supporting concerts and the Bonzos quietly went their own way for a second time.

CHAPTER SEVEN
HEIGH HO

Once more the Bonzos were solo performers. Vivian Stanshall began to appear on a variety of albums including 'Tubular Bells' by Mike Oldfield, which Vivian had narrated for no royalties as a result of a chance meeting with a struggling Mike Oldfield who had been hanging around the Manor Studios while the Bonzos recorded "Let's Make Up And Be Friendly". Vivian is also to be found on albums recorded by John Entwistle, Steve Winwood, with whom he co-wrote most of the lyrics for the best selling "Arc Of A Diver" album, and even Punk pioneers such as The Damned.

As a solo artist Vivian Stanshall also completed and released four albums, the first three of which were released on Tony Stratton–Smith's famous Charisma label. First came "Men Opening Umbrellas Ahead", which featured guest appearances by Neil Innes. The subsequent albums were "Sir Henry At Rawlinson End", followed by "Teddy Boys Don't Knit", which also featured Neil Innes, Roger Ruskin Spear and Sam Spoons. The final solo offering was "Sir Henry At N'didi's Kraal", which was a less than thrilling offering.

Vivian Stanshall also carved out a career doing radio and television voiceovers. He made a large number of radio show appearances with various collaborators and wrote and performed in his own stage production, "Stinkfoot". Vivian also found time to appear with Neil on the "Innes Book of Records" and record a track for the film "That'll Be The Day" which starred David Essex. More importantly Vivian was able to cajole Tony Stratton-Smith into financing a low budget British feature film, "Sir Henry At Rawlinson End". As well as writing and producing Viv also appeared briefly as "Hubert Rawlinson" and the Narrator. Vernon Dudley Bowhay-Nowell also appears as "Nigel Nice".

Rodney Slater eventually ended up being able to blend his new professional commitments with session work and eventually carving out quite a niche as a bass saxophone player. He also played in a couple of bands including The Infamous New Titanic Band and Whites Scandals. "I played very little bass saxophone in the Bonzo Dog Band", recalls Rodney. "The only thing I really did

was 'Jollity Farm'. I did sixteen years afterwards on bass saxophone, I was literally one of about four players of the thing in the country, or amongst the best four! I got a hell of a lot of work out of it. It can be made to look funny, but to me, personally, a tuba is a far more inherently funny thing. I always laugh at tubas and sousaphones much more than a bass saxophone, which plays the same role. A bass saxophone is much more flexible, you can use it as a bass, which I didn't in the Bonzo Dog Band. I did in later life because I played in things that needed that. And also you should be paid twice as much money as everybody else because you're a soloist as well. You're the second front line. I worked in a band called White Scandals, which was a bloody brilliant band, and they said, "Oh, we'll have you, Rodney, because you're bass and you're the second front line instrument". Two for the price of one! Which was fine because I was suddenly released. I was the key of the band, I was the lynchpin and I got loads of solo work so there I was after years of Bonzo repression, musically sort of blowing my bloody head off and I loved it."

Roger Ruskin-Spear continued with His Giant Kinetic Wardrobe" and eventually released two highly regarded albums, "Unusual" and "Electric Shocks". Roger was also involved in several Bonzo off-shoot bands such as "Tatty Ollity" with Sam Spoons, "The Slightly Dangerous Brothers" and also occasional appearances in "Bill Posters Will Be Band", with Sam Spoons and Rodney Slater. Among other recordings Roger also appeared on "God Is Mad" by "Albertos & Los Trios Paranoias". He also appeared on Vivian Stanshall's "Teddy Boys Don't Knit" album, and in the "Dog Ends" shows in 1991. Roger also taught art at Chelsea College of Art.

"Legs" Larry Smith seemed to spend a decade making guest appearances on a host of records and live shows including Elton John, Eric Clapton, John Cale and George Harrison to name a few. Larry finally released the single, "Springtime For Hitler"/"I've Got A Braun New Girl", which he had pressed Tony Stratton-Smith to release in 1970. Larry also sang the title track, as well as performing in the feature film "Bullshot". Larry also appears on George Harrison's "Extra Texture" album, on the song written by George in his honour, "His Name Is Legs, Ladies and Gentlemen". Larry has a number of projects including CD, film and theatre projects. In between times Larry has continued with his first love, painting.

As we have seen Rodney Slater took a very different course to everyone else. When the Bonzo's split up, he went back to college to train as a social worker. Rodney then spent the next fifteen years as a family therapist and as a semi-professional musician. The advent of the Margaret Thatcher years encouraged Rodney back to a full time music career in the wake of extensive budget cuts, which saw Rodney out of a job. Rodney has always much preferred live music to the studio, and stresses, "I'm not music business". Rodney toured with Vivian Stanshall on the 'Cranks'

tour as well as assisting Vivian with his 'Rawlinson Dog Ends' project at the Bloomsbury Theatre. But, the majority of Rodney's touring has been "for the enjoyment of it…" in his own bands; the New Titanic Band, Rodney Slater's Quality Serrenaders and Geezer.

Roger Ruskin Spear had perhaps the most eclectic career of all the Bonzos. For some 20 years Roger toured with his show "Giant Kinetic Wardrobe", which very much carried on where the Bonzos had left off. Roger toured with Fairport Convention, Hawkwind, Man and even King Crimson. There was also a short lived comedy duo with Thunderclap Newman and a series of television appearances with Marty Feldman, Kenny Everett, Michael Parkinson, Granada Television's "Rock Circus", "Saturday Banana" and "Motormouth" for TSW. Roger's television career peaked with the 13 part Channel 4 series "The Cut Price Comedy Show". The 1980's saw more comedy bands; The Slightly Dangerous Brothers and an involvement with Bill Posters Will Be Band as well as supplying robots for Crackerjack and the Design Council. The 1990's included a diversion into producing music videos as well as skateboarding videos and ramps.

Dennis Cowan joined the short lived band, "Abednego", which featured guitarist John Etheridge, Lynton Naiff, and future Neil Innes collaborator John Altman. Dennis then moved into theatre and was the original bass player for the new stage show, "The Rocky Horror Picture Show". Dennis can be heard on the original London stage show soundtrack album. Next up, he was part of another short lived band, "Darien Spirit". In October 1973 they released a single, "Rock Your Soul", and an album, "Elegy To Marilyn". The album was better promoted than many Bonzo offerings and is still remembered for its innovative album sleeve art of Marilyn Monroe with hologramatic lips. Sadly Dennis died in 1973 of peritonitis. Neil Innes and Vivian Stanshall were particularly close and were very strongly hit by this tragic event. Neil dedicated his "Recycled Vinyl Blues" album to Dennis whilst Vivian wrote the beautiful song "Vacant Chair", which was recorded by Steve Winwood, in his memory.

Neil Innes continued to enjoy the most success, both as performer and a collaborator. As well as his fantastic work with the Grimms alongside Vivian Stanshall, Neil is rightly renowned for his work on the television series "The Innes Book Of Records", "The Rutles" and his well earned reputation as "The Seventh Python". Neil Innes has a very successful solo career. After the Bonzos folded Neil went on to write with the Monty Python team. Much of his songcraft can be found on 'The Holy Grail' soundtrack. The Python and Beatles connection then spawned The Rutles project with Eric Idle and George Harrison, which grew from an initial sketch on Rutland Weekend Television. After a spell in children's television, Neil returned to a solo career, the latest incarnation being his 'Ego Warriors' project, a one man show drawing upon Neil's formidable catalogue of material as well as his latest CD, "Works in Progress".

By the late 1980's however, things were not progressing so well for Vivian Stanshall who was losing his battle against alcohol addiction and tranquillisers. Vivian was now somewhat in the wilderness living alone in a bed-sit at 21 Hillfield Park in Muswell Hill, North London. Alcoholism and deep, long periods of black depression blighted his life, but his old Bonzo mates were determined to rally round and organised the recording of a record to help lift Vivian's spirits.

NO MATTER WHO YOU VOTE FOR

So once more Neil Innes, Vivian Stanshall, Roger Ruskin Spear, Rodney Slater and "Legs" Larry Smith regrouped for the recording of one final song as "The Bonzo Dog Doo-Dah Band", and recorded "No Matter Who You Vote For The Government Always Gets In", a sharply pointed political song on which it was hoped to revive the idea of the Bonzos. Neil Innes recalls the genesis of the song. "The thing about "No Matter Who You Vote For The Government Always Gets In", is that by that stage Viv was starting to outnumber his good days with his bad days and he'd gone back to being in a sort of bed-sit where he was in the very beginning of the Bonzos. People like Stevie Winwood helped him enormously by getting him to write lyrics. Everybody helped him, but he became more and more of a liability to everyone. So this is my stage of like, "Let's help Viv", and I mean, where do you begin? I thought it would help to give him a focus if we built something around the old Bonzo unit."

Rodney Slater readily agreed to play his part in the session and drove Vivian Stanshall to the recording sessions. "I remember I drove down there in my then pink Capri with Viv. Viv was sort of half sober. We got to the studios. I saw Neil there, who I hadn't

seen for a long time, and he'd put on about seven stone! He's got a hell of bear hug and I thought bloody hell this guy's got strong, because he was like a stick insect in the band. In the old days I remember Neil sort of prematurely balding with this huge black cloud of depression around him, that was his trademark in those days. And he hated the first few weeks of being a pro, because he'd just got married, and he was always depressed and miserable. Anyway there he was this enormous fellow obviously enjoying life, who had started playing cricket for the village team. Eventually we got started he told me, "Yeah, get out there, Rodney, and play this." And it was out the range of my instrument. I couldn't get that low. He said, "Don't worry about that, just play it and we'll play it a bit faster or slower..." – (I forget. Whatever.) – "...so it comes out in the right key." And I did and that was it. He wanted a G below A flat on the bass saxophone. Well, there ain't one, you can't do it! The only way you can do that is by putting your knee over the bell and if you do it right you'll get away with it but not a whole scale. You only get that one note you know."

Neil Innes recalls how the song came about. "I got the line from picking up a hitchhiker coming out of Leeds who was off to do a Sealed Knot thing – the Roundheads and Cavaliers. So, "Oh, really? So are you a Roundhead or a Cavalier?" So he said, "Oh, a Roundhead." So, "Are you political then?" "No, no matter who you vote for the Government always gets in." I thought, "What a wonderful line!", so I said, "I might steal that one day", so I got Viv up to where I lived, up in Suffolk, to work on it. I've still got the tapes of the original demos and they're really great. I mean again Viv's earlier stuff, before he started fiddling with it, I thought was a lot funnier. On the day of the first sessions I got a phone call and I was expecting him to phone me from Ipswich station or something. So I go and pick him up. I get a phone call, I say, "Well, where are you?" "I'm in a house down in the village." "What are you doing there?" And he says, "I'm using the phone." I said, "Well, how did you get there?" "Taxi." "Taxi?! You came all the way from Chertsey to Suffolk in a taxi?!" "Yes, it's the agoraphobia, dear boy." And I go down the bottom of the lane, the taxi wouldn't come up, I live in a very remote thing it's up a river more or less and I met Viv and there he is in his sandals and his trousers at sort of three quarter mast, he's got this ring with the glass eye in it, he's got his beard with a

Bob Kerr: Cornet, Trumpet, Euphonium, Trombone, Saxes etc.
www.whoopeeband.de

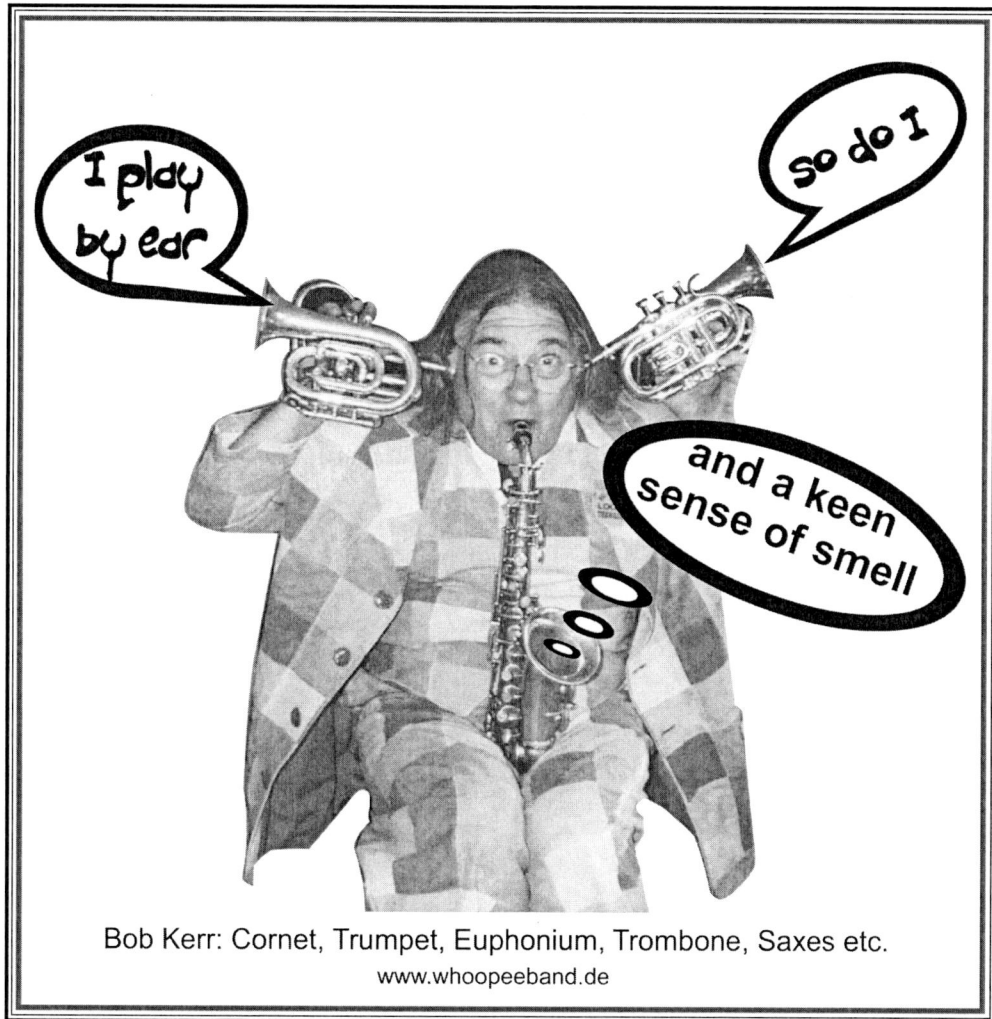

knot to keep it out of his soup or anything and he'd gone to the neighbour, – or to this house, and said, "May I use your phone?" They must have thought Aarrgghh! You know. So I pick him up to drive him up to the farmhouse and I said, "Agoraphobia? I didn't know you had agoraphobia." "Oh, yes, oh, yes." I said, "Well, how much did the cab cost?" He said, "Well, it was a hundred and twenty quid. Don't tell the wife!"

The single was a fun number, which deserved a much better fate. Unfortunately Neil Innes was unable to interest any of the major labels in the project. The "political" subject matter was considered beyond the pale by every record company and the single, which had been scheduled to coincide with the 1987 general election went unreleased.

Vivian Stanshall also staged what was essentially a live Bonzo re-union show in 1991, with "Dog Ends" featuring Vivian, Roger Ruskin Spear and

Rodney Slater. Eventually in time for the 1992 general election Neil Innes finally found a label to release the last Bonzo single with Vivian. Predictably, given the limited resources of the small independent China records label there was insufficient marketing clout behind the song and once more a Bonzo single failed to chart. "It was obviously disappointing," says Neil, "but anyway we had a very good three or four days working on this thing and they remain fond memories." The only thing that Neil was unwilling to join in were the late nights spent discussing the world with Vivian. "He would want to stay up late at night and I said, "No, I'm not going there, Viv, I'm not going there", and then he'd say complaining, "the bugger won't talk about life anymore."

Sadly there would be all too few opportunities for Neil Innes to talk about life with Vivian Stanshall. Vivian passed away in March 1995, in a house fire. His reputation and legacy shines on whenever the subject of the Bonzos is raised. "I take my hat off to him," says Neil. "He was unique. Absolutely brilliant and I'm privileged to have worked with him."

Sam Spoons also pays tribute. "Gradually he established a character and it became very apparent that he had this particular gift both with words and actions. He acted well and presented the song in a way that people really noticed, and obviously his whole persona was very appealing. I think the rest of us kind of recognised it as well."

For Rodney Slater, Vivian Stanshall will always be something of a renaissance man. "I mean he was a man of very many talents, which you will not get nowadays. You can't be all those things; – you can't be poet, writer, musician, entertainer, artist. He was all of those things in one. His brilliance was released in this crazy show, - and all the things that he did afterwards. He was too clever by half for people to understand what he was trying to say and his personality made him impossible to market and that was a collective at the end of the Bonzos, we were just impossible and Vivian was impossible too. Nobody could have done it."

"Legs" Larry Smith remembers Vivian Stanshall with great fondness. "There will never be anyone else like our Vivian, he was a great artist, poet and human being. Sadly the world is just too difficult a place for uniquely talented people like Vivian."

One of the great testimonies to Vivian Stanshall's genius is the intriguing body of work created by the Bonzos during his eight year tenure in the band. It is a remarkable body of work, which still has the power to delight and enlighten the bands enduring legion's of admirers both inside and outside the music business.

The last word on the Bonzos goes to its original co-founder. "I enjoyed it tremendously", says Rodney, "and I wouldn't have done anything else. You learn about life, don't you? University of life, ain't it? It's all there is you know."

164

CHAPTER EIGHT
I'LL REPEAT
THAT...

The sad passing of Vivian Stanshall in 1995 might well have marked the end of the Bonzo Dog saga, but there still remained one further chapter to be written. Once again no planning was involved and there was certainly no premeditated plan of action. Amazingly, in January 2006 most of the former Bonzos would once more find themselves on stage before an adoring crowd.

The catalyst for this unexpected meeting was a chance meeting in New York as Neil Innes recalls. "In March 2005, I did an interview with Bob Carruthers for a DVD called "Inside The Bonzo Dog Doo-Dah Band", which was part of a series featuring retrospective reviews on a number of rock bands from the Sixties and Seventies. I've never been one for living in the past but I enjoyed the rigorous approach and was agreeably entertained when I saw the end product. It brought back fond memories of bizarre days; like signing an autograph for a female lavatory attendant in Bremen airport who insisted on passing her book to me under the cubicle door. (She didn't know who I was. I just looked like someone in a "Beat Group") In those days, none of us had VCRs and good quality clips of our youthful exploits remain few and far between. It was also enjoyable to hear Rodney and Roger's version of events, bits I had forgotten, bits I never knew. So I was delighted when later that same year, in September, I met up with Bob in New York. He came to see a small off-Broadway show I was promoting, (called "Ego Warriors"), that included some music and reminiscences of the early Bonzo days, – when we used to scour the flea markets for silly old 78's."

"After the show, Bob mused that it would be great to get the band back together for a reunion concert. I immediately laughed out loud and declared the whole idea impossible: – "Vivian Stanshall is irreplaceable!" Bob heartily concurred and acknowledged that we couldn't hope to replace Viv. Nonetheless he persisted with the idea that the Bonzos material should be

I could leave the country and they'd never know

performed if nothing else to satisfy the huge number of fans who never got the chance to see the original band and suggested that a number of well known "younger men" would happily get involved thus avoiding the thorny question of a direct like-for-like replacement. Somehow Bob managed to persuade Chris Alexander of The Mean Fiddler that a celebration gig was a feasible economic reality. The original idea was to invite my own circle of musicians and any former members for a one-off concert to celebrate the material and the fun we had together. We agreed to put the idea to the others and invitations were dispatched."

A date in January 2006 was identified as a good opportunity. Of course at that stage there was no guarantee that anyone would be interested so initially the show was billed by Chris and his team at Mean Fiddler as 'Neil Innes and Friends - a celebration of the Bonzo Dog Doo-Dah Band'. Neil had invited all of his former band mates who were still active on the music scene in some capacity and had expected around half to take up his offer. One by one as the tentative offers to take part turned into acceptances it soon became obvious that with seven original members this really was as close to the real thing as the fans could get. So the show officially became 'The Bonzo Dog Doo-Dah Band 40th Anniversary Celebration – A Night To Remember', and took place in January 2006 at the Astoria in London. Tickets sold out within hours. It was indeed a night to remember with thunderous applause as the old stage favourites were wheeled out one by one in a two hour feast of nostalgia from the golden era of the Bonzos on vinyl. The show was recorded for Television Broadcast on BBC4 and also released as a DVD. The soundtrack later became better known as the double CD, "Wrestle Poodles …and Win!"

Given the enthusiasm for the band in the world of show business it was no surprise that a huge array of well known entertainers declared their willingness to take part. Sadly not everyone who was willing to take part could be accommodated and some potentially brilliant moments involving admirers as diverse as The Mighty Boosh, Bill Bailey and Lemmy had to be consigned to the "what might have been" pile, due to shortage of rehearsal time. It came as no surprise at all to the organisers that such a wave of goodwill existed, but the band members themselves were certainly taken aback. As Roger Ruskin Spear

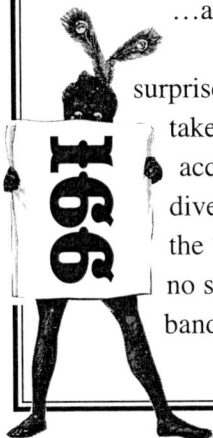

166

recalled, "What amazed us most about reforming the Bonzos was the enthusiasm of today's comedy entertainers. It would have been great to have everyone up on stage."

In the end the logistics of putting the show together intervened and the list had to be pared down to just four guests, Stephen Fry, Paul Merton, Phill Jupitus and Adrian Edmondson. Each of the guests represented a different aspect of Vivian's performing persona and each of the guests contributed in his own way to a highly memorable reunion gig.

Rodney Slater was another Bonzo who was pleasantly surprised by the warmth of feeling towards the band from some very high profile artists. "We were amazed that all these guys remembered us and wanted to join in. Not only that, but when they arrived at rehearsals they were word perfect. We looked up to Stephen, Paul, Ade and Phill as highly successful performers only to find out they, (for some reason), look up to us, even though we classify ourselves as unsuccessful performers!" The strength of the reaction certainly seemed to affirm the consensus view that the Bonzos are unique in successfully combining music, satire, humour and art. As such they are rightly celebrated as the originators of modern British comedy. The Bonzos reunion at the Astoria brought that salutary fact back to everyone's attention just how much affection there is for the band.

Phill Jupitus was happy to explain how the Bonzos had first touched upon his own life and career. "Imagine the scene if you will. It's 1967 in swinging London's glitzy Knightsbridge. Just around the corner from Harrods is a pub called The Paxtons Head, which at the time was managed by my aunt and uncle. During one particular visit I was called to the stairwell outside the bars by my uncle, "Phillip, this is "Legs", he's in The Bonzo Dog Doo-Dah Band..." I looked up at the vast hairdo of the Bonzo's erstwhile drummer. "Hello..." he seemed to boom, and he reached down and shook my hand. It was the first time I remembered shaking hands like a grown up. He was the coolest thing I'd ever seen in my life. I wanted to be him. Subsequently every time they were on telly or the radio, it was my proud if tenuous boast that "I know the drummer". I always kept an eye on the Bonzos but this being the days before I had a gramophone or money for records, I never got any... and so they faded from my sight, unconsciously replaced by Slade and The Sweet."

Adrian Edmondson was another celebrated performer who was influenced by the Bonzos at an early stage. "In 1974 I found myself abandoned in a very remote and exceedingly minor public school in the vast boringness of Yorkshire. I was seventeen and it was the time of the Three Day Week and power cuts; school was a drag and the masters were savagely boring; there was fuck all to do. (Certainly no fucking anyway.) After getting into slightly too much trouble I tried to run away to sea, but on reaching Hull docks found them closed because of the

167

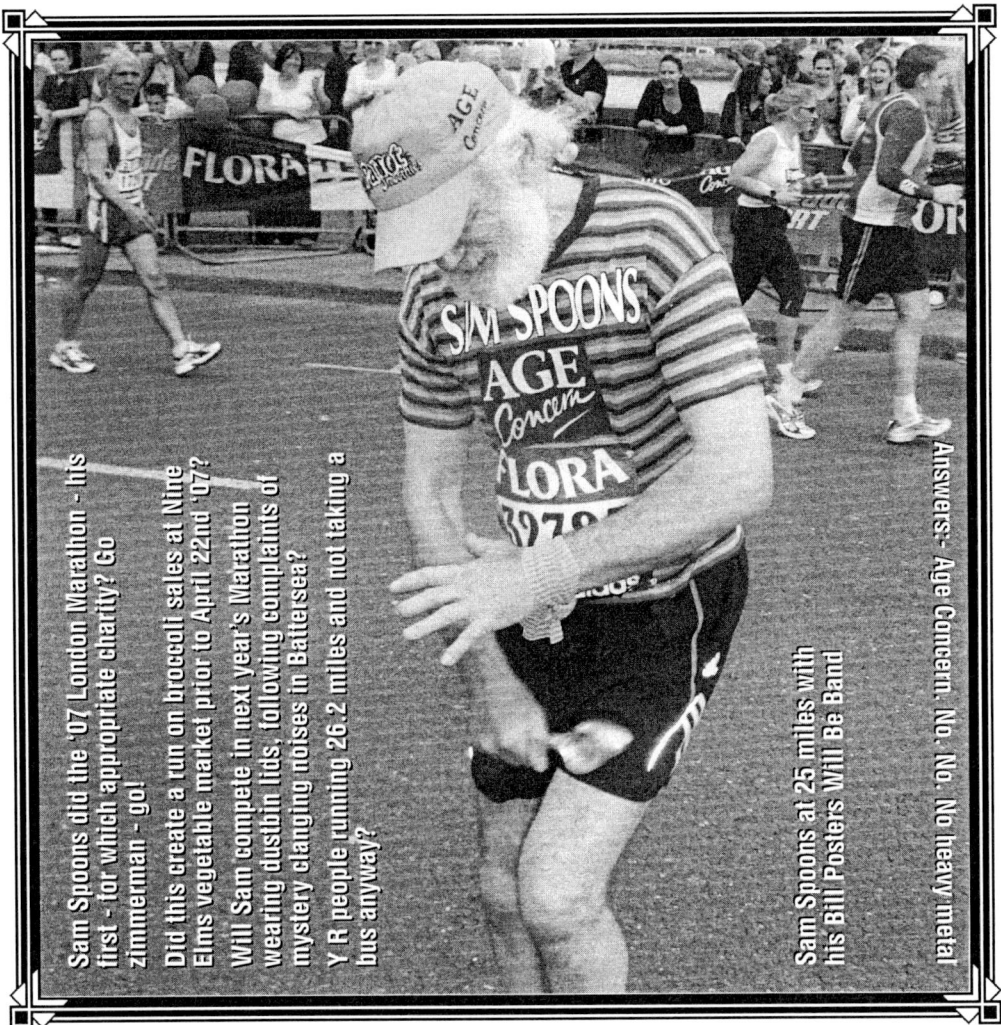

Sam Spoons did the '07 London Marathon – his first – for which appropriate charity? Go zimmerman – go!

Did this create a run on broccoli sales at Nine Elms vegetable market prior to April 22nd '07?

Will Sam compete in next year's Marathon wearing dustbin lids, following complaints of mystery clanging noises in Battersea?

Y R people running 26.2 miles and not taking a bus anyway?

Sam Spoons at 25 miles with his Bill Posters Will Be Band!

Answers: Age Concern. No. No. No heavy metal

recession. There was no escape. Everything seemed dead.

It was at this point that I stayed at a fellow inmate's house during half-term and found in his older brother's record collection… 'Gorilla'. It was, quite simply, life-changing. It was sensational. It was an escape. We played it non-stop whenever the power came back on, and when the power went off we sang it at the top of our voices all the way to the under-age pub and back: 'I'm BORED… Britannia you are cool, take a trip… I pass the swimming costume test… ruff ruff, ruff ruff… Hey, you have the same trouble with your trousers as I do… really wild general…' I know it was released seven years earlier, but it was new to us, and it seemed to fit the times completely, – blowing a great raspberry in the face of everything that was rotten and fetid and dull in 1974. It summed up all that

was brilliantly stupid about being English and gave us a new joy in our language that none of our insipid English teachers had ever managed to do."

As we have seen, Phill Jupitus was to be without the Bonzos and firmly locked in the embrace of glam rock until a radio broadcast reintroduced the Bonzos. "A decade or so later I was tuned in to John Peel's show on Radio One and off the back of some particularly challenging dub reggae, he played 'Mr Apollo'. I was sat in my bedroom and burst out laughing at Viv's phrase, "Wrestle poodles and win!" If it wasn't for Peely, I'd never have got the chance to reacquaint myself with their work. To me as a kid they were just that band on the telly. It never entered my head that they had actually made albums. So the first one I got was 'Gorilla'. I had it on all the time. I was especially taken with 'Big Shot's sleazy saxophone and piano groove. Then lines like "Whiskey wow wow I breathed, she was dressed as Biffo the Bear...", seared it into my brain. This ramshackle gathering of highly eccentric and musically gifted misfits had an off kilter approach to art and music that opened doors for me."

Like Phill Jupitus, the Bonzos continued to exercise their hold on Adrian Edmondson's young imagination. Adrian continued to find the Bonzos were in step with the events of his life. He takes up the story from where we left him at his minor boarding school. "The following year I went to Manchester University and met Rik Mayall. We were in the same year doing the same course. Our parents had identical jobs, our mother's had sent us with identical dressing gowns, we both smoked Player's No.6, both had crap haircuts, and we both had a copy of... 'Gorilla'. Still only seven years out of step with the rest of the world we then discovered 'The Doughnut In Granny's Greenhouse,' and in 1976 'Tadpoles'. We also discovered that playing 'Jazz, Delicious Hot, Disgusting Cold!' when we were completely pissed made it even funnier. (Please try it). In '77, our fellow student, Paul Bradley, alerted us to Viv's sessions on the John Peel show, and it not only blew us away, but also encouraged us to attempt our own recordings. This consisted largely of drinking anything and everything we could find, pressing record on a rudimentary cassette recorder, and doing Viv

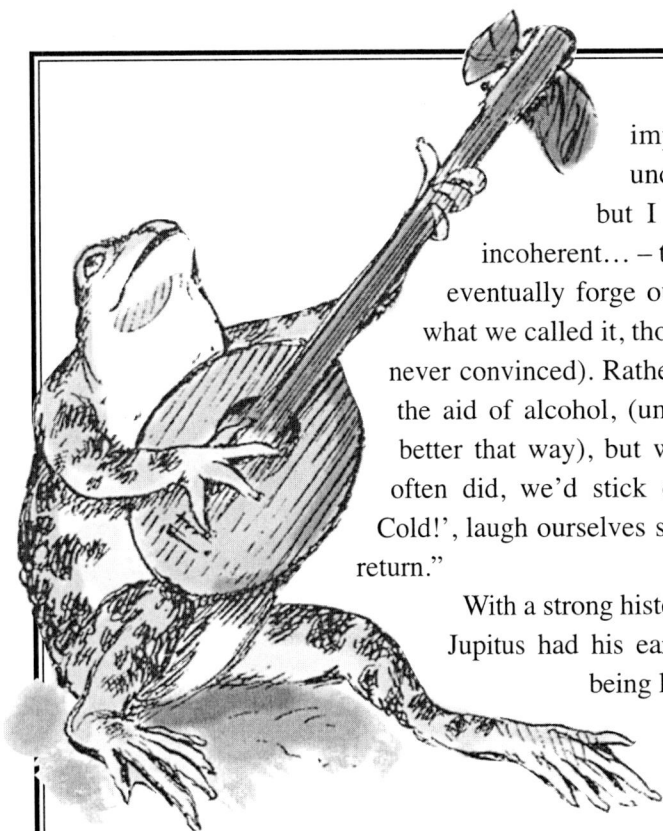

impressions until we fell into unconsciousness. I don't have the tapes, but I imagine they are spirited if a trifle incoherent… – they made us laugh at the time. We did eventually forge our own kind of comedy. (Well, that's what we called it, though certain sections of the press were never convinced). Rather daringly we began to write without the aid of alcohol, (unfortunately, sad to say, it does work better that way), but whenever inspiration failed us, and it often did, we'd stick on 'Jazz, Delicious Hot, Disgusting Cold!', laugh ourselves stupid, and the muse would invariably return."

With a strong historical commitment to the Bonzos, Phill Jupitus had his ear to the ground when the plans were being laid for the Astoria show. "A year or so back, the first rumours of a reunion gig began to circulate. Finally I'd get to see the songs I'd loved so much in my youth performed live. I frantically wondered how I could harness my negligible employment as a deejay into begging a couple of tickets. The next thing I know, I've been asked by Neil Innes to guest with the band at the show. It was utterly beyond my comprehension. To me these boys are bigger than The Beatles, and now I was going to be singing with them. Alongside Paul Merton, Ade Edmondson and Stephen Fry I took part in one of the most amazing nights. The band tore through a comprehensive history of their finest works. Songs that had seemed hysterical enough on record, performed live were utterly sublime. Myself and the other guest vocalists stood in the auditorium and watched open mouthed, grinning in delight as song after song awoke long buried memories of first hearing them. It was simply magical. So my thanks have to go to Uncle Graham, "Legs", Peely, Neil Innes and indeed all of the Bonzo's for making a little boy's dream come true."

Phill Jupitus' dream was to grow even more real when it was announced that in November 2006 the Bonzos would undertake their first tour for thirty five years. The re-union gig was judged a resounding success and thoroughly enjoyed by everyone who took part so Phill and Adrian Edmondson were roped in to do all the dates this time. Adrian even took up the trumpet in order to achieve a long ambition and actually play "Jazz Delicious" with a band. It seemed a shame to keep the fun to just those who lived inside the M25 ring so a national tour taking in most of England, along with dates in Scotland and Wales, was organised for November 2006 climaxing in two sold out nights at Shepherd's Bush Empire. Stephen Fry had other commitments

but Paul Merton again appeared at Shepherds Bush along with a surprise appearance by Bill Bailey who sang "Keynsham".

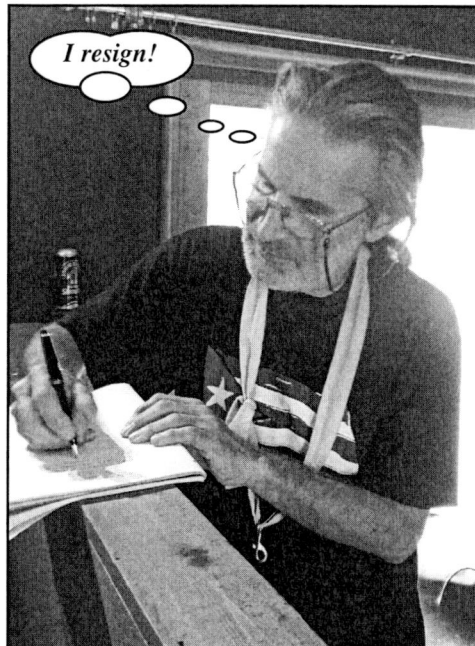
I resign!

Neil Innes picks up the story of how the 2006 tour came about. "So now we find ourselves on tour, and far from attempting some sort of "come back", (let's face it, we never really went anywhere), – the general mood was "let's do it... - one more time before we die!" Emphatically, we do not wish to tempt Providence, but as Diane Keaton once observed in a Woody Allen movie; "You know God is 'Dog' spelled backwards?" As Rodney is fond of saying, 'it's life, not books, that's taught me all I've learned' and in a world that more and more resembles a Hollywood Action Movie, I have begun to suspect that God does actually exist... - but only in one person at a time... – and this is why people move in mysterious ways!"

Altogether some 15,000 new and old fans took the opportunity to join in and celebrate with the Bonzos in 2006. The tour was a triumph and the press loved the shows with one Scottish journalist awarding the show six stars out of a possible five! That may sound a little like hyperbole but fortunately the second of the Shepherd's Bush Shows was filmed and recorded for posterity and presented for the first time with the first edition of this book so now you can judge for yourself.

POUR L'AMOUR DES CHIENS

With all of the interest in the revived Bonzos the inevitable question was could the Bonzos still cut it in the studio. The possibility of a studio album was certainly an intriguing subject and the issue was constantly raised by various journalists on tour. In the end Neil Innes and Mickey Simmonds were lent upon and agreed to produce the album with the input of Stephen Fry, Adrian Edmondson and Phill Jupitus. The announcement that the album would indeed be recorded was an exciting moment for Adrian and Phill who were now officially included in the ranks of The Bonzos. "When Phill and I were told that we were now officially 'in the band', (shiny new Bonzos!), we were like two schoolboys who'd just found a packet of fags and a porn mag. It's a real personal highlight for me. There's no way we could 'replace' Vivian. He was a comedy

171

god and totally unique. But when Phill, Stephen, Paul and I did the original reunion show we were paying homage, not only to Viv, but to the whole band. The back catalogue of Bonzo material is truly amazing and I think most people would agree it deserves to be performed, even though Viv is no longer with us. That said, we can't live in a museum either otherwise it's just a tribute band. If you want to keep it alive it has to be a proper living, organic thing, (apart from Vernon perhaps?), - and it needs to keep creating new things if it's going to be fun for band and audiences alike. So recording the new album was the obvious first stage of that process."

The album that was to become 'Pour L'amour Des Chiens', which was recorded over the summer of 2007 and released to an eager public in November 2007. Neil had managed to infuse a Baudrillard influenced polemic against the worst excesses of consumerism with some superb inspired comedic moments. 'Stadium Love' was a real treat as were the two short bookends, which all complemented wonderfully by Stephen Fry cameos, ("Salmon Proust" being one particular gem), and excellent contributions from Rodney Slater, Roger Ruskin Spear, Sam Spoons, Vernon Dudley Bowhay-Nowell, "Legs" Larry Smith and Bob Kerr.

Long term fans approached the album with some trepidation but once the disc was in the player any reservations soon melted away. 'Pour L'amour Des Chiens' was a triumph. The album had managed to hit the right balance between the jazz tinged world of the Twenties with the rockier side of the Bonzos, stopping off for a welcome pause for reflection here and there. The overall result was to combine the best qualities of 'Tadpoles' with 'Keynsham'. The album was a mature work in every sense and the combination of material from both new and old Bonzos was to prove a winning combination. Bizarrely this was to be Bob Kerr's first album with the Bonzos. "I really enjoyed making it", says Bob. "I was amazed at how well organised Neil is and I liked the way he gelled together with Mickey in the studio. I'm really pleased with the album and from what I've heard so are the fans and that's what matters, so it's job well done all round."

Neil Innes' vocal presence and his distinctive melodic approach gave the album a familiar Bonzo quality, which was so vital to the album and the running Fiasco gag would have been enjoyed by old Jean himself. With "Beautiful People", Adrian Edmondson was able to pull off the rare trick of writing a new song, which was instantly recognisable as capturing that indefinable quality, which can only be described as Bonzoesque. The public reception given to the song on 6th June 2008 by an audience, many of whom were hearing for the first time, was outstanding and once again the Bonzos had demonstrated just why the band is so unique.

Vernon Dudley Bowhay-Nowell takes up that thread: "We're all delighted that the new album has been so well received. I think it's

important to all of us that we are part of something that is dynamic and keeps moving forward. The Bonzos is not like any other band. Humour doesn't stand constant repetition like straight music does. Comedy demands a constant stream of new material and I felt the new material was certainly up to scratch."

On 6th June 2008 the Bonzo Dog Doo-Dah Band performed one last show together returning once more to the Astoria theatre. With Adrian Edmondson doing the whole show and Phill Jupitus sprinting to the Theatre fresh from performing in his West End play, the familiar line up was once again present. This final outing meant that the 'Pour L'amour' material was given a deserved outing before a live crowd. It was nevertheless a nerve wracking experience putting some of the new material through its paces in front of a live audience. Vernon Dudley Bowhay-Nowell recalls the importance of the show in relation to the album. "Presenting some of the new material at the Astoria in June 2008 for the first time was very exciting, but there was obviously some trepidation there because the back catalogue is so much admired by so many people. Audiences are notoriously unreceptive to new material and I was pretty

173

Hang on, nearly got it

pleased with how it went. We've now truly celebrated the Bonzo legacy from the past and the 15,000 people who joined us on the subsequent tour had a great time celebrating with us. We've also showed that we can do new things, which are well received by audiences."

Rodney Slater summed up the Astoria 2008 experience in his own inimitable fashion. "What we intended to do by adding the new material was to bring a different perspective to the live show and to build into the shows as much new material as we realistically could. It was certainly was not the idea to try and replace Vivian, that's why we again had Adrian and Phill along. Vivian was totally unique and the original idea behind the re-union show was to celebrate the great wealth of material, which is in the Bonzo back-catalogue. Having said that I thought making the album was a great idea. It adds a fresh dimension, which is essential if you are doing humourous material so things couldn't get stale and it becomes a museum. Having some new material to add to the old Bonzo legacy seemed like the right thing to do. Some of the material is brilliant and stands comparison with what went before. I'm glad we did it. In fact I'm glad I did all of it."

APPENDIX ONE
A BONZO DISCOGRAPHY 1966-1971
BY CHRIS WELCH

THE PARLOPHONE SINGLES

MY BROTHER MAKES THE NOISES FOR THE TALKIES
Released April 1966(Amber/Raymond/Bernauer)
UK SINGLES CHART: Did Not Chart
US SINGLES CHART: Did Not Chart

A cuckoo cry and the shattering roar of falling junk signalled to the world the Bonzo Dog Doo-Dah Band's arrival into the world of recorded sound. "'Ere, 'ere, 'ere, what's all that noise about?' 'Why don't you know, that's only my brother, he's practicing." This glorious racket was not only the band's debut single but a particular 'stage' favourite. The Bonzos had won a loyal and devoted following in the London pubs where they developed their act and were spotted by manager Reg Tracey in 1966. He booked them into the lucrative Northern cabaret circuit and also secured a record contract with Parlophone. Although the debut failed to chart, despite glowing reviews, 'My Brother' was a firm favourite among fans of the early Bonzos. Those were the days when they had an army of banjo, spoons and tuba players. The noise at the beginning however, was supplied by a 'Rowmonium', a box filled with bits of metallic junk. The song was written to celebrate the arrival of talking pictures in the 1920s and ironically the Bonzo's performance is now even older than the original version was at the time. Vivian Stanshall is besieged with sound effects from parrot squawks to steam escaping and cuckoo clocks. His diction remains perfect despite the barrage of burps and gunshots. Although accorded many radio plays, it is to the British public's lasting shame they didn't make this a Number One hit.

I'M GOING TO BRING A WATERMELON TO MY GAL TONIGHT (Conrad)

The fruity 'B' side to 'My Brother' was equally funny. How well these revivals compared to the 'originals' didn't matter because few remembered them by the mid-Sixties, when 78 rpm discs were already obsolete and only found in junk shops. The Bonzos, whose art student sensibilities ensured they appreciated the lyrics and their subtle messages, eagerly snapped up these gems and made them their own. Actually, the message wasn't so subtle when Vivian cooed his way through such lines as "I brought my girl bananas she let me squeeze her tight. I'm going to bring my girl a water melon tonight.' You can almost hear the saxophonist choke as he attempts to solo when a vexed Vivian announces that he's going to bring a rope 'and she can hang herself.' Although the single failed to chart it led to appearances on popular TV shows such as 'Thank Your Lucky Stars,' 'Blue Peter' and 'Late Night Line Up'.

ALLEY OOP (Frazier) October 1966

With their love of cartoon characters, superheroes and American pop culture, 'Alley Oop' made a perfect vehicle for Stanshall and chums. It was considered quite a departure for the band to switch from 1920s novelty songs to rock'n'roll pastiche. Yet it works as well as any of their other 'revivals'. The production is quite elaborate, with funky honks and splutters from the boys in the band, backing vocals and comic interjections. Maybe it was all too sophisticated for the masses. But then it had been six years since Gary Paxton, founder of the Hollywood Argyles, had recorded 'Alley-Oop' a song by Dallas Frazier written in honour of the comic strip character. The teenage pop pickers of 1966 wouldn't remember a 1960 hit let alone a 1926 classic. Damn fools! After two failed singles for Parlophone, the Bonzos switched to Liberty and as we have seen, enjoyed their first hit with 'I'm The Urban Spaceman', Number 5 in the U.K in 1968.

BUTTON UP YOUR OVERCOAT (De-Silver, Brown, Henderson) October 1966

The B side of 'Alley Oop' is a relatively straight forward reading of the jolly old standard whose appeal seems to have survived the decades and Viv's Twenties' crooner treatment. He advises dear listeners to "Keep away from bootleg hooch when you're on a spree. Take good care of yourself, you belong to me." A tap dancing interlude is accompanied by Neil Innes' energetic piano. This is a million miles away from 'Slush' the doomy final track on 'Let's Make Up And Be Friendly'. But these innocent, naïve and vastly entertaining singles epitomise the gentle, friendly humour of an organisation that eventually turned in on itself - no mean feat for a six-piece band.

GORILLA

(October 1967)

UK ALBUM CHART: Did Not Chart
US ALBUM CHART: Did Not Chart

Aficionados who delighted in the Bonzo Dog Doo-Dah Band's stage act eagerly awaited the Bonzos' debut album, which proved a great artistic success. In 1967 the band had moved to Liberty after two singles for Parlophone including 'My Brother Makes The Noises For The Talkies' and 'Alley Oop'. Music critics raved as 'Gorilla' proved a joy. The songs and arrangements were funny, witty and clever and revealed the Bonzos growing musical diversification as well as their skill at parody. Here was a team honed by hard touring in cabaret clubs. Let loose in the studio they had the freedom to experiment and indulge in an oblique sense of humour that saw 'normality' as just another aspect of surrealism.

It wasn't all biting satire and hard-nosed irony. The Bonzos humour was essentially good natured, jolly and almost cartoonish. Their songs and arrangements, sound effects, lyrics, dialogue and 'noises-off' celebrated rich veins of comic inspiration from 1920s novelty songs to 1950s rock 'n' roll as well as their own startlingly original compositions. Despite their anarchic streak and love of chaos The Bonzos aspired to be slick and cool. When they weren't, and their performances collapsed in 'Jazz, Delicious Hot,' or their ineffably cruel deconstruction of 'The Sound Of Music,' it was all the funnier.

Although much of the focus was on Vivian Stanshall and Neil Innes who shared the writing and singing duties and played many of the instruments, there were also vital contributions from Legs Larry Smith, Roger Ruskin Spear and Rodney Slater. As 'Gorilla' was being recorded the band was undergoing a change of style and line-up, but among those taking part were Martin 'Sam Spoons' Ash, Vernon Dudley Bowhay-Nowell and session bassist Dave Clague. The album was dedicated to cultural icon Kong 'who must have been a great bloke'.

COOL BRITANNIA (Trad Arr. Stanshall/Innes)

'Cool Britannia – Britannia you are cool. Take a trip. Britons ever ever shall be hip. Hit me hit me!' Vivian Stanshall, in his best Noel Coward tones, backed by the Bonzos in Jamaican Ska mode, launches a scintillating burst of mock patriotism. How ironic that New Labour should have adopted 'Cool Britannia' as a slogan in their 1997 election campaign. 'Swinging England' was still all the rage when Vivian and Neil Innes devised this rousing version of 'Rule Britannia' written by James Thomson and Dr. Thomas Arne in

1740, when Britain really ruled the waves. The band vanishes as the scene switches to a girl laughing hysterically at some gruesome activity, like limbs being chopped off underwater. Baffling, as Vivian was prone to remark. Pink Floyd later used manic laughter to great effect on 'Dark Side Of The Moon' and Ian Dury made the phrase 'Hit me, hit me' a telling feature of 'Hit Me With Your Rhythm Stick'.

THE EQUESTRIAN STATUE (Innes)
A charming Neil Innes ditty that utilises a harpsichord to imbue an 18th century mood to this tale of an equestrian statue coming to life and prancing through the town square. A man tasked to clean up any statuesque droppings in its wake, pursues this stony beast and its 'very famous' rider. Little old ladies stop and stare and feel gay at a sight 'guaranteed to brighten up your day.' Neil pays homage to Paul McCartney and The Beatles, making effective use of a high-pitched pocket trumpet, albeit in somewhat crazed Bonzo fashion. The piece was also performed in a 1967 Pathé newsreel devoted to the band.

JOLLITY FARM (Sarony)
One of the band's favourites, written by Leslie Sarony, the British songwriter and comedian who sang with Jack Hylton's band in the 1930s. It was typical of the novelty songs the Bonzos discovered on old 78-rpm records in junk shops and utilised in their stage act. It gave Stanshall a chance to introduce pigs, cats, dogs, birds, lambs, cockerels and all the beasts of the field in this glimpse of life in a raucous rural environment. A ukulele strums and the band has fun supplying farmyard noises. A cry of 'stuff it up your jumper, vo do de-o' became a catch phrase among fans. The jolliness concludes with a snatch of BBC Radio 4's 'The Archers' theme, courtesy of Rodney Slater's rumbling bass saxophone.

I LEFT MY HEART IN SAN FRANCISCO (Cross)
Anyone grown tired of this lachrymose ballad, would have welcomed Legs Larry Smith's quiveringly awful version, which brings new meaning to the phrase 'out of tune.' A highly sophisticated club audience languidly await the arrival in the spotlight of a famous crooner, come to entertain them. The genteel atmosphere is undermined by an irrelevant cry of 'fried rice'. Then loud applause greets Neil's delightful piano introduction as Larry, the tuba player and drummer turned cabaret star, breaks into song, pausing only to assure his fans they are 'very wonderful and very lucky'. He extols the loveliness of Paris and the glory that was Rome, but just as he is about to return to the 'city by the bay' his moment of showbiz glory is cut short by a peremptory crash on a cheap cymbal. It's hard not to hear this song again…without laughing.

LOOK OUT, THERE'S A MONSTER COMING (Stanshall)

'And three four' cries the MC, in the manner of Victor Sylvester, the famed dance bandleader. Adopting a Caribbean accent Vivian assumes the role of a 'lonely heart' in search of a girlfriend. During the course of this lilting calypso he tells how he tries to improve his image. He sends off for a 'deluxe Merseybeat wig', uses strong Aftershave, tries plastic surgery, has facial hair removed electrically and elocution lessons, learns to play the guitar and attempts to regain his virility. As his methods become increasingly desperate instead of turning himself into a desirable male, he becomes a monster, falling apart at the seams. It's a brilliant concept packed with demanding lyrics that Vivian delivers with deft accuracy.

JAZZ, DELICIOUS HOT, DISGUSTING COLD
(Stanshall/Innes/Ash/Spear/Slater/Nowell/Smith)

British traditional jazz never quite recovered from his glorious spoof that contains every blunder and cliché an amateur trad jazz band in full cry could muster. A relentless banjo, collapsing trumpet breaks, raucous slide trombone, clumsy clarinet and 'Ool ya ool ya' drum break complete a picture of musical incompetence masquerading as 'Trad.' When manager Gerry Bron asked Vivian Stanshall how they managed to play so badly, he affected to be insulted and claimed they were doing their best. Despite the Bonzos' worst efforts, their performance delighted Chris Barber, leader of the nation's premier traditional jazz band, who voted this one of his all-time favourite tracks.

DEATH CAB FOR CUTIE (Stanshall)

Elvis Presley impersonation has become an obsession in recent years, but Vivian Stanshall was one of the first and best to mimic 'The King'. Clad in a gold lame suit he amused and even outraged some punters at Bonzo pub gigs. 'I suppose you think that's funny!' yelled one affronted Elvis fan at the Tigers Head, Catford when Viv postured and sang in a sublimely camp ballad style. Neil sets up a rolling piano rhythm and the saxes riff in somewhat half-hearted fashion on a tune that harks back to 1957's 'Teddy Bear'. Although the lyrics are quite amusing, this is one of the weaker items on 'Gorilla', although it was performed by the Bonzos in the Beatles' 'Magical Mystery Tour' movie.

NARCISSUS (Nevin)

'How do you think it's going?' inquires Viv in concerned tones 'So so' says Neil. 'A lot of it's rubbish y'know' concedes Stanshall in a brief debate between the two protagonists on the progress of the album. A more disarming aside it would be hard to imagine, as they effectively neutralise any criticism. A 23 second gem, although quite what the 'trouble with trousers' has to do with anything remains a moot point.

179

THE INTRO AND THE OUTRO (Stanshall)

One of the Bonzos best loved and brilliantly constructed entertainments. Using the miracle of tape overdubbing Vivian creates a huge orchestra by introducing an increasingly bizarre number of guest musicians. After Legs Larry Smith sets up a swinging beat on drums, fellow Bonzos Vernon Dudley Bowhay-Nowell, Sam Spoons (on rhythm pole), Neil Innes, Rodney Slater and Roger Spear join in the fun. But henceforth the band swells to alarming proportions. Vivian as the courteous brilliantined band leader announces Big John Wayne on xylophone and 'looking very relaxed – Adolf Hitler on vibes.' Princess Anne makes a lugubrious appearance on sousaphone and Lord Snooty & His Pals enter tap dancing. Harold Wilson scrapes a mean violin and Eric Clapton is spied playing ukulele 'Hi Eric!' The Incredible Shrinking Man is among the first to arrive, armed with a euphonium, followed by General De Gaulle and J.Arthur Rank by which time the 'C Jam Blues' theme is overloaded to the point of cacophony, with only Val Doonican's cry of 'Hello there' still audible amidst the uproar. Priceless.

MICKEY'S SON AND DAUGHTER (Lisbona/Connor)

A merry celebration as the stork brings a son and daughter to Mr and Mrs Mickey Mouse. Vivian warbles that 'a million people are happy bright and gay' and reveals that Pluto is giving a party, steeple bells are ringing and that a public holiday has been proclaimed. Rod's bass saxophone adds comforting noises to a Disney cartoon period piece that typifies the charming innocence of early, youthful Bonzo material. Daft punk indeed.

BIG SHOT (Stanshall)

This homage to Mickey Spillane's pulp fiction is a cleverly wrought piece of scripting and acting. Certainly Stanshall as 'Johnny Cool' gave himself some tough lines to deliver. Innes plays discordant modern jazz chords as 'Johnny' makes his entrance and confides in shocked tones that party babe Hotsie has 'the hottest lips since Hiroshima'. It's the cue for lashings of crime story dialogue as the hero tells how he fought his way up from tough East Side New York. Hotsie warns him: 'Johnny this is a deadly game, have a few laughs and go home.' But the Big Shot is lured by a life of 'liquor, love and lies.' A demented sax solo gives the breathless narrator some respite before resuming his tale amidst squealing tyres and machine gun fire. Johnny Cool gets home late after a punk stops him on the street. 'You got a light mac?' 'No but I got a dark brown overcoat.' 'Big Shot' was left off the US version of the album. Perhaps it struck too close to home. Whiskey wow wow!

MUSIC FOR THE HEAD BALLET (Innes)

A serious interlude from Neil as he creates a hurdy gurdy

effect at his keyboard in an instrumental showcase designed to accompany one of the band's most stunning visual epics. It was used in the same Pathé short film that featured 'The Equestrian Statue.'

PIGGY BANK LOVE (Innes)
A Neil Innes composition that offers a gentle spoof of Sixties girl pop groups. The heroine saves Green Shield trading stamps for her wedding day and sings in high falsetto against rumbling saxophones played in unison with a surprising accuracy. Clearly Neil was determined to get a professional sounding performance out of his normally anarchistic colleagues. Not a duck call or klaxon horn to be heard.

I'M BORED (Stanshall)
An ode to boredom sung with surprising vigour by Stanshall in his best lounge lizard manner. He makes an inventory of all the things he finds boring such as the latest Julie Andrews' film and Frank Sinatra's LP. 'Quite apart from what one hears, I've been like this for years and years!' He hammers home the theme that he is 'bored to death – like mortar board' and then announces loudly 'This is boredom you can afford by Cyril Board!' This latter reference baffled American listeners, until it was explained that a contemporary advertisement for carpets assured TV viewers: 'This is luxury you can afford by Cyril Lord'. Vivian makes his final frank admission. 'The only thing that interests me – is me!'

THE SOUND OF MUSIC (Rogers & Hammerstein)
Gentle piano and then we find our beloved narrator in mid flow as he relates a particularly moving experience. 'Life's like that. Only the other day I was walking in the West End when suddenly I was set upon on by hordes of fans and admirers who wanted to touch my clothes. So I sought sanctuary in a nearby cinema. Normally I don't go in, but that day I saw something that really moved me. I want to share that wonderful experience with you. It was...the Sound of Music.' Cue trilling harp and then the most hideous, discordant row as singers wail and shriek like banshees and cymbals crash. What a finale. What an album.

181

THE DOUGHNUT IN GRANNY'S GREENHOUSE

(November 1968)
UK ALBUM CHART: UK Top 40
(Number 40 January 1969).
US ALBUM CHART: Did Not Chart

Major developments on the Bonzos' eagerly awaited second album, marked their progression from comedy cabaret act to experimental rock band. Psychedelic overtones to many of the performances baffled some critics but delighted and intrigued fans. Since 'Gorilla', original members Sam Spoons and Vernon Dudley Bowhay-Nowell had left. Bass guitarist David Clague took over, until replaced by extrovert American Joel Druckman, who was pictured on the new album sleeve, but not given a credit. Joel left the band in April 1969 and was replaced by Dennis Cowan. In December 1968 the Bonzos enjoyed a Top 5 hit with 'I'm The Urban Spaceman' produced by Paul McCartney under the pseudonym 'Apollo C.Vermouth'. The single wasn't included on the album, an omission that did not help its sales prospects. Even so, as a result of the hit single and appearances on ITV's 'Do Not Adjust Your Set' the 'Doughnut' slipped into the U.K. album chart at Number 40 in January 1969, their best result thus far.

'Doughnut' was packed with intriguing tracks, all composed by Neil Innes and Vivian Stanshall and engineered by Gus Dudgeon, who also worked with David Bowie and Elton John. The contrast between the Stanshall/Innes writing styles was very evident but the collaboration produced stunningly original work. Stanshall's sardonic asides and Innes' structured concepts resulted in a rare blend of satire and sensitivity. Among the highlights was 'My Pink Half Of The Drainpipe' a blistering tour de force for Stanshall, while Innes introduced more subtle and wryly witty pop songs, such as 'Beautiful Zelda' and 'Hello Mabel.' Richly comic moments remained throughout an album full of literate lyrics, bawdy gags and manic sound effects. Although well rehearsed playing prevailed, their anarchic roots often showed, notably on Roger Spear's delightfully dotty 'Trouser Press.' The meaning of the album's obscure title entirely escaped those unfamiliar with Cockney slang and euphemisms. Vulgarians well understood that 'Granny's greenhouse' was not a place for horticultural pursuits, but an outside toilet and clearly a noisesome place, unfit for casual visitors. Surprisingly, the Bonzos had heard the phrase, not on the streets, but on the 'Two Ronnies' a popular BBC TV comedy show.

WE ARE NORMAL (Stanshall/Innes)

'We are normal and we want our freedom!' chant the Bonzos, above a melange of frantic organ glissandos and stomping drums. 'Normal' makes for a dramatic overture, performed amidst wild whoops and yells in a frenzied atmosphere of abnormality. This is fitting as the 'freedom' message is taken from the cries of the inmates at Charenton, the French asylum where The Marquis De Sade died in 1814. 'We are normal and we dig Bert Weedon' adds Vivian Stanshall, a mischievous aside, which instantly subverts any serious intentions.

However, Neil Innes seems bent on opening the gates of perception in an awesome production that also features Joel Druckman armed with a tape recorder carrying out interviews with members of the public on the street outside the studio. 'He's got the head on him like a rabbit' responds one bemused Irish bystander. He was no doubt responding to the sight of a fugitive Bonzo, clad in a rabbit costume hopping past on the other side of the road. Jim Morrison would have been intrigued by this surreal, psychotic set up. It was Vivian who put on the papier maché rabbit's head, with one ear sticking up and the other bent. He leaned against a parked car a few yards away and told Gus Dudgeon his stunt would stop pedestrians in their tracks. However, only 'normals' could fail to laugh at the circus band style trumpeting and the voice of the cool young American adding to the fun. "Here come some normals. They look like normal... Hawaiians."

POSTCARD (Stanshall/Innes)

Soothing sounds of the seaside - waves and children laughing - provide a pleasing contrast to the uproar of the previous performance. 'I do like to be beside the sea' sings Neil wistfully, a view shared by Vivian who grew up in Southend and once worked at the resort's Kursaal funfair. It's a surprisingly restrained and tasteful arrangement played with due respect to the composer's intentions. One wonders how Neil managed to cajole the merry, disrespectful Bonzos into becoming serious musicians for this nostalgic piece. Even Vivien sounds duly sensible as he scribbles a holiday postcard to the folks back home, although he can't resist adding 'Dear Mum...I hope I get bronzed this year' suggests he is thinking of getting his kit off in public. An evocative soundscape, it works on several levels, from the beach to the promenade as it builds towards a sax fuelled climax.

BEAUTIFUL ZELDA (Innes)

This spirited paean to Zelda, a space goddess from Galaxy 4 is also a homage to cosmic Doo Wop of the Fifties and is full of amusing instrumental diversions that encourage the bright-eyed vocalist. Sympathetic backing vocals, brass riffs and a lively beat make 'Beautiful Zelda' sound like a contender for a Neil Innes solo album. It could even have been a

183

Eurovision Song Contest winner, given the right breaks Guv'nor. Not quite what one might have expected from a band famed for blowing raspberries and letting off smoke bombs, but then the Bonzos, they were a changin'.

CAN BLUE MEN SING THE WHITES (Stanshall)

'I need to have a shave cos I've gotta sing the blues' wails Vivian in this light hearted spoof of the deadly serious blues craze sweeping the nation in 1969. 'Hello boys I've got to mess up my hair and make some noise' says Viv sounding more like a head master addressing unruly pupils than Howlin' Wolf kicking ass. In fact Liverpool Scene's Adrian Henri made a better job of ridiculing the pretensions of white blues musicians on his group's parody 'I've Got Those Fleetwood Mac, Chicken Shack, John Mayall Can't Fail Blues.' Nevertheless, the Bonzos offer some seriously heavy guitar and drums from Neil Innes and Larry Smith.

HELLO MABEL (Innes)

A charming pastiche of a Twenties swinging love ditty starts with some armchair musing from Stanshall in avuncular mood. 'I can't help the way I feel' says Viv lighting a pipe and uncorking a bottle. He takes a swig before addressing Mabel, the love of his life. It's a return to vaudeville complete with glockenspiel and wah wah trumpet. 'That's nice' breathes Viv in pre-'Fast Show' jazz club mode. Tap dancing is accompanied by a menagerie of farmyard animals, before Vivian takes out the melody with a carefree 'Shoodle-oo bee, Shoodle-oo wasp, Shoodle-oo wah!' - one of those subtly silly gags of which he was inordinately fond and used to delight John Walters, his long suffering BBC radio producer.

KAMA SUTRA (Stanshall/Innes)

Two minutes of unmitigated pleasure in the hands of our guide, Vivian 'No Holds Barred' Stanshall. In an interlude whose brevity is all part of the joke, Stanshall sings of his sexual experiments based on cursory readings of the ancient Hindu text on erotic pleasure. His trusty aide Neil sets up a sexy, handclapping piano rhythm while girls chirrup encouragingly. Viv describes his very British approach to love making. 'We tried position 31 - yeah, yeah, yeah - it was terrific fun. In position 72 you were me and I was you. Oh!' 'Kama, Kama, Kama Sutra with me.' Then it's all over. The tune sounds oddly like Culture Club's hit 'Karma Chameleon' but that lay many years in the future.

HUMANOID BOOGIE (Innes)

Having already beaten Paul Whitehouse, New Labour and Boy George to the cultural punch The Bonzos anticipated the sounds of Gary Numan and Kraftwerk with this extraordinary robotic concoction. Neil's distorted voice looms, almost leers as he bellows 'Hi there!' and launches into a rap in which he envisions the human race turning rock 'n' roll into an electronic computer programme. That seems to be his interpretation of the future of pop music as viewed from the Sixties. He is suggesting that manufactured robot stars could somehow get to the top of the charts. Ridiculous!

TROUSER PRESS (Spear)

'One two three kick. Come on everybody clap your hands. Are you having a good time? Do you like thoul music?' lisps a camp dance instructor. 'No' snorts a curt Stanshall so dismissively you can almost see his lip curling. 'Well do the Trousers Press baby 1,2,3' says our host, cheerfully undaunted. Cue Roger Spear with his clattering contraption, the electric trouser press. No hotel room is complete without one. Nor was any recording studio when the Bonzos were in the mood for some fun. The noisiest and most unlikely rhythm instrument in the history of percussion is unleashed on what the band claims is the latest dance craze. 'You're so savage Roger.' 'Press those trousers!' The clumsy rattling noises purporting to provide the beat are so ridiculous that even Roger collapses with laughter and shouts a defiant cry of 'Raw meat!' The Trouser Press never quite achieved the mass acceptance of The 'Twist' but when DJs at pop concerts subsequently hoped to get crowds going with the once reliable battle cry 'Do you like soul music?' they were invariably greeted with groans of 'No!' This wonderfully daft divertissement lent its name to a highly respected American rock magazine. Technical note: The machine Roger used was a Corby trouser press wired up with contact microphones.

MY PINK HALF OF THE DRAINPIPE (Stanshall/Innes)

An affectionate but sharp observation of the absurdities of everyday life. Stanshall's strong vocal performance is enhanced by Innes' delightful arrangement that features a lilting Parisian piano accordion, supported by nifty drumming. Vivian, laughing before he sings a note, briskly sets out a bold riposte to the predictable life style pursued by the masses and most likely, his parents. He is aided and abetted by old pal Rodney Slater, who not only plays a saxophone solo 'as promised' but chortles through his holiday memories, in an artless celebration of working class joys. However, Viv's pink half of the drainpipe safely separates him from the tedious semi-detached banalities of his neighbours. He considers painting his social barrier blue, but remains clear that whatever happens, "I intend to be a freak for the rest of my life'. A defiant 'So there!' concludes with an incredibly long note. Not so much a feat of vocal endurance, it's a crudely spliced tape loop.

ROCKALISER BABY (Stanshall/Innes)

An intriguing Neil Innes concoction. We suspect it correlates the newly introduced traffic police breathalyser with the work of the rock police, aka music critics. There is a strong Beatles influence in the use of certain

emphatic piano chords and Liverpool accents abound in the various spoken asides. 'Don't you realise my friend you are bringing everybody down?' remonstrates Neil adding 'You're doing everybody wrong!' The piece also reflects the siege mentality of rock bands at a time of increased police surveillance on their activities. This mood is reflected in earthy dialogue between Roger Spear and Rodney Slater. Stanshall's contribution is to recite some completely irrelevant anecdotes about electric irons and seagulls.

RHINOCRATIC OATHS (Stanshall/Innes)

More eccentric tales told with ineffable charm by Mr. Stanshall reading from his collection of newspaper clippings and his own wild inventions. His description of a police officer disguised as a hippie doing the Twist as the 'Frug A Go Go Beir Keller' is priceless. A rapid fire series of character studies is accompanied by a highly sophisticated arrangement with tinkling piano, unison brass and swinging drums. 'Percy Rawlinson' makes an early appearance, a precursor of the character that would appear in the 'Sir Henry Rawlinson' saga Stanshall developed later in his chaotic career. When Percy spends too much time with his canine pal, friends tell him 'You should get out more, you'll end up looking like a dog.' Their worst fears are confirmed when Percy mistakes a policeman for a postman and tears his trousers off 'with his bare teeth' leading to a court appearance. 'It's hard to tell the difference when they take their hats off,' says Percy in his defence. Then there is the story of Ron Shirt and his feud with a neighbour who trims their garden hedge 'into the shape of a human leg.' Battle ensues as Ron responds with increasingly wild acts of topiary. It all ends with a brief 'hooray' and the snappy conclusion that 'sometimes you just can't win.' The song title is another of those slow burn gags. Hippocratic oaths? Aha!

11 MUSTACHIOED DAUGHTERS (Stanshall)

An eerie piece of work in which the Bonzos prove rather more successful in penetrating the dark arts of witchcraft and black magic than any number of heavy metal rock bands. Although bursts of laughter can be detected, the dialogue and madness seem rather too convincing for this to be mere parody alone. Vivian Stanshall is the master of the unholy revels as the drums set up a monotonous, menacing beat and Neil offers some dark, manic organ chords. You almost expected Christopher Lee to make a guest appearance in this Dennis Wheatley inspired saga. "Eleven moustachioed daughters, running in a field of fat" intones Stanshall his voice increasingly chilling and hypnotic. Then a witch enters the fray and devises a potion that will help him 'choose another form and make it thine!'

A trumpet blasts and Vivian sniggers as the blasphemy degenerates into an orgy. 'Doughnut' is an extraordinary album that

rewards constant plays. These highly literate fun and games are complemented by more hidden messages than might be found on any Beatles LP's stop groove. Apparently it was conceived and recorded amidst ferocious arguments that almost brought the band to its knees. But they had much more to do. The dance of the Trouser Press was far from over.

TADPOLES

(August 1969) UK ALBUM CHART: Number 36
August 1969 US ALBUM CHART: Did Not Chart

'Tadpoles' was billed as the soundtrack album to the band's regular TV spots. The original bright yellow LP cover with its cut-out graphics had the strap line 'Tackle the toons you tapped your tootsies to on Thames TV's Do Not Adjust Your Set.' It was an effort by the band's management and record label to promote the group, following the success of 'Urban Spaceman'. The eleven tracks include their hit single, although the song should have been on 'The Doughnut In Granny's Greenhouse' released the previous year. 'Tadpoles' is not really a 'soundtrack' but does include many songs featured on the TV series. This marvellously entertaining collection is more good humoured than the highly conceptual 'Doughnut' and is perhaps the best loved Bonzo album of them all. It encapsulates the essence of the early group that so appealed to pub, club and cabaret club audiences. Although there are some clever Innes-Stanshall productions, there also many vintage songs like 'Hunting Tigers' and 'Ali Baba's Camel'. These allow greater space for Roger Spear, who contributes the wonderfully manic 'Shirt' and 'Tubas In the Moonlight', more of which later. The band's third album was the last worked on by engineer Gus Dudgeon and for years afterwards he nurtured fond memories of the chaotic Bonzo sessions at London's Trident Studios. Amidst a welter of burps, Swanee whistles and out of tune guitars, the musicians and their attendants seemed to spend most of their time on the studio floor helpless with laughter. The band later embarked on a six week American tour to promote 'Tadpoles'. This was an exhausting, frustrating experience. Although hardcore U.S. fans loved them, it proved even harder to sell albums in the States than at home. But the six merry fellows peering out from the cover of 'Tadpoles' weren't ready to give up yet. They had a lot more shirts to press.

HUNTING TIGERS OUT IN 'INDIAH'

(Hargreaves/Damerell/Evans)

Tigers lack table manners it seems and Vivian Stanshall our jungle guide, warns 'they don't say their grace - after they

have eaten you.' They also 'bite, scratch and make an awful fuss. It's no use stroking them or saying puss, puss, puss'. A simple drum and bass beat thrusts along this delightful ditty which recalls the days of the British Empire and colonial India. A spot of snake charming doesn't calm the nerves of our hunting party. "Shaking? You silly goose, I'm just doing the Watusi" insists Legs Larry Smith. 'Hunting Tigers' was one of the band's most popular stage numbers and is ripping fun for all.

SHIRT (Spear)

The sound of Roger's wah wah rabbits' provides the introduction to this splendid addition to Mr. Spear's comical instruments and daffy dance crazes. 'The Shirt' is an unlikely rival to The Twist. But before the band rolls its sleeves and cuffs up, Vivian conducts another in the series of cheeky 'vox pop' interviews tape recorded with hapless pedestrians outside the Willesden Green studio. The resulting snatches of bizarre conversation are still gleefully recited whenever Bonzo fans gather. 'Shirts? I've got plenty at 'ome'. Viv capitulates in the face of public ignorance about the pressing subject of shirts and takes us to the 'shirt event'. Cue rock 'n' roll pastiche complete with out of tune guitar solo, Mr. Spear strains manfully over his electric shirt collar for a sparky solo to a chorus of 'Shaking the shirt.' Yes, this is all complete madness. Where is a trouser press when you need one?

TUBAS IN THE MOONLIGHT (Spear)

A charming and sincere tribute to the sort of orchestrated dance music that held sway in the 1920s, much admired by Roger Spear, who wrote this melodic arrangement. Vivian warbles in his best crooner style while the unison saxophone passage is reminiscent of the style pioneered by the Fletcher Henderson orchestra. The track was taken from a tape recording by one of Roger's early projects, the New Jungle Orchestra.

DR JAZZ (Oliver/Meltrose/Darewski)

A jazz standard beloved of British traditional jazz bands and given the ultimate Bonzo treatment complete with false start, a spoons solo and feature spot for the Swanee whistle, a bicycle pump style device destined to puncture musical egos. There are also chimes, whistles and a clarinet laboriously played in the lower register. If the Bonzos had sailed down Mississippi to New Orleans, they would have been sent right back again, to Willesden.

MONSTER MASH (Pickett/Capizzi)

When the Bonzos weren't crucifying Dixieland jazz they had a lot of fun at the expense of rock 'n' roll. 'The Monster Mash' was a Number One U.S. hit for Bobby 'Boris' Pickett and the Crypt-Kickers in 1962. Despite yet another false start by drummer Legs Larry, this is a well-meant tribute to one of Viv Stanshall's favourite records. Vivian sings in sepulchre tones of the ghouls and vampires and guest star Wolf Man, who appeared on the original

recording. But one wonders about the 'Poodle Stabbers' who sound suspiciously like a Stanshall invention. 'Igor, have you watered the brains? demands Viv as he embarks on a paroxysm of increasingly manic laughter. His echoing cries of 'hee hee hee' so amused Rodney Slater that he laughed until his sides hurt. Recalls Slater: "Viv didn't half alter some of the lyrics. I will always remember that manic laughter. I was sitting in the studio and the huge speakers filled the whole room with this unbelievable laughter. Of course everybody else started laughing and it was the kind where you almost can't breathe. The head starts to ache and a band tightens across your chest.'

I'M THE URBAN SPACEMAN (Innes)

Neil Innes' finest hour and the hit song that gave the band chart status and pop credentials. Paul McCartney, a keen Bonzo fan, produced the session under the pseudonym Apollo C.Vermouth. He showed the lads how to play the bass guitar riff that underpinned the theme and even plinked away briefly on Viv's ukulele. Lillian Bron, wife of producer Gerry happened to see Paul playing and asked 'What's that, a poor man's violin?' Replied McCartney: 'No, it's a rich man's ukulele.' Neil allegedly wrote the song in half an hour but it contains some clever imagery and ideas that lift it out of the realms of pop novelty. As the residual laughter fades away from 'Monster Mash', wooden recorders state the jaunty theme and Neil sings the line 'I've got speed'. This aroused the suspicions of Frank Zappa when he first heard the song played to him on a Melody Maker 'Blind Date' session. Yet it has nothing to do with drugs. The Urban Spaceman is the kind of perfect role model who peers out from glossy magazine advertisements, 'Here comes the twist. I don't exist' concludes Neil with a neat flourish.

ALI BABA'S CAMEL (Gay/Francis Day & Hunter)

Mr. Stanshall had to be on top form to cope with this wordy campfire saga. Our hero, Ali Baba, whose very name has become a byword for thievery, steals a camel from a zoo. The camel is grateful and forms an attachment to his master, a passion that sadly ends in tragedy. He enters a desert race, which leads to exhaustion and confusion. ' Its tail was pointing backwards, that's how a camel smiles' chortles Viv, clearly enjoying every minute of a lengthy but amusing tale interspersed with sound effects. Ali and his camel win the race, but are so exhausted and taken with their achievement they laugh themselves to death, a source of much lamentation by the entire company.

LAUGHING BLUES (Bradley)

More painful highlights from the Bonzo book of instrumental torture. A companion piece to 'Dr. Jazz' this was taped at what sounds like a rehearsal and commences with authentic blues piano followed by the strains of a phonofiddle, once described by Neil Innes as a 'singularly unrewarding instrument.' There are train whistles,

189

bird calls and a rather nifty trombone solo but the real agony begins when a clarinet starts 'laughing'. Oddly, its all done in deliberately po faced fashion, as if nobody is really amused by all these effects, which in any case are brought to a halt by the ancient tape recording breaking up. It's no laughing matter.

BY A WATERFALL (Kahal Fain/Feldman)

According to the late Gus Dudgeon, Viv Stanshall was beginning to lose control during these sessions. Gus: "On 'By A Waterfall' he was absolutely sloshed. You can hear it if you listen closely. He was completely paralytic. Halfway through the song he fell off his stool. I had to stop the tape, go down into the studio, pick him up, give him a cup of coffee and carry on.' This is a shame of course, although the unsteady delivery seems to suit the weak and watery nature of the song. The Bonzos do their best to support their singer by providing a barrage of responding love calls and all manner of irrelevant interjections, from xylophone solos to Hawaiian guitar and the return of the dreaded Swanee Whistle.

MR. APOLLO (Stanshall/Innes)

Charles Atlas, the bronzed Adonis who advertised his body building course in magazines throughout the Sixties, doubtless impressed the young Stanshall, just the sort of weakling who had sand kicked in his face by bullies on the beach. Mr. Apollo' was Neil and Vivian's variant on the Atlas theme. It seems that by following his methods in the appropriate postal course, (avoiding unpleasant bending) it was possible to 'wrestle poodles at will.' The super hero was meant to provide the follow up to 'Urban Spaceman' yet somehow when the track was released as a single it failed to chart. Sand was kicked in the Bonzos face by cruel pop fans. It's hard to see why. This is funnier and just as cleverly conceived as 'Urban Spaceman' but the production lacks the deft hand of Apollo C.Vermouth. A heavy metal guitar intro shows Jimi Hendrix was already a major influence but Neil's story of the 'strongest man the world has ever seen' doesn't quite have the allure of his predecessor. At any rate, it includes Vivian giving a bully a revenge beating to cries of 'Oh lor!' After taking the course you see, the four stone weakling is now 'two separate gorillas'. Priceless.

CANYONS OF YOUR MIND (Stanshall)

One of the Bonzo's funniest and most brilliant creations, this ultimate rock idol spoof can still induce tears of laughter 36 years after it was first conceived. Apart from the masterful performance by Stanshall as the agonised singer protesting his love, 'Canyons' also contains one of the greatest guitar solos of all time. While Vivian can be heard parodying Elvis the Pelvis, Neil Innes and de-tuned electric guitar embarks on a farrago of bum notes in a style that would actually compare to the work of any living musician. Stanshall takes the idea of comparing the human heart to the centre of love and desire to ridiculous

lengths. He explains how he will 'wander through your brain to the ventricles of your heart. 'Cross the mountains of your chest I will stick a Union Jack.' Whoops, screams and cackles accompany Neil's guitar nightmare then Viv returns to describe how his loved one's perfume reminds him of 'Sweet essence of giraffe.' While the Bonzo chorus sing blithely the hypnotic phrase 'frying pan, frying pan' Viv again professes his love, climaxing a series of sensuous grunts with an almighty burp, one of the skills he learned as a deck steward in the Merchant Navy. Ah, what rogues they were!

KEYNSHAM

(November 1969)
UK ALBUM CHART: Did Not Chart
US ALBUM CHART: Did Not Chart

'Keynsham' was the Bonzos' concept album they hoped would be seen as their 'Sgt. Pepper.' It was also their fourth album made within two years and although the songs were forged in the white heat of creativity, the production was rushed and there was only a cursory attempt made to explain the ideas behind the 'concept.' Nevertheless 'Keynsham' contains brilliant wheezes. Despite Neil Innes' continued efforts to make serious pop music, subversion remained at the core of the Bonzo oeuvre. Example. Just when a delightful instrumental interlude is successfully navigated, a dentist's drill shrieks and the sound of a tortured patient rents the air. It was ever thus.

The album has 14 original songs mostly short vignettes. The Bonzos could never be accused of labouring a point or succumbing to Prog Rock excess. Even when they did! Innes and Stanshall wrote all the material, although there were cameo contributions from Legs Larry Smith, Rodney Slater and Roger Spear, ranging from camp repartee to bizarre sound effects and wacky solos. The album was put together with the assistance of producer Barry Sheffield at London's Trident Studios. Their previous producer Gus Dudgeon had noticed a change in the band's writing methods during the making of 'Tadpoles'. "They used to jointly seek out targets. They'd pick out a particular thing they wanted to send up and do it en masse. Now they were indulging in individual send ups." Even so, there seemed broad agreement about Neil Innes' clever idea that underpinned 'Keynsham.' The group had been leading a crazy existence, touring and recording for what seemed like years. It got to the point where Neil concluded that none of what they saw around them was really happening. He guessed they were all were living in an institution, where everyone shared the same reality. Explained Neil: "It was an off-the-wall idea, but everybody

picked up on it and so 'Keynsham' was born." A similar theme would surface years later in Jim Carrey's fantasy movie 'The Truman Show' (1998).

The album's title would confuse American fans who had absolutely no idea what it was all about. Indeed, few Britons under the age of 60 now would remember Horace Bachelor and his 'Infra Draw' football pools winning method. It was advertised relentlessly on Radio Luxembourg in the Sixties, the droning Mr. Bachelor spelling out the address of his operational base near Bristol called… K.E.Y.N.S.H.A.M. Said Stanshall: "Keynsham seemed to me to be Never-Never land, a tangible Shangri-La where this disembodied man lived in." Vivian and Neil thought of 'Keynsham' as the fantasy village outside the asylum, where the band were inmates.

Neil: "Keynsham is our 'id' - our subconscious. The album itself splits off into many different directions and although there is an underlying theme, this is difficult for the average listener to detect or understand, because it is no more than hinted at in the lyrics."

Despite the album's promise, 'Busted' the track that should be the grand finale, only serves to illustrate the band's accumulating problems. Riven by argument, exhausted by hard work, the Bonzos, like their 'concept', were literally falling apart. It was a great disappointment when 'Keynsham' failed to chart and neither singles 'I Want To Be With You' and 'You Done My Brain In' were successful. Reality dawned. The angry patients fled the asylum. By January 1970 it was all over. But not quite. There was still a chance for the absconders to make up and be friendly.

YOU DONE MY BRAIN IN (Innes)

Described as 'an affirmation of madness' in the marginally helpful sleeve notes, this brief introduction to the world of 'Keynsham' begins with Vivian in best Horace Bachelor tones muttering: "I have personally won…" Ignoring desperately weak drumming and out of tune saxophone riffs, Neil perseveres with his carefully crafted lyrics, singing 'Don't kiss me with your silver lip" while the rest of the band blithely play the theme tune from 'Housewives Choice.' Madness indeed. "You done my brain in" was the sort of thing their loyal roadies Chalkie and Fred would say, as they wrestled with giant papier maché heads and smoke bombs at showtime.

KEYNSHAM (Innes)

"It's tragic magic" sings Neil Innes, a ringing phrase that concludes "There are no coincidences but sometimes the pattern is more obvious." Rarely had such literate lyrics been heard in pop, which only made the context seem odder. For all their musical imperfections, often deliberately introduced for their own anarchic pleasure, the Bonzos were secretly making some of the most satisfying and challenging records of the late Sixties. Most of their songs have endured and remain relevant, long after the most earnest fusion rock epics have taken their place in the vinyl dustbin of history.

QUIET TALKS & SUMMER WALKS (Innes)

"Let's talk about Keynsham," says Vivian in his best bedside manner as Neil sings an attractive ballad with fetching sincerity. It's really a thinly disguised tribute to his great idol Sir Paul 'Ukulele' McCartney although there is much that is pure Innes about the construction of an ode to lovers taking a rural path to intimacy. Recorders and strings create an oasis of calm before the next brainstorm.

TENT (Stanshall)

'Summer Walks' is disturbed by the sound of a dentist's drill and screams of pain, but there is even more violent upheaval to come. 'Tent' is one of Stanshall's most manic performances, whose angry, predatory violence pre-dates punk rock. There is no doubt about the plans Stanshall has for the hapless victim he lures to his lair. "Let's take a taxi to my tent, I'm gonna getcha in my tent where we can both experiment." Whatever else happens in this foetid canvas hellhole Stanshall promises to be eloquent in his depravity. "My love is so inscrutable, in a Stoic sort of way," he says airily. He is clearly the sort of man in shorts, beard and sandals best avoided on a hot summer's day. A Rotten saxophone solo adds to the paranoia engendered by Stanshall's Vicious vocals.

WE WERE WRONG (Stanshall)

From tent to bent. A gay love song only Vivian and Legs Larry could deliver with such convincing ardour. It was one of their great gags to pretend to be gay, usually in tough pubs, where their camp gestures and innuendoes caused great affront and outrage, as intended. This is a spoof of a rockabilly teen ballad done with heart-rending passion. "We were wrong…but so young and so very in lo-o-ve" sing the poovy pair, recalling shocking nights of drunkenness at the Oxford May Ball where 'we arrived in a punt – you fell down in the beer tent, unashamedly drunk.' There are obscure references to rhinos, leather, champagne and kedgeree, which make one shudder at Viv and Larry's misspent youth.

JOKE SHOP MAN (Innes)

As if to give Vivian time to recover from his tented orgy and outings with Legs Larry, Neil offers a vignette that is but 1.23 seconds long. And yet it neatly encapsulates the strange atmosphere at a shop where sneezing powder and rubber feet are sold in paper bags like so many sweets and humbugs. No doubt the Bonzos spent many morbid hours in such humourless emporia. The song has elements of 'world music', many years before the rest of the world discovered such resources.

THE BRIDE STRIPPED BARE BY 'BACHELORS' (Stanshall/Innes)

"So the boys formed a band, fate played the straight man and since then they've never looked back", narrates Stanshall in a strangled voice, an imitation of the band's first hardworking manager. Quite what the

famous work of art by Marcel Duchamp has to do with anecdotal stories about touring Northern cabaret clubs, only these former art students would understand. Maybe it is not a thousand league's distant from the French surrealist's own propensity for irony and satire. And of course there is the link twixt 'Horace Bachelor' and Duchamp's 'Bride'. "I've seen you on the telly with your long hair and pimples" says Viv, satirising the avuncular jollity of their hosts. "We arrived at the gig looking rough, we were tired and we'd all had enough," sings Neil, They recall the horrors of smelly boarding houses and backstage bullies who warn against scratching their precious pianos. The piece builds to frenzy amidst time-honoured phrases such as 'We've had 'em all here – your Buddy Greeky'. It's the closest the album gets to coherent documentary form.

LOOK AT ME, I'M WONDERFUL (Stanshall)

More camp theatre as the resolutely star struck and very wonderful "Legs" Larry Smith applies make-up in the seclusion of his dressing room. The singer and dancer practises his big opening number in front of a mirror to the sound of clattering tins of rouge. Suddenly Vivian's callboy is tapping on the door and announcing 'Ten minutes Mr. Smith'. The band strikes up a swinging introduction and Larry dashes for stage and spotlights. To rippling applause he launches into song. "I'm not a bit like you or you, I'm a super showbiz star!" Quite right too.

WHAT DO YOU DO? (Innes)

The Bonzos rock out. It's tempting to believe it really is Keith Moon on drums. Certainly the arrangement sounds like The Who in action, complete with Pete Townshend style power chords. Moon was a great Bonzo fan, so it is possible he took over the kit from Legs Larry. If not, Larry had been taking drum lessons. Neil proclaims "I do what I do…I am what I am." Which can be taken as a loose affirmation of their existence within the Keynsham 'id', if anyone is still paying attention to the story line. This mature piece hints at a yearning desire to be taken seriously. Indeed, the band would have been, had they stayed together and persevered for a few more magical years.

MR. SLATER'S PARROT (Stanshall)

Meanwhile, back in the asylum…Mr. Slater's parrot says 'Hello.' Squawks, whistles and the kind of repetitive talk favoured by parrots is accompanied by the sound of a washboard being scrubbed in rhythmic fashion behind a merry clarinet theme. Once heard this relentlessly jolly ditty is almost impossible to forget. It is dedicated to the parrot owned by the band's stalwart bass saxophonist. The talkative bird so delighted Mr. Stanshall that he wrote: 'We love to hear him squeak, we like to see him biting fingers in his horny beak." However, the noise so enraged Mr. Slater's neighbours he had to get rid of him, inducing one last squawk 'goodbye.' Whether this song inspired Monty Python's 'Dead parrot' sketch is a

194

horny problem.

SPORT (THE ODD BOY) (STANSHALL)

Stephen Fry, the great English comedic actor and televisual entertainer was still at public school when 'Keynsham' was drawn to his attention and he immediately fell in love with the sound of Stanshall's 'fruity' voice and this song in particular. He could identify with its sentiments, as an indolent schoolboy, exposed to the pitiless cruelty of games masters and their insistence on "masculine sport." Confronted by an 'odd boy' who couldn't play football or cricket or even wrestle poodles, they heaped scorn upon his head. In Vivian's song, his parents beg for their sickly son to be excused games. The icy response is 'give him a nice cold shower."

I WANT TO BE WITH YOU (Innes)

Neil Innes in particularly fine voice on this pleasant tune that could have been a hit single, if only fate had played the straight man and the cards had been tipped in their favour.

NOISES FOR THE LEG (Stanshall)

"No, no, please, not the leg." Vivian's latest fetish seems to concern amputations. He is clearly amused by the spectacle of a lone leg, possibly removed by stray cannibals. You can see a detached leg, pictured on the album cover, tied down like Gulliver on his travels. When Roger Spear devised his leg-shaped Theramin, Stanshall's joy was complete. The noises produced by this unique electronic instrument were enough to leave most audiences legless. Our story begins with Viv announcing: "I've found the men sir. God – I wish I hadn't!" The howling wolf cry that follows this announcement is so ridiculous as to be almost as funny as the great Leg itself. The Theramin Leg is one of Roger's best inventions, on a par with the Electric Shirt Collar and Trouser Press.

BUSTED (Stanshall/Innes)

Here's where 'Keynsham' takes a wrong turning. After a succession of ballads, mad rockers, amusing interludes the grand finale turns out to be a bit of damp squib. They stretch out an idea about teenage rebels being 'busted' by the police with a long bass guitar solo and even a spot of jazz trumpet. This would have baffled the great Marcel Duchamp himself, if he were still alive to hear it. Maybe he would retreat to his garret, there to rethink the whole concept of surrealism. Although the band seems to be at a loss for words and relapse into instrumentalism, 'Keynsham' still contains enough gems for it to be considered among their best works.

LET'S MAKE UP AND BE FRIENDLY

(March 1972)
UK ALBUM CHART: Did Not Chart
US ALBUM CHART: 199

Fans were bereft when the group broke up in January 1970. Melody Maker, the weekly music paper that had long championed the Bonzos, took up the clamour for a reunion. Eventually the lads succumbed to pressure and got back together in the Manor Studios, newly opened by Virgin's Richard Branson in November 1971. The line up consisted of Vivian Stanshall, Neil Innes, Dennis Cowan, Larry Smith and Roger Spear augmented by Bubs White (guitars), Andy Roberts (guitars and fiddle), Dave Richards (bass), Dick Parry (saxophone) and Hughie Flint (drums).

Melody Maker critic Roy Hollingworth gave Vivian a lift down to the studios. They set off from London in a hired ambulance, which broke down and the party eventually arrived in Oxfordshire by taxi. Because they had stopped off at various pubs en route, Vivian was in a bad way. "Thank you for bringing a dead artist" was Neil Innes tight-lipped comment as he greeted them at the studio. This did not auger well for sessions that resulted in a less than satisfactory album. The title sounded promising. The band had taken their name from 'Bonzo' the loveable character created by the artist George Ernest Studdy (1878-1948) A suitably lugubrious looking puppy dog, he was featured in a range of popular illustrations and postcards and even had his own 'Bonzo Annual'. Studdy's 'Let's Make Up And Be Friendly' postcard seemed an appropriate choice for an album cover.

Yet not all the Bonzos wanted to join in the reunion. Rodney Slater was there in spirit, but he had started a new life with a 'proper' job, in local government. His saxophone playing and perhaps more importantly, his support for old pal Vivian Stanshall was sorely missed. Neil Innes did all the hard musical work while Stanshall's best moments came when he was talking rather than singing. The efficient session men brought on board were mates and sympathetic to the cause, but the final result was a string of strangely uninspired performances. All the life and inspiration seemed drained out of the band.

The scheduled two week recording session took two months. Among those present in the studio was a young Mike Oldfield, working on an ambitious project called 'Tubular Bells'. He invited Vivian to participate, although by all accounts, Viv took little interest in the unknown composer's work, an instrumental album that eventually went on to sell millions and underpinned

Branson's expanding Virgin empire. The Bonzos' album, on the other hand, failed to chart. The band went their separate ways and there would be no further attempts to reunite, although their paths crossed in the years ahead. Neil Innes enjoyed a successful solo career, mainly through his work in television with Monty Python and film. Legs Larry aimed to become a super showbiz star, tap dancing his way onto shows with Elton John and Eric Clapton.

Roger Spear made solo albums and led his own groups such as the Giant Kinetic Wardrobe and Tatty Ollity before becoming a lecturer at Chelsea College of Art. Stanshall developed the 'The Rawlinsons', characters that first appeared on 'Let's Make Up' into a radio series and a bizarre film. He also released several solo albums and wrote a stage musical called 'Stinkfoot'. He seemed quite prolific but in his cups confessed that the Bonzo days were the happiest of his life. Sadly, his career was blighted by alcoholism and he died in a fire at his London home aged 52 in March 1995. His most lasting memorial is undoubtedly the succession of brilliantly funny performances that shone forth on the Bonzos' wondrous recordings.

THE STRAIN (Stanshall)

It certainly was a strain when Vivian Stanshall sat on the toilet at the Manor Studios in Oxfordshire, and recorded the sound of his painful attempts at bowel movements. While not the most edifying of subjects it was certainly original, although it does sound as though he is tastelessly equating soul music with one of the less attractive human functions. The band sounds startlingly heavy with their ranks of funky guitar players. Vivian sounds as if he has been incessantly smoking roll ups as he groans, coughs, wheezes and gasps his way through this experiment in 'scatological rock'n'roll'. It's hard to tell which is worse, his coughing or crapping.

TURKEYS (Innes)

Neil Innes tip toes away from the unpleasant scenes in the Manor lavatory facility and does his best to raise the tone of proceedings. His complex and neatly executed instrumental arrangement explores new horizons in sound. Saxophones hoot, pianos sparkle and the piece is redolent of some Parisian cabaret in the 1920s.

KING OF SCURF (Innes)

High pitched vocals from the composer are accompanied by the sound of dandruff being combed from someone's 'filthy hair' in this tribute to the Jan & Dean style surfing genre. Actually surfing fans might regard it as some kind of deadly insult, but its quite amusing in an irritating sort of way. "Guess I'll have to start from scratch" interjects Viv as a violin prolongs an over long and messy performance.

WAITING FOR THE WARDROBE (Spear)

Although Roger Spear was on hand to raise the banner of musical mayhem on behalf of the old Bonzo's tradition, this was not was one of his best works. The

main problem is the truly awful singing that is only partially alleviated by the businesslike lead guitar and saxophone playing. The owners of the Manor, had they chanced upon this session, might have wondered whether they might have done better converting the building into a hotel rather than a recording studio. And the wardrobe should have been crushed under a steamroller.

STRAIGHT FROM MY HEART (Innes/Stanshall)

The mysterious sound of rustling paper can be discerned during the saxophone solo on this waltzing ballad, sung by Vivian Stanshall who seems to have developed a severe head cold as well as asthma and memory loss. Maybe he was still sitting on the lavatory while recording this eminently forgettable ditty.

RUSTY (CHAMPION THRUST) (Kaye/Smith)

If 'Straight From The Heart' was bad, 'Rusty' was one of the most self-indulgent performances devised in the name of the Bonzos. It consists of a lot of incomprehensible cocktail party chatter about a pair of unsavoury characters and their exploits. It's hard to hear the dialogue and virtually impossible to understand. Maybe it's a tribute to Lou Reed and the New York glam scene. Whatever, it drags on for what seems like hours. Its authors are Legs Larry Smith, an otherwise charming and witty chap and Tony Kaye the ebullient Hammond organ player with prog-rock band Yes. Larry should have done a follow up to 'Look At Me I'm Wonderful', but seemed to get lost en route to the theatre.

RAWLINSON END (Innes/Stanshall)

The album's saving grace is a brilliant collaboration between Neil and Vivian inspired by the sort of BBC afternoon play the band might hear on the car radio en route to a gig. Vivian begins this nine-minute venture into radio theatre with a recapitulation of the story so far. Neil plays a sprightly piano accompaniment that perfectly suits the Home Counties flavour and Viv's collection of dotty suburban heroes.

"It's almost three years since Madge and Bobby Rawlinson pulled up roots and were arrested by the parks department. Jeremy Sphincter has sailed for Australia after the poultry scare. We won't mention HIM again…." Vivian continues his script in best Radio 4 tones and comes up with ever more extraordinary revelations about the Rawlinsons. "Sandra…smells. Randy has turned in on himself, no mean feat for a 40 stone man…now read on.' As the music stops, Vivian is alone and perfectly in control. His asthmatic, booziness gives way to the sharp-witted mind that once gave us 'My Pink Half Of The Drain Pipe' and 'Canyons Of Your Mind'. He becomes even funnier as he assumes the mantle of old Sir Henry, recounting his adventures with the natives in the jungle, although the wheeziness returns with such violent realism that Stanshall almost has to give up his narrative in a coughing fit. This radio parody is done with such

inventive affection it was no wonder Stanshall was to become a regular broadcaster, his further tales of Old Sir Henry's exploits enlivening the John Peel show. "He looks so sinister in that corset…" Indeed.

DON'T GET ME WRONG (Stanshall/Innes)

Back to rock 'n' roll and the mood is soulful Beatles, as Viv sighs woefully against Neil's bold lead vocals. It's a relaxed, carefully arranged piece complete with Voice Bag effects and a long jam session. Once musicians get to jamming in the studio its difficult to get them to stop, unless you are Yoko Ono, who once screamed during a John Lennon recording session 'Stop jamming!" 'Don't Get Me Wrong' combines early Merseybeat with Detroit vocal harmonies.

FRESH WOUND (Innes)

Nimble acoustic folk guitar ushers in Neil in pre-Rutles mode, singing like a former Beatle hoping to return to the group to claim four years back pay. That is Neil's own joke incidentally. It all becomes quite hysterical, but in truth has little to do with the group formerly known as Bonzo.

BAD BLOOD (Stanshall)

Gunfire ricochets off the canyons of Stanshall's mind as he intones this gory tale of a one eyed half breed amputee, crippled in his mind and out to settle old scores. Banjos and guitars take us way out West and you can tell Viv read lots of cowboy comics as a lad. "You can lick bad blood but it still won't go away," he sings gruffly, reaching for his six-shooter. Most of the laboriously crafted lyrics are buried in the hash of 'geetars', but the song develops into quite a successful piece, until Viv starts to laugh at his own lyrics and seems to give up on this saddle sore attempt to ride the range.

SLUSH (Innes)

Neil's haunting requiem for a faded dream, as the now exhausted band sinks slowly into the studio mire. A slow moving organ theme intertwines with the sort of repetitive manic laughter that Pink Floyd would use on 'Dark Side Of The Moon' to huge commercial success some three years later. The music stops but the laughter goes on. And that's the story of the Bonzo Dog Doo-Dah Band.

APPENDIX TWO
POUR L'AMOUR DES CHIENS
SLEEVE NOTES

POUR L'AMOUR DES CHIENS (Innes)
WARNING: If you are thinking, "this disc seems much smaller than I remember." Don't worry, it's not your misspent youth catching up with you. It's what they call a CD! Pop it in the drawer thingy and allow Musical Director and Master of Ceremonies Mr Innes to lead (ho! ho!) us all off and kick-start the proceedings with this short study of an equally short dog.

LET'S ALL GO TO MARY'S HOUSE (Trad. Arr. Bonzos)
A wash of nostalgia from an earlier altogether more innocent age flows from this engaging tale concerning a number of mature single men visiting Mary at her house at some late hour in pursuit of wholesome fun, companionship and a "good time". Vocal from "Legs" augmented by Mr Slater on non-chicken clarinet.

HAWKEYE THE GNU (trad. arr. slater/innes)
The Highlands come to Surrey. A reworking of a reworking of a traditional tune re-interpreted by Mr Slater, ably assisted by shiny young fresh new Bonzos Adrian Edmondson and Stephen Fry. Sure to be a stage favourite at some stage.

MAKING FACES AT THE MAN IN THE MOON
(Rich/Smith/Hoffman) Warner/ Chappell North America
Roger and "Legs" take the fore with this Mills brothers meets shirt-cleaning extravaganza.
Spear Speaks Out #1:
"I hope we can get away with another in the "Moon" series. This time, the tuba part is played by Bob Kerr (on the euphonium). Close

harmony, and an even closer shave for Larry, who gets carried away in the moonlight and is offered another chance to have his "shirt cleaned express". Rodney demonstrates his versatility on the clarinet. There are no dying chickens here, just a polished performance, and the careful listener may spot the "Acker Bilk" moment in the last few notes of the song. Thanks to our musical director, Mickey and his "quantising" skills, my Shoenberg-inspired vocal stylings have been rendered almost bearable."

FIASCO (Innes)

...and now a word from our sponsors. Well it is the 21st century after all.

PURPLE SPROUTING BROCCOLI (Ash)

Sam Spoons takes the spotlight with this wonderful pean to the charms of a sadly underrated vegetable. Has stage favourite written all over it.

OLD TIGE (Burke/Burke/Reeves) Sony/ATV Music Publishing (UK)

And next up on stage is brand new millennium Bonzo boy "country" Phill Jupitus. Originally a "B" side of a Jim Reeves single, Phill chose this as "probably the best song ever written about a ghost dog." Watch out for that dam Phill!

WIRE PEOPLE (Ash/Innes)

Sam Spoons and Adrian Edmondson return with this classic introduction to the legendary non-existent TV series of the same name. Unsuitable for children ...or adults.

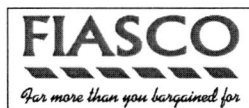

SALMON PROUST (Innes)

Literary smugness from Mr Innes fruitily voiced by Mr Fry.
NB A microwaveable pre-owned version of this dish is available at all branches of Fiasco, two for the price of one until February. *(Terms: Under certain circumstances actual purchase date may post-date original sell-by date displayed on packaging).*

DEMOCRACY (Innes)

Every album needs a calypso and here it is, courtesy of Mr Innes. He really isn't that keen on our beloved leaders is he?

I PREDICT A RIOT * (Hodgson/Wilson/Rix/ Baines/White)
Rondor Music (London) Ltd

Hard to predict the plot of this one, as Mr Spear and Mr Edmondson are let loose on this Kaiser Chiefs classic. Planned and unplanned studio incursions by Mexicans, Wurzels, that bloody chicken clarinet and HM constabulary.

Spear Speaks Out #2:

"This one came to me in a dream, whereby Kaiser Wilhelm III had a night on the town and assaulted a policeman with a ukulele. I called it -

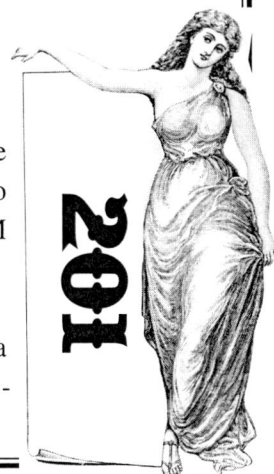

"I foresee a banjo solo". Unfortunately, I awoke to discover that some talented chaps had already had the same dream. Such is life. Fuzz banjos and electric spoons - all part of a night's work for the Leeds city police. Mr Slater finally nails that chicken and Ade lets rip on the trumpet. Neil brings along that guitarist from "Canyons" and we all have a jolly good time on a Saturday night, including the Mexicans.

SCARLET RIBBONS (Danzig/Segal) EMI Harmonies Ltd

Yes, there was a time when this was the choice of an entire nation. Vernon Dudley Bowhay-Nowell attempts to wind the clock back by introducing a new generation to the hitherto highly resistible charms of the musical saw.

PAWS (Jupitus)

You may have noticed that side 2 is in fact blank, dashed clever these CDs.

AND WE'RE BACK (Innes)

You didn't really think we'd leave you did you?

STADIUM LOVE (Innes/Heatherington/Fraser-Simpson/Milne)

Mr Innes, ably assisted by Phill Jupitus, invites us all on a musical journey of exploration. Our mission is to discover just how big a stadium chorus can grow. The answer is very BIG indeed. Lighters aloft - who needs amnesia - unforgettable.

MORNINGTON CRESCENT (Simmonds)

The trad world intrudes with Bob Kerr on cornet and the one note solo is not to be missed. OK so it's the old underground station routine, but the last time we made a record, 35 minutes was all you needed to fill two whole sides... and we would have been back at the pub by now!

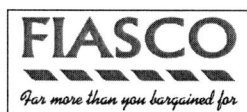

FIASCO
Far more than you bargained for

L'ESSENCE D'HOOLIGAN (Innes)

Does what it says on the tin. Buy one get three free at Fiasco (may cause some skin peeling, flaking, burning agony and extreme irritability). External use only, not to be taken in the event of a West Ham defeat. Consult Sports Desk before use.

EARLY MORNING TRAIN (Innes)

An impassioned and frankly rather soppy Innes ballad brought to earth by Adrian Edmondson on behalf of selfish bastards everywhere.

MY FRIEND'S OUTSIDE (Spear)

Electro Bonzos for the last century. Sadly we missed the eighties as a fully functioning ensemble, (funny how you turn your back and a decade slips by) but if the Bonzos had been around in the years of bad mullets and synth pop, this is what you may well have missed ...or not. Inspiration from Mr Spear.

Spear Speaks Out #3:

"Recorded live at Murrayfield Stadium, that third chorus goal was a cracker - quite remarkable! Mickey again, this time having a synth-fest! I forget now - is it Barry Neuman, "Legs" Larry Neuman, or even Nannette? One thing is certain, for this recording, the vocals were by the Arthur Mullard male voice choir, again with caustic interference from Ade Edmondson (and we didn't let them in, either).

We've now fixed the fault at the end so we can play you the full eight hour version (perhaps on the next CD?)"

FOR THE BENEFIT OF MANKIND (Innes)

Gilbert and Sullivan would never have written a song like this; but Neil Innes did. Good to see disinfected aubergines finally taking their place in rock mythology, and about time too we hear you cry.

203

BEAUTIFUL PEOPLE (Edmondson)
Adrian Edmondson contributes a beautiful melody married to an entirely unsuitable lyric. Pure essence d'Bonzo. The people of France appear courtesy of President Nicolas Sarkozy.

EGO WARRIORS (Innes)
The obligatory crusading number, standing up for the individual in the face of a relentlessly homogenised society, a cause popularised by the unstinting efforts of Neil Innes - with no noticeable effect so far.

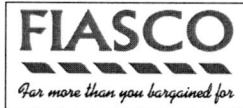

FIASCO
Far more than you bargained for

COCKADOODLE TATO (Innes)
Sorry to disappoint, but just when you need one, there's no actual chicken clarinet solo in sight. Sale on pre-owned items now on. Buy one get two free* from all branches of Fiasco. (*Standard terms and conditions apply. Your standard rights are affected).

TIPTOE THROUGH THE TULIPS (Burke/Dubin) B.Feldman & Co Ltd
Yes, it is the same Tip Toe through the Tulips. You've heard the faux soprano version which was a minor hit for Tiny Tim. This is the basso profundo version re-imagined by Sam Spoons featured here on vox humana. Surely destined to be an even more minor hit than last time round.

SWEET MEMORIES (Smith)
"Legs" proves that nostalgia isn't what it used to be with this canter down memory lane. Yes it was really that grim up north. "Legs" turns the screw by setting it all to a Euro pop synth background with sitar interlude. Now you don't hear that every week.

SUDOKU FORECAST (Jupitus)
If you need this, you really should get out more. Didn't you get enough maths in school?

NOW YOU'RE ASLEEP (Stanshall/Catlin-Birch) EMI Music Publishing Ltd
Thoughts of the late, great Vivian Stanshall are never too far away when all things Bonzo are considered. This time Vivian is also here in spirit with this track, co-written with David Catlin-Birch and released on CD for the first time. Wonderful stuff. We do miss you Vivian.

JEAN BAUDRILLARD (Innes)
Ask yourself, if old Jean correctly postulated that society is organised around consumption and display of commodities through which individuals gain prestige, identity and standing... why exactly did you buy this worthless item? One born again every minute, eh?

APPENDIX THREE
THE ANSWERS

1. Page 11: The Bride Stripped Bare By Bachelors
2. Page 12: Death Cab For Cutie
3. Page 18: Tent
4. Page 20: Shirt
5. Page 22: The Intro and The Outro
6. Page 26: We Were Wrong
7. Page 30: The Strain
8. Page 38: Noises For The Leg
9. Page 40: Mr Apollo
10. Page 46: Sport (The Odd Boy)
11. Page 48: Piggy Bank Love
12. Page 54: Rawlinson End
13. Page 58: Slush
14. Page 60: Dr Jazz
15. Page 63: My Brother Makes The Noises For The Talkies
16. Page 66: Bad Blood
17. Page 70: Trouser Press
18. Page 77: Urban Spaceman
19. Page 82: Postcard
20. Page 83: Waiting For The Wardrobe
21. Page 86: I'm Bored

22. Page 88: Look At Me I'm Wonderful
23. Page 90: What Do You Do?
24. Page 93: Don't get me wrong
25. Page 95: Busted
26. Page 98: The Equestrian Statue
27. Page 101: Music For The Head Ballet
28. Page 104: Cool Britannia
29. Page 106: Mickey's Son And Daughter
30. Page 111: Narcissus
31. Page 114: Rhinocratic Oaths
32. Page 118: Turkeys
33. Page 123: Beautiful Zelda
34. Page 133: Hunting Tigers Out In Indiah
35. Page 141: Pour l'Amour des Chiens
36. Page 150: Rusty Champion Thrust
37. Page 152: Old Tige
38. Page 156: Hawkeye The Gnu
39. Page 160: Purple Sprouting Brocoli
40. Page 162: Morning Train
41. Page 169: The Sudoku Forecast

YOUR SCORE

1-5 You appear to know nothing about the Bonzos, no wonder you needed this book!

6-20 You are The Odd Boy.

21-25 You are Normal

26-30 You are in danger of becoming an anorak. Consider a cold shower.

31-35 You really should get out more!

36-40 Are you David Christie?

41 You cheating bugger!